CW00351699

Fabulous Creatures, Mythical Monsters, and Animal Power Symbols

A Handbook

CASSANDRA EASON

GREENWOOD PRESS
Westport, Connecticut • London

Library of Congress Cataloging-in-Publication Data

Eason, Cassandra.
  Fabulous creatures, mythical monsters, and animal power symbols : a handbook /
Cassandra Eason.
    p. cm.
  Includes bibliographical references and index.
  ISBN 978–0–275–99425–9 (alk. paper)
  1. Animals—Mythology. 2. Animals—Folklore. 3. Animals—Symbolic aspects. I.
Title.
  BL325.A6E27 2008
  398'.469—dc22   2007035367

British Library Cataloguing in Publication Data is available.

Library of Congress Catalog Card Number: 2007035367
ISBN: 978–0–275–99425–9

First published in 2008

Greenwood Press, 88 Post Road West, Westport, CT 06881
An imprint of Greenwood Publishing Group, Inc.
www.greenwood.com

Printed in the United States of America

The paper used in this book complies with the
Permanent Paper Standard issued by the National
Information Standards Organization (Z39.48–1984).
10   9   8   7   6   5   4   3   2   1

Contents

Introduction   vii

Chapter 1 ∾ Animal Worship   1

Chapter 2 ∾ Serpents in Myth   19

Chapter 3 ∾ Dragon Power   35

Chapter 4 ∾ Fabulous Birds and Other Winged Creatures   51

Chapter 5 ∾ Unicorns, Lost Animals of Legends, and
                    the Magic of Animals   81

Chapter 6 ∾ Monsters and Weird Creatures   103

Chapter 7 ∾ Clan Animals   121

Chapter 8 ∾ Creatures of the Waters   135

Chapter 9 ∾ Animals and Prophecy   153

Bibliography   167

Index   175

Introduction

From early times humans have been fascinated by the animal and bird kingdoms. From the fabulous real-life creatures described by voyagers from Ancient Egyptian and Greek times onward, a strong mythology of mystical and mythical creatures has developed. These creatures may once have roamed the earth, only to become extinct. Among indigenous societies, animals and birds have been and still are accorded great respect. Creatures that are hunted for food are considered gifts from a generic and universal Mistress of the Animals, Birds, or Fish, or a Lord of the Animals. By studying Paleolithic cave painting and artifacts from these sites, one can speculate that traditional hunting rituals were accorded almost magical significance. These hunting practices have remained relatively unchanged for many centuries among such people as the Innu of North America and the Sámi reindeer people of Lapland.

For example, in the British Museum in London there is a small wounded bison image on stone that is 12,500 years old, engraved during the Upper Paleolithic age. It comes from a cave in the Tarn et Garonne region of France. The diagonal lines on the animal's side are believed to represent spears thrown at the creature, and the wavy lines on the animal's lung area represent blood, made with red ochre. Such charms may have been carried for luck; perhaps the user believed it would bring about, by some kind of mental or telepathic power, the successful conclusion of the hunt by drawing the animals to the hunters and at the same time guiding the hunters to the herds.

Life for the Innu or Montagnais–Naskapi people of Quebec and Labrador, even today, depends on the caribou migration. Before the hunt, according to tradition, the leaders dreamed of caribou migrations and saw the route the herds would take. The women once decorated caribou skin coats, showing the design of Caribou Mountain where the Caribou Master of the Spirits was said to live, and the route that the dreams indicated the animals would take. Hand-sewn and hand-painted, the colorful caribou skin coats of the Innu are now rare, though one is on display in the British Museum in London. There are estimated to be about 150 Innu caribou skin coats surviving in museums in the world, dating from 1700 to the early 1900s. Hopefully, with the revival of indigenous arts, the coats may become more commonplace again. The Mokushan feast at which these coats were once worn is a ritual that honors the caribou through the ritual consumption by elders of caribou fat and bone marrow. The women prepare the carcass of the first caribou caught, splintering the long bones to create broth. The broth is drunk carefully so as not to spill a drop.

On the northwest coast of America, local tribal fishermen pray and hold ceremonies each year to ensure the return of salmon and candlefish to the rivers. Fish represent wealth in that society, and salmon are the color of copper, the highest-value metal in that society.

The first salmon of the year is eaten at a ceremonial feast, and thanks are given to the Salmon people. Salmon bones are then returned to the water so they might regenerate into fish (a practice that is ecologically sound because it adds minerals to the water).

This natural rhythm, common among indigenous people, is just one of many ritual actions to ensure that humans live in harmony with animals, birds, and fish, and it is a kind of magical offering in the belief that sufficient food supplies will be given to the people in return. This respect, based on dependency on the animal kingdom for food, may explain the creation of idealized or especially intelligent and spiritually wise members of different animal and bird species as helpers of the nature gods and goddesses in many lands, called Animal or Bird Clan leaders in the Native North American tradition. These imagined, wise, and often larger-than-life creatures were described in myth as bringers of gifts, such as fire, to humanity, and they were regarded as messengers of the deities. Some high-ranking families in cultures throughout the world, from the Innu to the ancient clans of Scotland, claim symbolic, or in some cases, actual ancestry from the wise animals.

THE PSYCHOLOGY OF MAGICAL CREATURES

Magical creatures represent, in a pure and undiluted form, strengths and qualities that humans desire in their own lives: the courage of the lion, the selfless devotion of the dog, the single-minded focus of the hawk, and the protective fierceness of Mother Wolf toward her young and her clan. In modern urban society, where daily contact and observation of animals is not so frequent, the spiritual focus of these creatures can have symbolic and psychological significance and can draw people closer to nature and activate their own innate natural instincts. This could occur by reading old legends of these creatures or by studying the actual creatures described in the myths, such as the wolf, in conservation areas.

The Ancient Egyptians linked these higher animal qualities with specific deities. The sacred animals and birds embodied the most positive characteristics of their ruling gods and goddesses. Each Egyptian town and region, called a Nome, had its own local sacred animal, centered on the place where the related deity was most venerated. It is hard to imagine the huge scale of this veneration, but archaeologists have excavated vast acres of cat cemeteries at Bubastis, Bast's cult center on the Nile delta, where it is estimated that many hundreds of thousands of mummified cats were buried over centuries. Although sacred animals have always been central in Ancient Egypt, animal temple cults developed into their most popular and widespread form during the Late and Ptolemaic periods, between 664 and 30 BCE.

The goddess Bast in her cat form, or Bastet in her cat-headed form, was the goddess of music, dance, children, women, and fertility, and is still adopted by some young business women as a power symbol because of her fierce protectiveness to her kittens.

FABULOUS CREATURES AS POWER SYMBOLS

Totally mythical beasts can also act as psychological power icons. For example, the phoenix, common to several cultures, is said to burn itself on a pyre of fragrant incense every 500 or 1,000 years, whereupon a new bird rises from the ashes as a symbol of renewal and transformation. Medieval heraldry adopted a number of mythical creatures such as the unicorn and the griffon as family crests, engraved on armor and shields to express values that typified a family or clan. Native North American clans engraved their family clan animals, whether idealized beavers or mythical thunderbirds, on their totem poles.

SHAPE-SHIFTING INTO ANIMALS

Changing into an animal or bird form was common among myths of pre-Christian deities in a number of cultures, a strategy adopted, according to the stories, when the ancients wished to travel swiftly or undetected by humans.

For example, according to Norse myth, the fertility and love goddess Freya, often took the form of a falcon by putting on a falcon skin that gave her the power to fly. Bronze Freya falcon necklaces are still sold in Sweden, where there is a revival of interest in the pre-Christian religions, especially among younger people. I asked a businesswoman I met recently in Central Sweden about this. She was wearing a Freya charm, and she said that it reminded her of the courage of Freya in her fierce battle aspects.

Shape-shifting was also associated with exceptionally powerful humans, for example the Viking berserkers or bear men. The term comes from the Old Norse word *berserkr*, a wild warrior or champion. Such warriors wore bearskins, and the origin of the word was probably *bera* (bear) and *serkr* (shirt or coat), or it might have meant *bare of shirt*, that is fighting without armor. According to eye witness accounts (albeit recorded later) the Berserker warriors, who were dedicated to the father god Odin, went into ecstatic trance in battle and howled like animals, foamed at the mouth, and seemed totally fearless and unaware of pain. The enemy saw them as wild animals; they were sometimes described as wearing wolfskins or bearskins. The warriors thought of themselves as bears, and because of the power of the mind, in this psychological sense, they appeared, in the heat of battle, like wild animals to the enemy, who no doubt had heard stories about them turning into bears. Because of all of this they struck terror into all who opposed them.[1]

THE SHAPE-SHIFTING SAINT

Shape-shifting accounts may also be found in Celtic myth, among the stories of their deities, including the intriguing account of the Celtic Christian, Saint Patrick. There is little hard evidence about the precise dates of Patrick's conversion of Ireland, but it seems to have been during the second half of the fifth century. Celtic Christian chroniclers seem fairly liberal about events and dates. It is told that Saint Patrick and his men were travelling to the king's court, when he discovered that the Druids (Celtic priests) had prepared an ambush for him. As they walked, the saint and his followers chanted the sacred Lorica, or Deer's Cry, that later became known as the St. Patrick's Breastplate Prayer, claimed, again with some uncertainty, to have been created by the saint. According to the myth the Druids did not see the saint and his followers pass, but saw only a gentle doe followed by twenty fawns.

One explanation is that there were deer present and that Patrick, who was supposedly gifted in the powers of illusion, like some modern-day magicians, somehow lowered his and his followers' profiles psychologically, or distracted the enemy. It may have been that he and his followers went unseen, perhaps behind bushes, while the Druids were watching the procession of deer, an animal sacred to them. Many stories of the amazing deeds of Christian saints were probably created to win over pagan worshippers by convincing them that the new deity was more powerful than the old ones. I can describe this ability apparently displayed by St Patrick only as being similar to when there is a confrontation, and some people are not picked on by the troublemakers, while others stand out as victims, maybe because they are transmitting unseen waves of fear. We do not really understand how, or indeed whether, people can send out certain energies to prevent attack, or whether there is some kind of illusion. In Irish the Deer Cry is called Fáed Fíada. There exist a variety of versions, written in both Irish and Latin.

Most of these versions have an openly strong Christian and anti-pagan theme and seek God's protection against such dangers as "black laws of pagan-ism, against deceit of idolatry, against spells of women and smiths and druids."[2]

Though Saint Patrick was crusading for Christianity in a pagan land, the version of the Deer Cry I use is generally more nature based, and it is included in all the other versions. I learned this shortened version when I was working with some Irish women who lived in a dangerous part of Ireland and so were interested in the whole idea of psychological profile lowering. (There are a number of versions of the Deer Cry in books and online.)

Today I put on
The power of Heaven,
The brightness of the sun,
The radiance of the moon,
The splendour of fire,
The fierceness of the lightning.

Today I put on
The whiteness of snow,
The swiftness of the wind,
The depth of the sea,
The stability of the earth,
And the hardness of rock.

Christ with me, Christ before me,
Christ behind me, Christ in me,
Christ under me, Christ over me,
Christ in every eye, which may look on me,
Christ in every ear, which may hear me.

The Saint Patrick account is also quite unusual because shape-shifting into deer is more usually associated with myths about Celtic goddesses. I have written about this more in Chapter 1 on Animal Worship and Chapter 7 on Clan Animals, and it is a theme that recurs frequently throughout the book.

THE PSYCHOLOGY OF SHAPE-SHIFTING

Of course no one is suggesting that even a saint can change into an animal. But because the belief still exists among some indigenous people, it may have some enduring psychological significance. Supposing people were able not just to imagine they had the courage of a lion, but to take into their own energy field the sensation of feeling as though they were lions, while at the same time retaining the necessary restraints of humanity. I know of no scientific experiments into the effects of such visualization, either to dismiss it as pure imagination on the part of the person projecting leonine energies, or to suggest that shape-shifting might be a valuable psychological technique in confidence or assertiveness training.

SHAMANIC SHAPE-SHIFTING

Shamans, the priest/healer/magicians of both sexes in tribal societies in areas as far apart as India; Australia; Japan and China; Siberia and Mongolia; and in Africa; among the Bedouins in the Middle East; and in North, Central, and South America, frequently put on bird or animal headdresses, animal skins, or feather cloaks as part of their rituals. According to numerous eye witness accounts, they enter into trance to travel in their minds as birds or animals, visiting the spirit worlds to seek healing for individuals and blessings or help for the people from the Mistress of the Herds or the Sea Creatures. This would seem a very old tradition.

Painted in black on the cave walls of Les Trois Frères in the French Pyrenees is a shamanic figure that may portray a specific man dressed in animal skins and mask, dating from about 14,000 BCE. He stands high above the animals that throng the walls. Only his feet are human; he possesses the large round eyes of an owl or lion, the antlers and ears of a stag, the front paws of a lion or bear, the genitals of a feline, and the tail of a horse or wolf. Similar costumes can be seen in African seasonal rites and rites of passage ceremonies today.

Aztec priests would also assume such animal guises with headdresses and skins or feather cloaks to signify the power of the deities, many of who had animal or bird characteristics. At an Aztec exhibition at the Royal Academy of Arts in London in 2005, I saw a headdress of a priest of the god Ehcatl with his birdlike beak, who generated wind, the precursor of rain. Once the priest assumed the role and the bird headdress, he ritually *became* Ehcatl, and it was believed that his bird spirit flew through the skies generating in ritual what the people believed were the necessary energies to herald the rainy season that was so necessary for the crops to grow. As with other shamanic practices, the inert body would lie below as if dead, or dance so fast it was easy for onlookers, in the excitement of the ritual and perhaps moving fast themselves to a drum beat, to imagine that the priest was flying.

A number of New Age practitioners and traditional spiritual teachers of shamanism and indigenous religions instruct others to achieve this mind flight using a variety of techniques including drums, rattles, dance, and chanting.

WEIRD CREATURES

In recent years there has been a great revival in interest in werewolves and other strange creatures not currently recognizable as existing species. Some are hypothesized in the more popular forms of the media to be of paranormal or even extraterrestrial origin, and sightings of some of the strangest are often accompanied by increased anecdotal reports of UFOs in the area.

Cryptozoology, the science of hidden or unknown animals, from the Greek words *kryptos*, *zoon*, and *logos*, which mean *hidden*, *animals*, and *discourse*, aims not to research the paranormal, but to discover and explain previously unknown and unclassified creatures. Of course this is not a new study. For example the unicorn was first described in 398 BCE by the Ancient Greek naturalist Cresias. He travelled throughout Persia and the Far East and told of a creature he encountered that seems remarkably similar to the fabled unicorn, with a white horse body, a dark red head and dark blue eyes, and a three-colored, pointed horn about one-and-a-half feet long. It may be that unicorns died out because their powdered horns, as Cresias reported, when powdered, were considered to have healing properties and so were highly prized. Of course we have of no way of proving that unicorns existed outside the realms of myth. However in parts of the Far East the tiger is threatened with extinction because its paws and other body parts are prized for medicinal purposes and as an aphrodisiac. European Medieval bestiaries are filled with accounts and illustrations of strange creatures such as the unicorn, seen during journeys by Greek and Roman philosophers and chroniclers. These bestiaries formed fascinating early cryptozoology books.

In popular culture the term *cryptozoology* has been widened to include creatures that are not explicable in terms of the nature of the planet earth. Of course it may be that some we consider paranormal may be animal mutations or the survival of creatures from much earlier times. With new methods of detection, some of these weird creatures may one day be found in an as-yet-unexplored remote rainforest, or a much-less-exotic but similar creature may emerge to provide the basis for myths to grow up over time like Chinese whispers.

WHY THE REVIVED INTEREST IN WEIRD CREATURES?

The interest in strange creatures, especially in what appear to be (in current terms of reference) other worldly encounters, may be partly due to conventional religious declines in a number of westernized societies, in which people are desperately looking for some proof that there is life beyond the material world, and that we are not alone in the universe. This of course does not make the sightings objectively true or paranormal.

What is more, with advanced, computer-created graphics, special effects in films such as *Jurassic Park* and the recent *King Kong* and programs like the *X Files*, it becomes easy to blur the lines on an unconscious level between what is actual and what is fantasy. Therefore a lake monster or a Yeti in the remote parts of Tibet suddenly seems more possible; the boundaries of possibility have extended within the mind because of this media simulation.

The frightening nature of many of these creatures may also reflect a primitive instinctive terror of being harmed by forces beyond our control, and this is not a recent phenomenon. In the Christian religion these terrifying forces are focused on the devil himself, often pictured as horned and cloven-footed, and still believed by some to be an actual, physical being. The werewolf, for example, reflects a fear of being eaten alive, of bloodletting, hints of which can be detected lurking beneath the surface of unedited versions of so-called fairy stories, as in, for example, the German Brothers Grimm Red Riding Hood written around 1812.

WEREWOLVES

The werewolf, or wolfman or -woman, appears throughout the literature of Northern Europe, with Germany being a particularly rich source of werewolf legends. The first werewolf accounts are found in the Babylonian Epic of Gilgamesh, written about 1800 BCE. Throughout the Middle Ages there were numerous accounts and legends, especially in Western Europe. Through the ages people have believed in werewolves and the legends of people turning into wolves on the night of the full moon have grown up around certain areas. There may have been an original attack or a series of attacks by a huge ferocious wolf that stood on its hind legs. These may have occurred more frequently around the full moon, when people were more likely to be out at night walking in the countryside because the increased natural light made travel easier when the moon was bright.[3]

Any other attacks in the same place might thereafter be interpreted in the same way, and unscrupulous, strong, hairy men might have dressed in wolf-skins to avoid detection and hide behind the superstitious fears of werewolves to attack females out at night alone. The most recent reported werewolf sighting, or at least one considered locally to be a werewolf sighting, was in 1998 at Hahn Air Force Base, Germany, just outside the village of Wittlich, the last town where, it is said, a werewolf was killed in the late 1880s. There is a shrine just outside town where a candle always burns. Legend has it that if the candle ever goes out, the werewolf will return. One night during 1998 the candle went out, and security policemen investigating alarms at the base saw a huge wolflike creature seven or eight feet tall, who jumped a twelve-foot security fence after taking three immense leaps. I have written more about werewolves in Chapter 6.

MOTHMAN

Perhaps the strangest creature, the subject of a popular film in 2002, *The Mothman Prophecies*, is called *Mothman*. He has been sighted in a number of places in Virginia and West Virginia, most commonly near an abandoned ammunitions dump dating from World War II, close to Point Pleasant, West Virginia. The strange creature was called Mothman after a fictional Batman enemy, Killer Moth. The majority of sightings were between 12 November 1966 and December 1967, though there have been occasional reported sightings as recently as 2005.

Mothman has been consistently described as a grey figure with large hypnotic red eyes that glowed in the dark, which were set right into his shoulders or chest. He had wings folded against his back, and it was reported that he chased cars at speed approaching 100 mph.

A number of hypotheses have been presented to explain eyewitness accounts of Mothman, ranging from misidentification and media hype to a huge bird or some kind of paranormal creature. There are numerous abandoned and collapsed tunnels that could in theory harbor such a creature were it to exist. Mothman's appearances also coincided with anecdotally reported UFO sightings in the Point Pleasant area during the same period, and sightings of the mythical Native North American thunderbird, to which Mothman was reported to have similarities. Cases like this are curious, even allowing for media hype and hoax reports, and the intense distress felt for months afterward by those involved seem out of all proportion to the experience.[4]

THE FOUR CELESTIAL ANIMALS OF *FENG SHUI*

The four celestial animals of *Feng Shui*—a bird, a tortoise, a dragon, and a tiger—were once called the four celestial palaces and were associated with major constellation groupings in Chinese astrology. They demonstrate how archetypal or idealized animals have become central to a major belief system of energy balancing that has spread from China to the West in recent years. *Feng Shui* is a popular, worldwide energy-directing method adopted on business premises and in homes alike, apparently to ensure that the *Qi*, or universal life force, is directed through the home or office in the most beneficial way. It may be useful to study these four creatures, regardless of whether *Feng Shui* is an objectively valid system, because the animals have moved far beyond their original role of lucky or protective creatures to become part of the way a considerable number of people measure and try to manipulate energies within their homes.[5]

WHAT IS *FENG SHUI?*

Feng Shui, which means *wind and water power*, may have been practiced in some form for up to 6,000 years. A Neolithic grave from that time, excavated in the Henan province of China, showed on either side of the buried body two of the four *Feng Shui* celestial animals etched on clam shell, the dragon on the east side and the tiger on the west. The first actual discovered writings about *Feng Shui* do not appear until the fourth century CE, however, in a sacred Chinese text called the *Book of Burial*, written by Guo Pu (276–324 CE) during the Jin Dynasty. It is suggested here that the universal *Qi* life force is carried on the wind (Feng), representing change and transformation in nature. *Qi* is held or contained within water (Shui), which provides a more stable form of the life force. The *Book of Burial* described how, by finding a place where the four animals were in harmony according to the characteristics of the landscape, the best site might be identified for imperial tombs, the original purpose of *Feng Shui*.

The Form or Shape method, the more intuitive of the formal *Feng Shui* Schools or traditions, involves visually assessing and identifying, rather than measuring, the form and nature of the landscape, the site, and the specific location of the building, according to traditional principles set down by the early *Feng Shui* geomancers. The founder was the Imperial *Feng Shui* master Yang Yun Sung in Kwangsi province, China, about 840 to 888 CE. The method was inspired by the dramatic nature of the landscape in that area.

THE RED PHOENIX OR BIRD

The red phoenix is associated with the south point of the compass. It was in the ideal Chinese location, positioned in front of the main entrance door to a home or business. Chinese front doors traditionally face south, the direction of the sun, even in apartment blocks. More populist westernized *Feng Shui* practices site the red phoenix in front of the main door regardless of the compass orientation of the door, and they locate the other three creatures accordingly. The phoenix is said ideally to need an open space at the front of the site or house, on a small hill gently sloping down, but not too steeply, or the phoenix will fall off. A small pool here, or a winding stream, is considered good, so that the water transmits the *Qi* gently.

The phoenix, whose name means gracefulness, represents the sun and the summer, the season of warmth and time of harvest. It symbolizes fame and good fortune. In Chinese mythology the body of the phoenix is said to signify the five human qualities. Its head represents virtue; the wings represent duty; the back portrays ritually correct behavior; the breast stands for humanity; the stomach represents reliability.

The red phoenix of the South is often depicted as the mate of the celestial dragon of the East. It is linked to the Chinese element of fire, which is portrayed as dynamic and energetic. Its prosperity- and success-bringing energy, *Yang Qi*, comes from the south.

BLACK TORTOISE

The black tortoise is sometimes called the *Dark Warrior*. He stands in the North (or the back of the house in modern westernized practice). The tortoise needs enclosed protective sheltering land such as low hills at the back. It is the creature of the moon and the winter, and a symbol of long life, the family, strength, and endurance. Its element is water and it is mysterious, intuitive, and compliant.

Its slow gentle power *T'sang Qi* comes from the north, flowing slowly and gently, bringing harmony and tranquility.

THE GREEN DRAGON

There are nine Chinese dragons that control the various universal elements. The green dragon is the Earth dragon.

The dragon stands on the east (or in modern westernized adaptation, to the left) side of the house as the practitioner faces the front door. Traditionally the land of the dragon should be higher than that of the tiger in the West. The balance between the dragon and tiger is considered an important one in *Feng Shui* practice. Too powerful a tiger is said to be reflected in disruptive energies and maybe in power struggles in the family.

The dragon represents the East, the springtime, the direction of sunrise. It is associated with thunder and the Chinese element of wood, which signifies health, ambitions, and growth. Its energy is called *Sheng Qi*, the power that is believed to stimulate new beginnings, fertility, and an increase in everything positive in the home or workplace.

THE WHITE TIGER

To the Chinese, a white tiger symbol is considered inauspicious, especially in matters of gambling or speculation. However, in *Feng Shui*, the White Tiger is an icon of strength, disruption, or more positively necessary change, and protection against evil intentions from strangers. It traditionally stands to the west of a building (or in modern westernized adaptation to the right side) as a practitioner faces the front door.

The white tiger symbolizes autumn, the Chinese element of Metal, which represents determination, unyielding powers, and unpredictability. The *Sha* or Tiger *Qi* is very fierce *Qi*, and it is believed to rush in straight lines through a home, overwhelming other energies if unchecked.

ABOUT THIS BOOK

Unusually perhaps, for a resource book, a large proportion of the material comes from the oral tradition. The legends and myths about a number of the creatures in the following chapters have been collected orally in my travels and research during more than twenty years, from people of different cultures, from their family, or from local traditions. I have collated these along with material from written and Internet sources into a private database of millions of words. Because of this there are variations in legends and chants, such as the Saint Patrick Deer Cry, and the anecdotal oral versions are part of a living and evolving tradition, which is what mythology should represent.

So that you can follow up the references and use them for more in-depth study if you wish, I have suggested in the reading list at the end of each chapter a great number of books that deal with each subject separately.

DEVELOPING THE MATERIAL

Rather than giving you specific page references to read out of context, I have focused more on high-quality books to be read in more detail. These will expand your knowledge on those topics that fascinate you and act as reference sources for project or reference work. If you do want a quick follow-up of any details I have given, the Internet is also an excellent source of material. It may include research in the field, or direct you to people who have visited the areas associated with the legends, or who have gone back to ancient sources in old languages, as well as presenting more academic papers. You can also find traditional sites of indigenous wisdom that may tell myths and legends in different versions so you can decide which one seems best to you to typify the creature concerned. In this way you will understand what it was that prompted our ancestors to write about the animals and to describe what they had seen in dreams, or through rich imagination that embellished or changed the stories over time.

Perhaps an elderly relative mentioned an even older relative who once saw a strange creature in a remote country. As new species are discovered in remote rainforests, and as other species die out, our descendants may marvel at the mythical white Siberian tiger or polar bear unless we seriously begin to tackle global warming and take responsibility for worldwide conservation.

Begin your own journal of mystical and mythical creatures. Keep your journal on your computer, or use a handwritten one, and collect material online of old drawings that can be downloaded for noncommercial purposes. Look on Web sites for unusual accounts and legends build your own database for creative work and for handing on your favorite stories to your descendants.

BIBLIOGRAPHY

1. Sturluson S. (Author), Magnusson M. (Translator), and Palsson H. (Translator). *King Harold's Sagas from Snorri Sturluson's Heimskringla*. London: Penguin, 1976. Recorded from a late ninth-century poem describing the berserker troops of King Harald Fairhair, ruler of Norway. Sturluson was an Icelandic Christian historian, poet, and chronicler dedicated to recording the earlier oral myths. He was born in 1179 and died in 1241. *Heimskringla* is a history of Norwegian kings.
2. Alexander, C. F. *St Patrick's Breastplate*. Belfast, Ireland: Appletree Press, 1995.
3. Hall, J. *Half Human, Half Animal: Tales of Werewolves and Related Creatures*. Bloomington, Indiana: Authorhouse, 2003.
4. Coleman, L. L. *Mothman and Other Curious Encounters*. New York: Paraview Press, 2001.
5. Zhang, J. *A Translation of the Ancient Chinese Book of Burial (Zang Shu)*. New York: Edwin Mellen Press, 2004.

CHAPTER 1

Animal Worship

There is a long and close relationship between animals and deities in pre-Christian societies. This relationship still exists in hunting societies where practices are largely unchanged over the centuries. They reflect the dependency of hunting and fishing societies on the coming of the herds and shoals. They also reflect the link between a Mother goddess figure as the creatrix and animals who could be entreated for food. Excavated artifacts, art, and sites are the main source of information, but their meaning is open to interpretation. Other information from preliterate time comes from folk stories handed down in the oral tradition for many centuries. For example, few Native North American myths were recorded before the nineteenth century. However, there is a growing body of writings from indigenous teachers, especially in the Native North American world.[1]

The world's earliest cave paintings were discovered in Fumane Cave, near Verona in northern Italy. They are between 32,000 and 36,500 years old and were originally painted in red ochre. Though faded and covered in calcite, they show a four-legged beast and a man with an animal head. These paintings may have had some significance in the ritual of worshipping early earth deities.

THE MISTRESS OF THE ANIMALS

The Mistress of the Animals or Herds or the Lady of the Beasts is a generic term used in different cultures and ages for an Earth goddess. She was believed to be responsible for the care of and release of animals to the hunters. (The early Bird goddesses are covered in Chapter 4 and the Sea Mothers in Chapter 8.)

Like the Caribou Master or Spirit of the Montagnais-Naskapi people of Quebec and Labrador, the Mistress of the Herds and her male counterpart, the Horned Hunter, in different cultures, transmitted rules through messages. These messages were believed to have been given by the gods or spirits to wise huntsmen and shamans. These safeguards ensured that the forest or land would not be overhunted, and that respect for the animals would be maintained. Though these laws were practical, such as restrictions on killing breeding females, they had more weight because they were considered divine edicts.

Even in more complex civilizations like the Ancient Greeks, Artemis, the goddess of Hunt, punished hunters who killed pregnant or nursing animals with death by her silver arrows.

WHY A MISTRESS OF THE HERDS?

Early people, who witnessed human and animal life cycles and the seasonal variations in plants and trees, assumed that a Mother or Earth goddess gave birth to all forms of life, and so human and animal remains were returned to the earth after death. Even today, among some existing hunting peoples, the Earth Mother is offered the most precious body parts of the first animal killed in the hunt. In Sweden, as a relic of this folk custom, even sophisticated moose hunters from the cities leave the entrails of the slain animal on a rock in the forest as an offering to the Earth Mother, though none I have interviewed have any idea why.

The historian Anne Baring describes in her book, *Myth of the Goddess*, how at a burial site at Mal'ta, near Lake Baikal, Siberia, twenty mammoth ivory figures of goddesses, carbon dated between 16,000 and 13,000 BCE, have been excavated.[2] One is dressed in lion skin. Found within a child's grave, the small goddess figures were surrounded by six ivory birds, either geese or swans with wings in flight, an ivory fish, and the skeletons of fourteen ritually buried animals. The tiny lion-skin goddess may have been an early representation of the association between the goddesses and animals. Her feet were tapered so she could have been originally carried while hunting and set in the ground as a good luck charm.

In Siberia, indigenous hunters still pay respect to Bugudy Musun, Siberian Mother Goddess of the Animals, an old but very physically powerful goddess who sometimes assumed the form of a huge elk or a reindeer and controlled all food supplies. Even today, she is offered the finest part of the first animal killed. Another Siberian Mistress of the Herds, Zonget, ruled all birds, animals, and the people who hunt them. According to folk custom, birds and animals would allow themselves to be trapped if she ordained it. The shamans today still give her offerings and make sure the creatures are treated with reverence. Zonget, it is believed, appears to mortals in the form of a gray Arctic bird.

THE NEOLITHIC MISTRESS OF THE WILD ANIMALS

Çatal Hüyük, a very large Neolithic settlement in southern Anatolia, now part of Turkey, dates from 7500 BCE. The site was inhabited for more than a thousand years.[3]

A small terracotta goddess statue, dating from 6000 to 5800 BCE, sitting on a rocklike throne, was excavated from a grain bin. She may have been a charm to encourage a good harvest. She is shown giving birth while resting her hands on two leopards or lions and has a big head, hip, and legs though she is only four-and-a-half inches (11.2cm) tall. Leopards seem to be a goddess symbol in this part of the world because in another statue, two goddesses stand behind leopards and are portrayed wearing leopard-skin robes. This statue dates from 5800 BCE. As part of the same statue, a young boy is riding on the back of a leopard. Perhaps, it has been speculated, he is the young god born from the Mother goddess.

MINOAN CRETE

The Mistress of the Animals also features in the civilization of Minoan Crete. Because evidence of the culture is largely through artifacts and ruins, there is again room for interpretation. A seal dating from 1500 BCE was excavated in 1900 by the UK archaeologist and onetime director of the British Museum in London, Arthur Evans, in the area identified as the former royal complex at Knossos on the Isle of Crete. The goddess is shown standing on a mountain in front of a shrine of a pile of bull horns. Two guardian lions rise up on either side of her. The bull horns are a symbol of the Minoan bull cult. Bulls were sometimes identified in myth as the son/consort of the Mistress of the Animals. Other similar images of the goddess with lions or griffons continued after the invasion of the Mycenaeans from southern Greece who conquered Crete in 1400 BCE, after it was weakened by tidal waves. The images may also be seen in necklace plaques, decorated with the Mistress of Animals from the second half of the seventh century BCE in Thebes. She has wings and is variously surrounded by lions and bees. Gradually, she became associated with the Greek huntress goddess, Artemis.[4]

ARTEMIS

Artemis, the virgin huntress goddess, was entreated for safe childbirth by humans. She also was said to release women from suffering and pain with her silver arrows. She was very much a women's goddess, and men were not allowed to attend her rituals.

Artemis as the Great She Bear was worshipped in this form by her virgin priestesses at the New Moon as well as during festivals. Bear worship is said to be the most ancient of all known forms of religion, and this suggests she may be a pre-Hellenic Greek goddess associated with animals.

At Ephesus, on the west coast of what is now Turkey, her worship merged with that of the Virgin Mary whose tomb was said to be located there, with the establishment of the church of Our Lady of Ephesus in ad 431.

Artemis was also associated with the Bee goddess, another ancient goddess symbol. At the temple of Artemis at Ephesus her statues were adorned with bees. The priests would become eunuchs to serve the Bee goddesses. These priests were called *essenes*, which means drones, the name given to the male bee. It is said that a virgin can walk through a swarm of bees and not be stung.

THE CELTIC ANIMAL GODDESSES

There is still debate about the origins and dates of the Celtic invasions or migrations in Western Europe. However, the traditional view of historians is that the ancestors of the Celts were the Proto-Indo-Europeans who lived near the Black Sea circa 4000 BCE.

Two waves of Iron Age Celts spread throughout Central Europe, the first, known as the Hallstat culture from 800 to 500 BCE and the second, the La Tene culture from 500 to 100 BCE. They colonized Britain and much of Western Europe. They underwent great changes as they came into contact with indigenous cultures and those they regularly encountered on their extensive trade routes. By the first century AD, the Romans had overcome most of the Celtic tribes and destroyed the heartlands of Druidry, the Celtic priesthood. The most accurate accounts of the Celts—apart from the more biased references by hostile classical chroniclers such as Julius Caesar—come from the oral native Celtic mythology. The remains of this oral tradition, preserved over the centuries by Celtic Bards and minstrels, were recorded by Christian monks from the eighth to thirteenth centuries. They were also collected as folklore in areas where Celtic descendants remained, from the seventeenth century onward.[5]

Many of the Celtic deities were specifically related to animals and it was believed that the Mistress of the Animals could take an animal or a bird form like a number of other Celtic goddesses. Until influenced by the Romans, who combined indigenous deities of the people they conquered with their own, the Celtic goddess forms were not recorded as statues or on seals.

According to myth, Celtic goddesses were able to shape-shift or change into animal form to signify their particular qualities. For example, Epona the Horse goddess was beloved by the Celts and later the Romans. The horse signified power because they were very important in battle. Therefore, Epona, the goddess who in her humanlike form gave sovereignty of the land to chiefs, was either pictured riding on a white horse or as a horse with foals. She was an icon of the fertility of land, people, and animals. She is recalled in the great white chalk figures of horses etched on hillsides throughout England, such as the White Horse of Uffingham in Berkshire. The Uffingham horse is close to the ancient Ridgeway track that connects various sacred sites such as Wayland's Smithy, a Neolithic long barrow through southern England. The horse is 374 feet long and 110 feet high and a foal accompanied it in the twelfth century (though the foal is no longer there). In 1996 Oxford University Archaeology Research Unit dated the horse between 1400 and 600 BCE, which suggests that this was a pre-Celtic figure adopted by the Celts and may have influenced the creation of Epona. Epona was known as Macha to the Irish and Rhiannon in Wales.

THE CELTIC MISTRESS OF THE ANIMALS

In Ireland and Scotland, the Mistress of the Animals was given a generic name *Cailleach* meaning the *Veiled One*. In Scotland, this powerful sorceress, also called Scotia, is depicted with the teeth of a wild bear and a boar's tusks.

As the Scottish Cailleach Bhuer, meaning the *Blue Hag*, she manifested herself as an old woman wearing black or dark blue rags with a crow on her left shoulder and a holly staff that was said could kill a mortal with a touch. She cared for the moorland animals in winter.

In Ireland she was also identified with Garbh Ogh, a giantess who lived for many centuries and who used to hunt the mountain deer with a pack of seventy dogs, all of whom had the names of different birds.

As cattle and sheep became important to the tribes, the Cailleach assumed the role of protectress on remote moorlands in Scotland and Ireland during winters, breaking the ice so the animals might drink and making sure they had food and shelter.

According to myth, Cailleach also took the form of a deer as one of her animal guises. In later Christianized stories, the Celtic goddesses were downgraded to fairies and, it was said, they would assume the form of a deer to escape pursuit of a powerful hunter magician who sought to possess them.

Another related Celtic Irish animal goddess was Flidais, a huntress goddess who could shape-shift into any creature she desired. She is described as riding in a chariot pulled by stags and as having possessed a cow who could give milk to thirty people at a time.

THE DIVINE SOW

The sow, especially the female wild boar, was another important goddess symbol. To the Celts the wild boar was an icon of courage. They were depicted on banners, and a special longhorn with a boar's head was blown in battle to strike terror into enemies. Arduinna or Ardwinna was the French Gallic goddess of the Wild Wood and the Boar goddess. She demanded an offering for every animal she allowed to be hunted and was described riding on a wild boar. She was entreated as a wood spirit at the beginning of the annual boar hunt even after the coming of Christianity.

The Welsh Cerridwen, Crone goddess of the Moon, was called the White Sow goddess because the sow was a symbol of divine fertility and rebirth. Sows are the symbol of nourishment, and in Celtic times, their carcasses were sometimes buried in the graves of important people to feed them in the afterlife. There was a mythical cauldron or pot in the otherworld or afterlife that was believed always to be filled with cooked pork. When the bones were discarded the pigs were miraculously reincarnated, so the warriors living in the otherworld could hunt them again.

Cerridwen was called the Mistress of Shape-Shifting. The ultimate shapeshifting saga tells of a young boy Gwion, who was left to guard Cerridwen's Cauldron of Inspiration and Wisdom. Cerridwen had created a brew intended to compensate her own son for his ugliness. But Gwion *accidentally* got three drops of the brew on his fingers and when he licked them, he absorbed the energies meant for the other boy. Cerridwen was furious and to escape from her, Gwion turned himself into a hare. Cerridwen shape-shifted into a greyhound to hunt the hare. When he becomes a fish, she turns into an otter. He turns into a bird and she a falcon. Finally, he metamorphoses into a grain of corn, but she becomes a hen and swallows Gwion. Nine months later he is born as the bard Taliesin, the Shining Brow.

There was an actual sixth-century Welsh bard called Taliesin who claimed a series of spectacular past lives and said he had attained immortality being reborn from Cerridwen's womb. He is mixed with the earlier mythological Taliesin and a later mediaeval one, who collected and maybe added to the original poems of Taliesin that may be of Celtic origin.[6]

THE LORDS OF THE HUNT AND WILD ANIMAL GODS

Horned deities appear as bulls, stags, and goats in a number of cultures and are, it would seem, linked with the son/consort of the Earth goddess. From Neolithic times, bulls were ritually sacrificed for offerings as a symbol of the god offering himself as a sacrifice of the land. For example, in the worship of the Anatolian Mother goddess Cybele, a bull was ritually sacrificed on March 24 (from around the eighth century BCE each year, and certainly until the fourth century CE), and his testicles were offered to the goddess to symbolize the castration and death of Attis her son/lover and his resurrection on March 25 so that life might return to the world and the crops could grow.

HORNED OR ANTLERED GODS

In Celtic times, *Cernunnos* seems to have been a generic term, meaning Horned One given for the various horned gods of this tradition. Attempts have been made to link him mythologically with shamanic figures such as the Shaman of le Trois Freres mentioned in the Introduction.

In modern Celtic spirituality, Cernunnos is called Lord of Winter, the Hunt, animals, death, male fertility, and the underworld. According to twentieth-century myths, he died at the end of summer and was reborn in the spring. This could refer to the offering of the first stag killed at the beginning of the hunting season in mid-September in parts of Europe and Scandinavia.

During the first century CE, the Romans assimilated some of the native deities of lands they conquered, and so the head of Cernunnos occasionally appeared on monumental pillars that supported a Roman god. For example, a Roman pillar of a statue of Jupiter was discovered under the choir of the cathedral of Notre Dame during the eighteenth century. It is now in the Museum of Cluny, Paris. The carvings on this pillar depict, among other native gods, the horned god Cernunnos and the Celtic thunder god Taranis emerging from a tree. In Celtic-Romano imagery, Cernunnos is also shown with a ram-headed serpent and a stag or holding a bag of money.

Another famous image we have of Cernunnos is on the side of the silver Gundestrup Cauldron, a religious vessel found in Himmerland, Denmark in 1891, in a peat bog. It is believed to have been produced in the late La Tene

Celtic period after 120 BCE. It can be seen in the National Museum in Copen-hagen, Denmark. The Cernunnos figure on the cauldron resembles the one in the Museum de Cluny.

THE NORSE HORNED GOD

The Norse Freyr or Frey was the Norse hunting god who had a dual role as an Earth agriculture god in Scandinavia and Germany. He was the twin brother of Freya, the Norse fertility and love goddess, although some myths say he was son of the Earth goddess Nerthus. One of the order of the old Vanir nature gods, according to Norse myth, Freyr ruled over the weather and fertility and was frequently depicted in earlier images with horns. The earliest images of Freyr date from the Bronze Age on rock carvings in Östergötland, Sweden. It would seem that from Sweden his worship spread to Norway and Iceland. His power animal was the golden boar called Gul-lenbursti.

Freyr's boar was also a symbol of the rising sun, and according to Norse myth, Freyr rode his boar through the skies around the Midwinter Solstice, the darkest and shortest days around December 20/21. It was believed he brought the sun and light back into the world.

The boar was, in pre-Christian times, sacrificed at Yule to Freyr so that he would bring abundance in the months ahead. It was also dedicated to the thunder god Thor as Lord of Winter. Freyr lived in Alfheim where he ruled over the Light Elves. It was said that the last battle he fought with an Elk horn as his weapon was at Ragnarok. (Ragnarok was the last battle fought that ended the old order of Norse gods.) Freyr was also invoked in Viking times for abundance, ships and sailors, oaths, and bravery in battle.[7]

THE CHRISTIANIZATION OF THE HORNED GOD

The role of Cernunnos as Lord of the Forest was split with the coming of Christianity. In France, the Divine Huntsman became the late seventh-century-CE St Hubert, patron saint of hunters. According to legend, he was converted to Christianity by a stag with a cross between his antlers while Hubert was hunting on Good Friday. The saint converted to Christianity instantly and became patron saint of hunting, though it could be argued he is also an antihunting saint. He died in 727 CE.

On November 3, St Hubert's Day, huntsmen in red jackets play a fanfare on hunting horns outside churches and cathedrals in France, (including

Amiens Cathedral), before going in to celebrate the Mass. St Hubert is a popular saint in modern Scandinavia.

BULL GODS

The most famous mythological semideity bull was the Minotaur, half-bull and half-man, who was kept in a labyrinth, beneath the palace of King Minos at Knossos in Crete. Greek myth recounts that the Minotaur was created when the Sea god Poseidon enchanted Pasiphaë, queen of Crete, to mate with the snow white bull he sent to her husband, King Minos. King Minos had angered Poseidon by refusing to sacrifice the white bull.

Minos, who was at the time very powerful, demanded that seven Athenian youths and seven maidens, drawn by lots, be sent every ninth year to be eaten by the Minotaur. Theseus, son of the Greek king Aegeus, offered to go as one of the sacrifices to try to kill the Minotaur. Ariadne, daughter of Minos, fell in love with Theseus and helped him get out of the labyrinth. She gave him a ball of thread, allowing him to retrace his path. Theseus killed the Minotaur and, according to myth, led the other Athenians unharmed back out of the labyrinth.

It has been suggested that the bull was actually a warrior priest with a bull headdress or mask who was part of a goddess cult where the bull represented the male god principle.

It was not until 1900 that British archaeologist Arthur Evans unearthed the huge palace at Knossos on Crete. He found evidence of a bull-worshipping cult and murals depicting the fantastic activities of bull dancers trained in the art of bull dancing and wrestling, a ritual form connected with bull ceremonies, culminating perhaps in the annual sacrifice of a bull to the goddess.[8]

The complexity of the layout of the palace—actually a number of palace buildings that had been built on each other over the centuries—would have made possible the construction of a labyrinth beneath the palace. Evans concluded that this labyrinth was probably connected with bull and goddess worship rather than imprisoning a monster. But some archaeologists argue that the labyrinth may simply have been a reference to the warren of passages on different levels.

If the Minotaur myth refers to the bull-dancing cult, the victory of Theseus over the Minotaur could symbolize the overthrowing of Minoan Crete by invaders from the mainland and the replacement of goddess/bull-worshipping culture with the worship of Zeus, the Greek Sky god in the region.

Certainly, the seven-coil labyrinth design appeared on Minoan coins and seals around 1500 BCE. In the Mediterranean area, earth tremors were said in folklore to be the Bull god roaring beneath the ground.

6

GOAT GODS

The greatest of the Goat gods that, along with the Horned Cernunnos, contributed to images of the Christian devil was Pan. Pan was the Ancient Greek herdsman's god of forests, flocks, and fields. He was portrayed as half-goat, with the horns, legs, and feet of a goat. Too wild to be allowed on Mount Olympus with the other deities, he roamed the groves of Arcadia, playing his magical pipes and protecting the herds. Sometimes considered to predate the Olympian gods, he was said to have given Artemis her hunting dogs.

The Greek satyrs, horned semideities or nature spirits who also followed the wilder Greek gods Bacchus and Dionysus, were associated with Pan and were described as having the body, arms, and sex organs of a man, combined with slanted eyes, flat noses, pointed ears, cloven hooves, the horns and tails of goats, and bodies that were covered with coarse hairs. They were said to love music, dancing, women and wood nymphs, and wine and so symbolized instinctive behavior at its worst, a horror to the civilized Greek world. The satyrs were considered disruptive, scattering herds of grazing sheep, causing horses to bolt, and terrifying travelers.

Saint Jerome wrote an account of St Anthony the Abbot meeting St Paul the apostle in the desert, in the *Life of Paulus the Hermit*. This was written in the year 374 or 375 CE during Jerome's stay in the desert of Syria. Jerome describes how Anthony at ninety, while walking through the desert, met first the mythical hippocentaur, a half horse–half man. Then in a small rocky valley, shut in on all sides, he saw a satyr with a hooked snout, horned forehead, and extremities like a goat's feet. These creatures apparently submitted to the saint, and so it may be that the experience was not actual but symbolic of Christianity's dominance over the pagan gods. However, it does show that belief in such creatures existed at the time Jerome was writing.[9]

ANCIENT EGYPTIAN ANIMAL DEITIES

A great deal of knowledge has been transmitted from Ancient Egypt, both as sacred texts and artifacts, sometimes preserved in the sand for thousands of years. A number of American universities have rich collections of Egyptian artifacts and statues, including the Smithsonian Institution in Washington, D.C., Boston Museum of Fine Art, the Metropolitan Museum of Art in New York, the Harvard University Fogg Art Museum, Yale University's Art Gallery, and the University of California–Berkeley's Robert H. Lowrie Museum of Anthropology.

However, I would recommend a visit to Egypt itself. The Museum in Cairo is said to take nine months to see everything, and I found I was falling over precious artifacts that show the animal-headed deities. You can also see their statues in situ in the ruined temples at Luxor and Karnak. As mentioned in the Introduction, each deity had its own sacred animal, and live animals of this species were kept in the appropriate temples. One of these living creatures was believed to be home of the *Ka*, part of the soul essence of the deity. It was treated as royalty. One example is the Bull of Apis, who lived a pampered existence as a manifestation of the creator god Ptah on earth. When this creature died, another chosen bull would become the shelter of the god's soul. The apparent divinatory powers of the Bull of Apis are described in Chapter 9.

Some animal and bird mummies received special treatment. It may be that this particular creature was one who had demonstrated special signs of being possessed by the divinity. The animal mummies were buried in bronze or even gold boxes which carried the animals' images on them. For example, in the case of a cat which was believed to house the life of the Ka of Bastet the cat-headed goddess, the mummy was adorned with jewelry such as the ankh, a scarab, and gold earrings. The image of the totem deity appears on the coffin. There is a fine collection of cats with gold earrings and ornate coffins in the Ashmolean Museum in Oxford, England.

In Ancient Egypt it was also believed that after death a human spirit could assume the form of animals or birds and temporarily return to this world. A number of chapters in *The Book of the Dead* gave formulas whereby the deceased's spirit, the *ba*, could transform itself into a hawk of gold, a heron, a swallow, or a serpent. For example, in the Wallis Budge translation of *The Book of the Dead*, the following formula was given in the papyrus of the scribe Ani so that his deceased hawk-headed spirit or *ba* might recite them and assume the form of a swallow at will:

> The Osiris Ani, whose word is truth, saith: "I am a swallow, I am a swallow. Hail, O ye gods whose odour is sweet—I am like Horus (the falcon headed god),—Let me pass on and deliver my message—although my body lieth a mummy in the tomb." [10]

POWER ANIMALS AND THEIR DEITIES

Egyptian sacred animals and birds embodied the most positive characteristics of their ruling gods and goddesses. So central to worship were the animal symbols of power that many, though not all, deities were portrayed either in animal form or with an animal head or headdress. Indeed, animal associations were a good way for ordinary people to understand the different characteristics of the deities. Whether through a creature they feared but admired, such as the desert lioness Sekhmet, lion-headed goddess not only of fire, battle, and vengeance but also of medicine and healing, or one who was famed for nurturing mothering qualities such as the cow imagery of, for example, Hathor, a Mother goddess form, all were a basis of learning. Of course, no one actually worshipped Hathor as a cow. Rather, it was a strong metaphor to express that just as a cow provided milk for its calf and for humans so Hathor would eternally suckle humankind in death as well as life.

Some theorists believe that animals mirror or reflect the untainted forms of valuable human qualities and strengths because in Egyptian creation myths, animals were made from the primal material from which humankind came in a more evolved form. Indeed, the original deities of Hermopolis, an early creation myth from before 3100 BCE, were themselves depicted as frogs and serpents.[11]

ANCIENT EGYPTIAN DEITIES AND THEIR ANIMAL ASSOCIATIONS

Hathor was represented as a cow or as a goddess with cow horns and the sun disk between them, showing her solar and lunar links. She was called the Mother of All. Hathor was especially associated with the rising sun.

Most spectacularly, she is shown as a large cow covered with lotus flowers or ankhs in the tomb of King Amenhotep III. His image is painted black, the color of death, and he is depicted in the position of prayer under the head of the cow. There is also a small statue of him in red, the color of the living, that is, as a reborn king, drinking from the teat of the cow. This suggests that the goddess had adopted him as her chid. These statues are from Deir el Bahar in the eighteenth dynasty (after 1570 BCE) and can be seen in the Cairo Museum.

Hathor continued the role of mother cow in the afterlife. Many wealthy tombs contained a golden cow to suckle the owners when they were reborn. At Memphis, near Cairo, and in other temples her human head with cow ears emerges from a pillar.

One of the most fearsome and yet protective creatures was the jackal, a predatory wild dog who came from the desert in search of prey and who consumed the bodies of those who had died in the desert, animal or human. They were often seen around the tombs in the Valley of the Kings and Queens and their nocturnal howling was interpreted as protection of the deceased. Some jackals were tamed and became fierce guard dogs. Who more protective to guard against hostile forces in this world and the next but Anubis, the black jackal-headed god?

Anubis, the alter ego of Horus the Sky god and whose father, Osiris, he shared with Horus, guided the deceased through the underworld, having embalmed and prepared their bodies as he did for his murdered father. Black and gold statues of Anubis as a jackal were set to guard the tombs of kings and queens and the wealthy from grave robbers. Tuamutef, the jackal-headed son of Horus, protected the lungs in his canopic jar. Sacred jackals were kept at Anubis shrines. A more sensationalized reworked myth from a recent film *Return of the Mummy* showed that as a jackal Anubis hunted down the unrighteous, the jackal-headed warriors of Anubis were sent magically against powerful enemies. No doubt this will soon enter future folklore.

ANIMAL GODS IN THE AMERICAS AND AFRICA

Whereas evidence from papyri, statues, and spells recorded on tomb walls document myths from Ancient Egypt and detailed written Greek myths exist, few Native American myths were written down before the late nineteenth century and African myths were also traditionally oral. Therefore, there are various versions of myths that appear among different nations. With the exception of Anansi the Spider trickster of Africa, this chapter primarily focuses on Native North American goddess forms associated with animals.

WHITE BUFFALO WOMAN

The character of White Buffalo Woman comes mainly from the myths of the Plains tribes, especially the Lakota, and Sioux. The following is a generic version that includes the main points from a number of myths. It tells that before the Lakota Sioux people had horses to hunt buffalo, there was little food. All the different tribespeople met together to discuss the crisis and two young warriors left the camp in the early morning to find meat. At last, as the sun rose, they could see in the distance a brilliant white light that gradually became a white buffalo calf. As the calf came closer to them, it turned into a beautiful woman dressed in white.

One of the men was lustful and when he reached out to touch her, was instantly reduced to a pile of bones with snakes in them. White Buffalo Woman told the remaining warrior that she had come with a message from the Buffalo nation (the archetypal spirit buffalo and the Clan Leader who released the animals for hunting). She ordered that a special tipi be prepared for her, large enough so everyone could enter and said she would return in four days.

After four days as promised, White Buffalo Woman materialized as a cloud from the sky among the assembled people. A white buffalo calf stepped out from it. It rolled over and became White Buffalo Woman, who opened a sacred bundle and took out a pipe. She explained how the adornments on it represented all the children of Mother Earth and she described how smoking the pipe when meeting together while making decisions would bring peace and wisdom. She also brought the women corn and wild turnip, taught them how to make a hearth fire, and to cook. White Buffalo Woman also taught the people seven sacred ceremonies, including the Sweat Lodge purification ceremony, the Sun dance, and the Making of Relations ritual, in which a family adopted as their own the orphaned children of men and women who had died. She promised that she would return. The sign of this return would be the birth of four white buffalo calves. These calves would herald peace and harmony in the world. As she left walking toward the setting sun, she sat down in the prairie and rolled over four times. First she became a black buffalo; then brown, then a red one, and finally, a white female buffalo calf. After she had gone the buffalo herds returned to give the people enough food, skins for clothing and their tipis, and bones for tools.[12]

Joseph Chasing Horse, traditional leader of the Lakota Nation, dates the appearance of White Buffalo Woman as two thousand years ago. The first white buffalo calf was born in 1933 in Colorado, the second in 1994 in Janesville, Wisconsin, and a third on May 9, 1996, a silvery white buffalo calf on the Pine Ridge reservation of South Dakota. A fourth calf was born at the end of 1996 but did not survive. Another calf was looked for. These calves are seen as a sign that the old ways will be restored and that peace may return among all nations.

SPIDER DEITIES

The most powerful Spider goddess in mythology is the Native North American Grandmother Spider Woman. She is a Holy Woman/creatrix goddess found in a number of indigenous spiritualities including the Navaho, Hopi, and Pueblo Indian mythology. In some myths she wove the web of the world and peopled it with figures from the earth made from four different clays: red, white, yellow, and brown. Her creation was very gentle. In Hopi legend, Spider Woman and Tawa the Sun deity, created the earth between them and brought forth life with magical songs, from the thoughts and images in Tawa's mind. From these animated thoughts, Spider Women fashioned from clay wonderful animals, birds and finally man and woman. Man and woman were given life as Spider Woman cradled them in her arms and wrapped them in a soft blanket, while Tawa breathed life into them. Grandmother Spider then led her creation from the womb of the earth into the light in a symbolic act of childbirth, an act repeated in every human and animal birth. Spider Woman chose women to be her representatives as the homemakers and ordered that the family name and property would descend through them to avoid quarrels.

After creation, the sun remained in the sky, but Grandmother Spider has returned many times to teach and guide in many guises: as the Navajo White Shell or Changing Woman who controlled the seasons, as Selu the Cherokee Corn Woman who allowed herself to be dragged along the ground to fertilize the soil with corn, and even as White Buffalo Woman.

Grandmother Spider Woman taught many crafts: how to cultivate food, the power of herbs, how to smudge, ways of healing, and how to weave dream catchers to stop children having nightmares. In Cherokee myth she brought the sun and fire, pottery, and weaving whereas among the Hopi she is said to have created the moon and gave and took life with the cutting of a thread in her web.[13]

THE SPIDER MAN IN AFRICA

In the West African tradition, Anansi the spider man, regarded as a semi-deity, could climb higher than any other mortal. He ascended (or in some versions of the myth he wove) the celestial web into the heavens. He returned to earth after meeting Nyambe, the supreme Sky god. By performing various tasks such as catching the jaguar with teeth like daggers and the hornets that sting like fire using ingenuity, Anansi was rewarded with the gift of stories for humans. In return Anansi gave Nyambe the sun. Anansi serves the role of a trickster who stirs up change and prevents stagnation and who encourages ingenuity and enterprise to find a way round problems. He also acts as a helper on earth for Nyambe, sometimes called his father, and sends rain to prevent drought or destructive fires. Anansi taught the knowledge of farming. He is described in various legends either as a spider or human with long legs and great dexterity. The origin of his stories that spread throughout Africa and as far as the West Indies may have originated from Ghana. In various myths Anansi whose name means spider, was also credited with creating the sun, the moon, and the stars. The vital trickster role is associated with the fox and coyote in the European and Native North American tradition.[14]

THE AZTEC ANIMAL DEITIES

Animals, birds, and even insects were an essential part of worship in the world of the Aztecs. According to their oral mythology, the Aztecs came from the island of Aztlan, the land of the god Huitzilopochtli who was called the Humming Bird of the South. The Aztecs were nomadic for two centuries, but were promised by Huitzilopochtli that they would find their homeland where they saw an eagle perched on a nopal, a prickly pear cactus that was growing out of stone. This happened and Tenochtitlan (the place of the stone cactus) was founded in 1325. The first temple was built here (now Mexico City), in honor of Huitzilopochtli.

The only known representation of the god was made in greenstone around 1300. It was three-dimensional and identifiable by a hummingbird costume and serpent head on his left foot. I saw it in 2004 in an Aztec exhibition at the Royal Academy of Arts, London.

The most powerful predator of the region, the jaguar, was associated with the omnipotent Aztec god Tezcatlipoca and was the form the sun took on its nightly journey through the underworld Mictlan, to fight off the dangers so it might emerge triumphant the next morning. The eagle was the sun by day. Each night the jaguar lost part of his flesh in the nocturnal battle.

Black jaguars live in the north and central areas of the South American continent, especially in the forests around the Amazon and of Central and Southern Mexico. Some in the deeply forested regions have developed dark coats through which the spots faintly shine.

The Mayans, who occupied southern Guatemala and Mexico's Yucatán Peninsula from about AD 200 until AD 900, worshipped the war god Cit-Chac-Coh, whose name means *twin of the red lion*. This refers to the cougar or mountain lion that is similar to the jaguar. He was very protective and guarded villages from harm, and he was called the Earth Father, Lord of all the forest. His jaguarlike roar formed, it was said, the roar of thunder.

Throughout South America in folklore it is still told that the jaguar taught humans to use bows and arrows and gave them cooked meat from his own fire. But men stole the fire and killed his wife, and so the jaguar lives alone in deep forests and is now their enemy.

Tiny creatures were also part of Aztec spirituality. The mysterious moth, the scorpion, and the centipede struck terror and reverence among the fierce Aztec warriors. The Aztecs dedicated altars to these feared creatures on which their images were carved and where they made offerings to propitiate them. The night owl, the scorpion, the bat, and the spider were associated with the Aztec Mictlantecutl, Lord of Death, and so might not be killed.[15]

BIBLIOGRAPHY

1. Alexander, H. B. *Native American Mythology.* London and New York: Dover Publications, 2005.
2. Baring, A., and J. Cashford. *The Myth of the Goddess: Evolution of an Image.* London, Arkana: Penguin, 1993.
3. Balter, M. *The Goddess and the Bull: Çatalhöyük, An Archaeological Journey to the Dawn of Civilization.* New York: Free Press, 2004.
4. Higgins, R. *Minoan and Mycenaean Art.* London: Thames and Hudson, 1997.
5. Ellis, B. P. *Celtic Myths and Legends.* New York: Caroll and Graf, 2002.
6. Matthews, J. *The Song of Taliesin: Stories and Poems.* Illustrated by L. Stuart. London: HarperCollins, Mandala, 1991.
7. Sturluson, S. *The Prose Eddas.* London: Penguin Classics, 2005.
8. See note 4 above.
9. Cardinal Farley, J., Archbishop of New York. *The Catholic Encyclopaedia,* Vol. XI. New York: Robert Appleton Company, 1911.
10. Budge, E. A. Wallis. *The Book of the Dead.* New York: Gramercy Books, 1995.
11. Weidermann, A. *Religion of the Ancient Egyptians.* Boston: Adamant Media Corporation, 2001.
12. Drysdale, V. L., and J. E. Brown, eds. *The Gift of the Sacred Pipe.* Norman: University of Oklahoma Press, 1995.
13. See note 1 above.
14. Parrinder, G. *African Mythology.* New York: Bedrick Books, 1991.
15. Miller, M., and K. Taube. *The Gods and Symbols of Ancient Mexico and the Maya.* London: Thames and Hudson, 1993.

CHAPTER 2

Serpents in Myth

A number of myths about animals and other creatures are rooted in the observation of nature. Snakes hold a certain fascination for humans. They have the ability to shed their skins and seemingly emerge reborn, so they are identified with the symbol of regeneration and immortality. The snake or serpent, as it is usually called in mythology, was also associated with the idea of giving birth and mothers. The serpent image, therefore, was considered as magically endowing both living and deceased with powers of rebirth and fertility.

This image of a snake can be seen at the Serpent Mound, Ohio, east of Cincinnati. The Serpent Mound, stretching a quarter-mile long, is the largest American coiling snake effigy. The head of the serpent is aligned to the summer solstice sunset. The bottom of the Serpent Mound is made of clay and rock and the soil covering the rock is four to five feet high. The huge undulating snake is either interpreted as a serpent with its mouth open, about to swallow an egg, or as a horned serpent, a symbol popular in Native North American mythology.

The site was probably created and used for worship by the Adena Indians, somewhere between 800 BCE and 100 CE. Some researchers date the snake effigy to the tenth century CE and believe it may have replaced an earlier one.

Some other serpent images, carved on stone tablets, have been excavated from nearby burial mounds.[1]

THE DANGEROUS SERPENT

Snakes can poison humans and animals and so can be life takers. Snake goddesses hold the dual role of a protector and a destroyer. This role of Serpent goddesses is described in myths such as that of the Ancient Egyptian Cobra goddess Uadjet, who was both protector and destroyer of the pharaoh, and spit poison at anybody who would do the pharaoh harm. She was also said to administer the death sting when his appointed time on earth was over.[2]

Of course pharaohs died for a lot of reasons but snakebite-related deaths were relatively common among the Ancient Egyptian population. In olden times, this may have appeared a more dramatic and acceptable way for a pharaoh to leave earth, rather than his getting older and weaker or dying of some common disease, because he was considered the earthly representative and manifestation of Horus the Sky god.

SERPENTS AND EVIL

Over the millennia the less positive aspects of the serpent as a tempter or temptress toward evil was more prevalent in lands influenced by Judaism and Christianity with the Garden of Eden serpent story. This again has some physiological basis, for a snake's forked tongue darts in and out of its mouth and a poisonous snake could spit venom at anybody that could be equated with the lying or spiteful words of a human. Because snakes do not have eyelids it stares fixedly before striking, making the prey feel uncomfortable. However, in indigenous cultures, the Serpent Father or Mother is still regarded with affection and respect. For example, according to myth, the Australian Aboriginal Rainbow serpent, who can be male or female, brings the life-giving rains.[3]

THE COBRA GODDESSES OF ANCIENT EGYPT

The cobra or Uraeus is still one of the most feared snakes in Egypt because of its winglike hood outstretched to strike. Uadjet, Buto, or Wadjet was the Cobra goddess of the prehistoric kingdom of Buto and was considered a goddess of the underworld, justice, and truth. Because many snakes live in underground holes, they were equated with death and the underworld. Uadjet's erect cobra symbol, called the Uraeus, became that of Lower Egypt (the northern area of Egypt that ended at the Nile Delta and northernmost coast). Uraeus formed one of the two main power symbols of the pharaoh, and it was worn on the headdress of the pharaoh to offer protection against enemies. Another symbol was the Vulture goddess Nekhbet.

Uadjet was called the mother of the sun and the moon. She was linked with the eye of Ra, the Sun god, fixing the enemies of the pharaoh with her fiery eyes and then spitting poison into their faces. She was also called the Lady of the Heavens and associated with the heat of the sun because cobras were most often seen sunning themselves in the heat.

Wings were protective images among the goddesses of Ancient Egypt. Uadjet was usually pictured as winged and crowned, rising to strike. She was sometimes shown as a snake with a human face. In myth she protected the infant Horus among the reeds while his mother Isis was looking for the body of her husband, Osiris, who had been murdered.

Another important Cobra goddess in Egypt was Renenet, a fertility goddess who was sometimes depicted as nursing children and as protector of pharaoh. Like Uadjet she too administered the death sting to the pharaoh when his time on earth was over. According to myth, she ended the life of Cleopatra, the last of the Ptolemy (Greco-Egyptian) rulers of Egypt. Cleopatra committed suicide by allowing the sacred Uraeus snake in the form of the asp to administer the death sting in 27 BCE. Renenet was depicted as a winged, crowned cobra or in the form of a snake with the face of a woman.

THE HINDU SERPENT GODDESSES

In India the Serpent goddess is fierce but revered and associated with fertility: as the creating mother and with rebirth. Ananta, goddess of infinite time, is a creator Serpent goddess. Brahma, the Hindu Creator god, and the other gods were believed to sleep between their incarnations on her coils. She was identified with the Serpent goddess Kundalini who, in Far Eastern spiritual philosophy that has become popular in the Westernized world, is said to symbolize the life force that resides like a coiled serpent at the base of the human spine.

According to myth, Khadru, the Serpent goddess, gave birth to all the cobras in India as well as the nagas, the divine water snakes, which are discussed in Chapter 8. It is told that the wise man Kasyapa had two wives, Kadru and Vinata. Each wife was granted a wish. Kadru asked for many children. In contrast Vinata asked for few but powerful offspring. Each got her wish. Kadru laid 1,000 eggs, which hatched into nagas—the divine water snakes. Vinata laid two eggs, one of which became Garuda, king of the birds, who is discussed in Chapter 4.

Manasa, a Serpent goddess identified with the moon, reflects the dual role of preserver and destroyer. She is very popular in Bihar and West Bengal, India. She inflicts bites on those who offend her but guards her devotees against poisonous snakes. She is usually depicted with a child on her knee, who is protected by the hood of the cobra.[4]

THE RAINBOW SERPENT IN ABORIGINAL AUSTRALIAN CULTURE

The Rainbow serpent creation stories are popular throughout Australia, especially in Arnhem Land in the Northern Territory around Darwin. In Arnhem Land, there are a number of representations of the Rainbow serpent in rock art. The first rock art was created before 6000 BCE. The art is being revived now.[5] The male Rainbow serpent is called Ngalyod by the Kunwinjku people in western Arnhem Land. Yingarna, the female Rainbow serpent, is the mother and creates all life—people, plants, and animals, while Ngalyod is the transformer of the land. Storms, drought, and floods are seen as punishment from the Rainbow serpent/s for those who defy laws and codes of conduct.

THE RAINBOW SERPENT AS MOTHER

In Australian aboriginal culture, the female Rainbow snake is sometimes called the Mother of All. Uluru (Ayers Rock), the vast mass of red rock in the Northern Territory which is the largest monolith (single stone) in the world, is called the navel of the earth. The serpent-shaped umbilical cord of Fertility Mothers has contributed to the legends of Uluru.

Eingana is another Rainbow Serpent goddess whose sacred animal is the kangaroo. According to myth, Eingana had no means of giving birth. Her children grew inside her, but she was unable to deliver them. The god Barraiya pitied her pain and threw a spear at her, enabling life to pour forth. She also brings death to her children, holding the umbilical cord that is joined to each creature. When she breaks it, the person dies. According to myth, if she herself died, existence would end.

In another version of the same legend, Eingana asked the Kingfishers, one of the first tribes to come forth from her womb, to shoot an arrow at her head. This allowed the rest of creation to be freed. Her rainbow scales flew into the air to become the colorful lorikeet tribe and the reflection of the colors became the rainbow in the sky.

THE MALE RAINBOW SERPENT CREATION MYTHS

The male Rainbow snake is frequently called Jarapiri in northern and central Australia. According to some myths, the Rainbow snake battles for water with the sun on behalf of the people. In other accounts, the water in the form of the monsoons results from the coming together of Earth Mother Kunapipi with the Rainbow serpent. An image of the Jarapiri serpent with humans on its back may be seen in a rock painting near Djukuita Cave, Ngama, central Australia. Aboriginal guardians still repaint the image to ensure that his power continues to bring water.[6]

The black-headed python is also sometimes associated with the Rainbow serpent. In one version from the Northern Territories that establishes a link between them, Jarapiri came from the sea or underground and gave form to the land. In this version, Jarapiri or Kunukban is given a challenger or trickster role. Jarapiri wanted to capture Ekarlarwan, another name for Balame, the All Father or supreme creator, to obtain from him the secrets of the people, law, ritual, and ceremony. But instead Jarapiri chased after Ekarlarwan's dog, Djaringin, who acted as a decoy. The dog made a winding track all over the country, and as the snake followed him its slitherings and turnings created landmarks, rivers, and waterholes.

The Rainbow snake finally obtained the secrets and then travelled throughout the continent, teaching the law and creating landmarks as he went. The angry Ekarlarwan sent the butcher bird Jolpol after the Rainbow snake. Jolpol used trickery to push Jarapiri's head into a campfire to burn him to death. However, the storm bird Kurukura, who was Jarapiri's protector, attacked the butcher bird and drove him away.

The storm bird was burned all over by fire, Jolpol was partially burned, and the Rainbow snake received burns to his head. This was taken as a sign that evil and suffering had now entered the world. Because of this, Aboriginal people say, the storm bird is black, the butcher bird is black and white, and there is a black-headed python.

THE SERPENT GODDESS IN CLASSICAL MYTH— THE JOURNEY FROM POWERFUL MOTHER TO EVIL TEMPTRESS

THE MINOAN SNAKE GODDESSES

A Neolithic seated terracotta Snake goddess dating from 4500 BCE was found in Kata Ierapetra, Crete. The 14.5 cm-high figurine has the body of a snake. There is a great deal of controversy about the significance of the Minoan Cretan Snake goddess statues dating from around 1600 BCE that were excavated by Sir Arthur Evans in 1900. Two goddess figurines, with bell-shaped flounced skirts of the late Minoan period, are made of faience and were found in a stone pit beneath the ruins of the palace at Knossos. The first figurine holds a snake between her hands, and its body draped round her shoulders and back. Two other snakes coil round her waist and arms, and one of them becomes part of her headdress. She has bare breasts. The other figure holds a snake in each hand. It was suggested by Sir Arthur Evans that the goddess figures represented a protective household deity.

It may be that small nonvenomous snakes were welcomed in Minoan homes and temples as luck bringers and for the protection of the goddess. This is not known from archaeological finds in Crete, but certainly the practice of luck-bringing domestic snakes is found in another part of the world— Lithuania. Aspelenie, the goddess who ruled the corner of the house behind the stove, had as her special animal a little ringed snake. The snakes were encouraged indoors because it was believed if the protective snake left your home, your luck would end.

The wisdom of the snake and its positive and magical role in Crete is suggested in the Greek legend about Glaukos, the son of King Minos and Queen Pasiphae. According to the story, as a small boy, Glaukos was drowned. A serpent was discovered crawling near the corpse, and it was killed by the wise Greek seer Polyeidos. Another serpent brought the first serpent back to life by carrying a seemingly miraculous herb and setting it on top of the dead serpent's body. Polyeidos set the same herb on the drowned boy (Glaukos), and he too was restored to life.

MEDUSA AND THE SNAKE WOMEN OF ANCIENT GREECE

Athene or Athena, the Ancient Greek goddess of wisdom, is sometimes linked, like Artemis the huntress goddess, with the Serpent goddesses of the Minoans. This is represented on the snake-wreathed figurines of Athena.

Athene carried on her shield the image of the serpent-haired Medusa. Medusa was killed by Perseus, apparently at Athene's request. It is recorded that sacred nonvenomous snakes were kept in temples in Athens. This forms an intriguing story and cannot be proved any more than any other myth can be linked to fact. However, early Greek myth tells us Medusa was not always a hideous monster as described by the patriarchal Greeks. It has been suggested that Medusa was once part of the Libyan Triple goddesses (sometimes called Ath-enna—associated with the Egyptian Neith), the primal goddess of fate and weaving whose name meant *I am sprung from myself*. It is said that Medusa, in this earlier form, was Athene's true mother because another name for Medusa was Metis.

Metis was the goddess Zeus swallowed so that he himself could give birth to their daughter Athene through his head (a male virgin birth, when Hephaestus the blacksmith god split Zeus' head open to release the child).

Athene, according to myth, was born from Zeus's head fully grown and armed for war. She became the ideal Greek goddess: impartial; patroness of art, science, literature, and learning; symbol of wisdom, justice, and intelligence; patroness of the city of Athens; a creature without emotion or weaknesses.

Ancient Greek art depicted Medusa and her sisters the Gorgons as serpentine monsters, born of Echidna, half-woman, half-serpent. The Roman poet Ovid (43 BCE–18 CE) in his *Metamorphoses*, described how Medusa was once a beautiful woman but was raped by Poseidon in Athene's temple.[7] In revenge against Medusa, not Poseidon, for the defilement of the temple, Athene changed Medusa's golden hair into hideous yellow serpents. Medusa became so ugly that it was said any man who looked at her would be turned to stone.

The hero Perseus killed Medusa while she slept, by looking at her reflection in a mirror, and from her blood sprang the magical winged horse Pegasus. In some versions of the myth Medusa had two sisters, Stheno and Euryale. All three sisters had snakes as hair.

The Greek Scylla, which is discussed in Chapter 8, had twelve snakelike heads. According to some legends, Scylla was once a beautiful sea maiden, also seduced by Poseidon.

THE SERPENT AS EVIL IN JUDAISM AND CHRISTIANITY

A serpent is associated with the Tree of Knowledge in the books of Genesis of the Old Testament, the Torah, and in most sacred books in Judaism. It was the serpent who is blamed for tempting Eve to eat the fruit of the Tree of Knowledge of Good and Evil and so brought evil into the world. As his punishment the serpent was said to henceforward crawl on his belly and be hated by humans.

> And the Lord God said unto the serpent, Because thou hast done this, thou art cursed above all cattle, and above every beast of the field; upon thy belly shalt thou go, and dust shalt thou eat all the days of thy life.

> "He (man) shall bruise your head, and ye shall bruise his heel." Genesis 3: 14 and 15[8]

In Christianity, the Church fathers' writing in the fourth and fifth centuries CE identify the serpent with Satan and women as daughters of Eve. It also identifies the serpent as a temptress of men. Indeed this doctrine of original sin and the culpability of Eve was enshrined by the Church Father St Augustine (354–430 CE) who referred to Eve as the Devil's gateway.

According to Hebrew Rabbinical lore, the serpent that tempted Eve was Lilith, Adam's first wife, motivated by jealousy and her daughters, the Lilim. The Lilim were regarded as half-serpent and like their mother as temptresses of virtuous men.

LILITH AND THE LILIM

The biblical Lilith is conspicuous by her absence and her negative connotations as seductress of innocent males and slayer of children. The Lilith legend is derived from Hebrew folklore that was recorded during the Middle Ages from an earlier oral tradition.

A more female-friendly explanation is that Lilith was a version of the ancient Earth Mother defeated by the Sky Father Yahweh and thus demonized. According to this theory, Adam represented the nomadic herdsmen who invaded the matriarchal agricultural lands and met resistance.

The belief that Lilith gave birth to a hundred children a day, originally with Adam and later by consorting with demons, came from the Alphabet of Ben Sira, written between the sixth and the eleventh centuries CE. Lilith is associated both as the temptress of virtuous men and slayer of infants. It is said that she refused to submit to Adam's will, specifically sexually, by refusing to lie beneath him. All manner of abominations were thereafter attributed to her.

In the story, Lilith fled to a cave near the Red Sea, where she had sex with the Archangel Samael, the Dark Angel, and with unspecified demons. Three angels were sent to force Lilith back to Adam: Senoi, Sansenoi, and Sammangel. She was told that unless she obeyed, 100 of her offspring would die every day. Lilith responded with the counterthreat that she would slay a 100 of Adam's children every day. The image of Lilith as slayer of young children comes from this story.

Lilith is portrayed in the Sistine Chapel, Rome in Michelangelo's *Temptation and Fall* as the serpent in the Garden of Eden. In the painting, Lilith's tail is coiled round the Tree of Knowledge and has a beautiful female face. There is another example of Lilith as the serpent carved in stone over the west façade of Notre Dame Cathedral in Paris, dated around 1210 CE.[9]

In later times Lilith was linked, in myth and literature, with another serpentine temptress. In myths of Ancient Greece, Lilith was identified with Lamia who had the head and body of a woman, and a serpent's tail for the lower half of her body. Lamia was also associated with the daughters of Lilith and like Lilith herself, these Lamiae were said to steal and eat children and tempt and destroy virtuous men. These Lamiae could assume lovely mortal form but would drain their lover of his life force. English poet John Keats (1795–1821) wrote a poem *Lamia*, in which a young and innocent man Lycius is seduced by the beautiful Lamia. She is unmasked at their wedding feast by the penetrating stare of his old teacher Apollonius because, as a snake woman, she had no eyelids and so could not turn away.

> "Fool! Fool!" repeated he,
> "from every ill
> Of life have I preserv'd thee to this day,
> And shall I see thee made a serpent's prey?
> —Then with a frightful scream she vanished:
> And Lycius' arms were empty of delight,
> As were his limbs of life, from that same night."[10]

Similar seducing serpents are found in the folklore of the New Hebrides Islands; here they are called the *Mae* and assume many forms, including that of local village maidens, wreathed in flowers. The theme of the sexually insatiable female serpent and the helpless male is one that recurs in many forms throughout patriarchal mythology, philosophy, and religious writing.

THE EVIL SERPENT IN CELTIC CHRISTIANITY

One of the most fascinating appearances of the evil serpent found in folklore surround the early Christian saints, St Patrick of Ireland and St Hilda of Whitby in northeast England. They both cast out snakes, a variation on the dragon-slaying myth that may be a way of describing overthrowing the pagan practitioners. In Ireland, in the fifth century CE there was a known serpent cult, dedicated to an ancient Sun god Cromm Cruaich, the Crooked or Bent One of the Mound.

St Patrick, according to legend, stood on a hill and drove all the serpents into the sea with his wooden staff, maybe the priests of the old god or the Celtic Druidesses whom he regarded as particularly evil. Patrick was helped by showers of meteorites that coincidentally arrived at the right time during preaching in asserting his divine authority.[11]

St Hilda in 657 CE founded a double monastery for monks and nuns at Streaneshalch, near Whitby in northeast England. The land was, according to legend, infested with snakes which she turned into stone and cast over the cliff. When they fell on Whitby Beach as ammonites, their heads broke off. Souvenir ammonites with painted snake heads are still sold in the area to tourists. Of course it may be that St Hilda had practical rather than religious reasons for her grandiose gesture if the land really was snake infested and so unsuitable for building. However, the Celtic saints were very good at providing crowd satisfaction to win over a largely indifferent population.

THE SURVIVAL OF THE SNAKE IN CHRISTIANITY

The early fifth century Irish and Welsh St Bridget (or Bride) who took over the role of the pre-Christian goddess Brighid, like the Pagan goddess, was associated with snakes. The serpent was one of her sacred creatures. St Brigit's snake comes out of its hibernation mound on February 2, the saint's day that coincided with the early spring festival of the Celtic goddess of the same name. February 2 is shared by Groundhog Day in America. The serpent coming from its hole on this day seems linked with the coming of spring. But this is a little early for actual snakes to emerge from hibernation in Celtic Western European lands such as France, Ireland, Scotland, and Wales. Maybe for this reason a clay snake was used, and it was smashed to signify the shedding of the snakeskin and rebirth, a seemingly strange action in connection with the verse's promise not to harm the snake.

Today is the Day of Bride,
The serpent shall come from the hole,
I will not molest the serpent,
Nor will the serpent molest me.

I first heard this rhyme when I used to spend time in southwest Wales around the Tenby area where there are links through the huge Neolithic burial at Pentre Ifan with pagan tradition. However, the rhyme is also sometimes changed to say, *"The Queen shall come from the mound"* presumably referring to a fairy queen/goddess as the queen of the springtime. It was believed in Ireland that fairies lived in the old burial mounds and the fairy king and queen, Finvarra and Oonagh, were linked with the ancient gods of Ireland, the Tuatha de Danaan, which means *the people of the mounds.*

THE HEALING SERPENT

The caduceus or healing staff of the Ancient Greek and Roman worlds, entwined with twin snakes, may be symbolizing the Tree of Life. It is still seen as a logo in modern medicine, along with the healing staff of Asclepius that has a single entwined snake. In 1902 the U.S. Army adopted the caduceus as its logo for the medical corps. However, the concept of the healing double serpentine staff, the true caduceus, may date back earlier than Greece to Ancient Babylon.

A green steatite vase, which can be seen in the Louvre Museum, Paris, was excavated from the ancient Mesopotamian city of Lagash. The vase contained an inscription dedicated to the Serpent god of healing and the underworld, Ningizzida.[12] In Sumerian, the language of old Babylon, his name means *lord of the good tree*. Ningizzida was said to be the ancestor of the semidivine Gilgamesh. Ningizzida, according to *The Epic of Gilgamesh* (dated around 2650 BCE), brought the plant of everlasting life from the depths of the sea. However, a serpent ate the plant as Gilgamesh slept and became immortal instead. On the vase is a figure of two entwined snakes on a rod, said to be a representation of Ningizzida, who protected the Tree of Life.

The twin serpent-healing staff or caduceus is, however, most associated with Hermes, the Greek god of medicine who assumed many of the attributes of the Ancient Egyptian god Thoth (whose myths were, in turn, influenced by the earlier Babylonian culture). The caduceus is often topped with wings, because Hermes is also the winged messenger, carrying messages between the underworld, earth, and heavens.

The single serpent round the rough wooden staff is the symbol of Asclepius, the healer demigod of Greece and Rome whose healing dream temples spread throughout the Roman Empire. This staff became equally popular as a symbol of healing the classical world. The snakes on both staffs symbolized healing as the god protecting deceased souls in the underworld, as the Babylonian entwined-Serpent god Ningizzida did.

Asclepius, the son of the god of light Apollo, and a mortal woman, Koronis, acquired his serpentine symbolism when Asclepius learned the secrets of overcoming death. He saw one serpent bring another dead serpent back to life with a magical herb. This has remarkable similarities to the Cretan Glaukos myth.

Although, Zeus killed Asclepius to prevent him from making the human race immortal, Asclepius became a god as compensation. For this reason nonvenomous snakes were encouraged in his healing temples.

Curiously the Gorgon sisters are sometimes shown as having belts or girdles on which the entwined caduceus is shown.

STRANGE SERPENTS FROM THE MEDIAEVAL BESTIARY

The concept of the bestiary appears several times in the book.[13] There are a number of bestiaries, collections of descriptions of fabulous real and imaginary animals, birds, and reptiles, some apparently seen by the philosophers and travelers of the Ancient world. The sources are Greek, Roman, Egyptian, Hebrew, and other Middle Eastern and North African chronicles. The bestiaries first appeared highly illustrated, in England and Western Europe during the twelfth century. The material for the bestiaries came partly from the Physiologus, a collection produced in Alexandria, Egypt, a great center for classical learning during the fourth century CE. Each of the creatures described was used to make a Christian moral point about how people should live. The Physiologus was written in Greek, probably in Alexandria, in about the fourth century. It consisted of forty-eight or forty-nine chapters about beasts, birds, and stones used as a vehicle to explain Christian dogma. However, material was added as people traveled farther into the Far East and creatures from Northern Europe were added. This suggested bestiary is very useful, but additional works can be found on line.

One of the most fascinating bestiary serpents that almost certainly never lived is the Amphisbaena. Its name in Ancient Greek means *going both ways*, because this serpent apparently had a head at both ends. It ate ants, but also was strangely called the mother of ants, perhaps a reference to the rebirth/skin-shedding theory, as it was giving ants the chance of rebirth. The original Amphisbaena in Greek myth was created from the blood of Medusa's head as Perseus flew over the Libyan Desert on the winged horse Pegasus, holding it. Its eyes were said to shine as bright as lamps, and unlike other snakes it would appear even in frost. It was the first to come out of hibernation, maybe a herald of spring like Bridget's snake.

But most famous of the serpents described in the bestiary is the Basilisk or Regulus. This fearsome and deadly beast was called the king of serpents because it had a white crest on its head. Quite small, only about six inches (15 cm) long, it was described as covered with white spots. Sometimes it is described as a cockerel with a serpent's tail, and indeed the Roman writer and naturalist Pliny the Elder (23–79 CE) believed it was hatched from a cockerel's egg (obviously a rarity).[14] It could, it was claimed, kill other serpents by its odor, humans if it looked into their eyes (like Medusa), and birds by projecting fire from its mouth. Only a weasel could kill it.

Natural ways of avoiding the basilisk's powers are suggested in the bestiary. If a person sees the basilisk before being seen, the basilisk will die. However, once seen, humans have a very short time to defend themselves by holding up a glass bottle so that the poison flowing from the basilisk's eyes can be caught and thrown back.

THE SERPENT'S EGG

The Serpent's egg or Aguinum appeared in Celtic myth as well as classical texts including the Roman Pliny and continued to fascinate people during the Middle Ages. The Celts called the egg *glaine neidre*, the adder stone or *gelini na Droedh*, the Druid's gem. The continuing fascination with the serpent's egg was partly due to what was said in the bestiaries, as reported originally by Pliny the Elder: that it would bring success in matters of justice and also a welcome in the court of kings and leaders.

WHAT IS A SERPENT'S EGG?

About 20 percent of snakes, for example the python, give birth to their young live (the eggs hatch inside the mother), but many others, including the cobra, do lay eggs. But these were not ordinary snake eggs, and undoubtedly over the centuries many crystal geodes, shiny giant whelk shells, ammonites, and sea urchinlike fossils, even a dull ruby, have been sold as serpents' eggs. Pliny described the Celtic or Druid's egg as about the size of a small apple with a bonelike pock-marked shell. He complained that the Celtic Druid priests wore or carried them for unfair advantage in dealings with the Romans. Pliny reported that Claudius Caesar ordered a Romanized Gallic noble of the Vecontian family to be executed because he brought one of these eggs into court and so was seen to be attempting to corrupt justice.[15]

In Celtic myth the serpent's egg, made from adder spittle, could be found on the morning of the Spring Equinox, another rebirth festival, and would endow the finder with great prophetic powers.

Another unsourced version says that the egg is instantly created by mating serpents as it flies into the air. This egg should be caught in a cloak but the person catching it must ride off on a horse and cross water before the angry snakes retrieve it.

SNAKE HANDLERS IN MODERN
AMERICAN TRADITION

Snake spirituality has survived in diluted form in the modern world. It may be that snake handling was part of a number of religious cults worldwide and the snake charming still demonstrated to tourists in India and the Middle East may be a relic of this. However, snake handling still forms part of church services in a few hundred Pentecostal Churches in the United States, usually in rural locations. The practice is based on verses from the St James's Bible in the gospels of Mark and Luke, "They shall take up serpents; and if they drink any deadly thing, it shall not hurt them; they shall lay hands on the sick, and they shall recover" (Mark 16:17–18). And "Behold, I give unto you power to tread on serpents and scorpions, and over all the power of the enemy: and nothing shall by any means hurt you" (Luke 10:19).[16]

Snake handling, therefore, in mastering the serpent, became linked with the power to overcome Satan and his evil. In 1910, inspired by these verses a member of the congregation, George Went Hensley in Grasshopper Valley in southeastern Tennessee, took a rattlesnake box into the pulpit, lifted the snake out and challenged the rest of the congregation to hold snakes as a test of faith. He was unhurt and remained so until 1955, when he died from snakebite. The practice of snake handling in church spread in the area for ten years and was revived more widely in 1943 by Raymond Hayes, one of Hensley's converts. The practice has continued in spite of various laws forbidding it.[17]

Existing congregation members of the Oneness Pentecostalism, who handle rattlesnakes, cobras, and copperheads and who are bitten, often have other causes given by relatives on death certificates as the reason for any subsequent deaths. Only those who are anointed as chosen ones during the ceremony and so considered protected by god will handle the snakes .They may allow more than one venomous snake to slither over their bodies and may enter an ecstatic trance in which prophecy and healing powers may apparently emerge.

Snake-handling churches today, which number several hundred with about 5,000 snake handlers in total, are based mainly in Kentucky and Tennessee. But there are congregations in Florida, Georgia, Alabama, the Carolinas, Virginia, West Virginia, Ohio, and Texas. Since 2004, four snake-handling congregations have been established in Canada in Alberta and Columbia. Once it was the traveling preachers who spread stories of the healing miracles of the snake handlers. Now (the) media has helped fuel interest among the public. Some church members also handle fire and drink water to which strychnine is added, in accordance with biblical verses promising protection against poison.

BIBLIOGRAPHY

1. Woodward, S., and J. McDonald. *Indian Mounds of the Middle Ohio Valley.* Granville, Ohio: The McDonald & Woodward Publishing Company, 1986.
2. Wilkinson, R. *The Complete Gods and Goddesses of Ancient Egypt.* London: Thames and Hudson, 2003.
3. Isaacs, J. *Australian Dreaming: 40,000 Years of Aboriginal History.* Sydney: Lansdowne Press, 1995.
4. Kinsley, D. *Hindu Goddesses, Visions of the Divine Feminine in Religion.* Berkeley: University of California Press, 1988.
5. See note 4.
6. Mountford, Charles P. *Winbaraku and the Myth of Jarapiri.* Adelaide: Rigby Publishing, 1968.

7. Ovid, *Metamorphoses, Books 1–V111.* Translated by F. J. Miller. Cambridge, MA: Harvard University Press, 1916.

8. *Holy Bible, King James's Version of 1611.* Peabody, MA: Hendrickson Publishing, 2003.

9. Hurwitz, S. *Lilith, the First Eve: Historical and Psychological Aspects of the Divine Feminine.* Translated by G. Jacobson Einsiedein, Switzerland: Daimon Books, 1992.

10. Keats, J. *Complete Poems (Lamia).* New York: Random House, 1994.

11. Rees, E. *Celtic Saints in Their Landscape.* Gloucestershire: Sutton Publishing, 2001.

12. Michael, J. *Encyclopedia of Gods.* London: Kyle Cathie Limited, 2002.

13. Barber, R. *Bestiary.* Rochester, NY: Boydell and Brewer (Boydell Press), 1993.

14. Beagon, M., trans. *The Elder Pliny on the Human Animal: Natural History, Book V,* Clarendon Ancient History series. Oxford: Oxford University Press, 2005.

15. See note 14.

16. See note 8.

17. Sims, P. *The Snake-Handlers: With Signs Following, "Can Somebody Shout Amen!"* Lexington: University Press of Kentucky, 1996.

CHAPTER 3

Dragon Power

Dragons are mythical creatures that have fascinated humans in many cultures and ages. Until about 1500 CE it would seem that people still believed in their existence. Accounts of the dragon-slaying saints and heroes were probably taken literally. It was assumed that the lack of existing dragons could be explained by the fact that they had all been killed by the saints and heroes at some unspecified time in the past.

The only known existing dragons in the world today are Komodo dragons, the world's heaviest living lizards. Komodo dragons are very aggressive. The male dragons can grow to a length of 10 feet (over 3 meters) and weight of 200 lbs (91 kg.). They may still be found on islands in central Indonesia. Accounts of these creatures may have been carried back to the west by early travelers who circumnavigated the globe. Of course, their actual size and ferocity may have been exaggerated.

Dinosaur bones may also have been mistaken for dragon bones. For example, *Hua Yang Guo Zhi*, a book written by Zhang Qu around 300 CE described dragon bones being excavated at Wucheng in Sichuan Province. It would seem to anyone unearthing dinosaur bones that the living dragon must have been gigantic.

The Latin word *draco*, after which the northern constellation Draco the dragon was named, is derived from Greek *drakōn* which means huge serpent.

Though descriptions of dragons differ, in myth they are generally depicted as huge reptilian or lizard-like scaly creatures with claws, legs, and a long scaly tail, sometimes with huge leathery wings. Scandinavian and European traditions describe them as breathing fire. The dragon, in the Oriental tradition, hatched out of gem-like eggs. And they believed it took 1,000 years for the dragon to hatch out and a further 3,000 years for it to reach maturity.

THE BENEVOLENT DRAGONS OF CHINA AND THE FAR EAST

As mentioned in the Introduction, the dragon in China has always been considered a bringer of luck, and it was associated with the power of the emperor. The dragon is associated with the I Ching trigram Chen which means thunder. The thunder is pictured as bursting from the womb of he Earth Mother in the form of the first azure or green dragon at the Spring Equinox (around March 21 in the Northern Hemisphere) scattering the seeds of new life. In the season of drought, the dragons are thought to slumber under the ground or in pools or wells. As the dragons rise in the spring and fight or mate, creating welcome rain, it is believed that they scatter pearls and fireballs on to the earth.

Yuan Tan, the Chinese New Year, is held at the first Full Moon in February, on the fourth day. It is celebrated in every region of the world where Chinese or other Far Eastern people have settled. The celebration begins with the procession of the Golden Dragon, made of paper, linen, and bamboo. The Golden Dragon is worn by a number of people. It holds a red envelope, called *Ang Pao*, tied to a pole. This envelope is filled with coins. The procession ends with the dragon scattering the coins to the waiting crowds. This signifies good luck for the year ahead. People give red envelopes of money, especially to the young, to transfer the dragon's luck. Store owners on the procession route let off fire-crackers to attract the dragon's attention in order to make their businesses prosperous in the year ahead.

The Dragon Boat festival is an ancient summer sun festival, still celebrated in southern China, Hong Kong, and Malaysia on the fifth day of the fifth moon. The Dragon Boat festival is held to procure a rich harvest and seek good health from the dragon gods. People also celebrate this festival in commemoration of the famous poet and politician, Chu Yuan, who lived around 343–279 BCE. He was disillusioned by the warring lords of China and drowned himself to bring about reform. Boats decorated with dragons take to the water and offerings are cast into the rivers.[1]

According to Chinese astrology, a Year of the Dragon occurs every twelve years. Years of the Dragon are considered especially prosperous and dynamic. People born in the Year of the Dragon are considered lucky. Joan of Arc, Salvador Dali, and Che Guevara are Dragon people. Dragon years include 1928, 1940, 1952, 1964, 1976, 1988, 2000, 2012, 2024, and 2036.[2]

Chinese dragons are often portrayed with a fiery pearl in their mouths, said to give them the power to fly to the heavens, for they do not have wings.

BECOMING A DRAGON

In China and the Orient becoming a dragon signified blessing; unlike the West, where becoming a dragon was considered a punishment for greed or evil doing. One Chinese legend tells of boy called Nie Lang, who lived with his mother in the Szechuan province of China. One day, at the time of a drought in Szechuan, the boy found a dragon's pearl in the dry grass. He hid it in an empty rice jar, and the jar was filled overnight. The boy used the pearl wisely to give his family and friends enough to eat; however, the fame of the pearl spread. According to some versions, a rich man, or in other versions, his master Lord Zhou, tried to steal it. The boy swallowed the pearl and was transformed into a dragon. The thief or Lord Zhou was washed away as the transformed dragon rose out of the river. The dragon protects the province to this day or so the legend promises.

Another Chinese legend says that if any carp succeeds jumping over the mythical Dragon Gate he will become a dragon. One possible location for this Dragon Gate is a huge waterfall on the Yellow River in Hunan Province in northern China. The Yellow River is a possible location because someone saw a carp who did manage to make it way up the waterfall. For this reason, carps caught near waterfalls are said to bring health and long life to whoever eats them.

DIFFERENT KINDS OF CHINESE DRAGONS

Chinese dragons are generally described without wings and with 117 scales. The Chinese dragon is made up of nine creatures, including the horns of a deer; the neck of a snake; the scales of a carp; the claws of an eagle; the paws of a tiger; and the ears of an ox.

The dragons were seen as central to agricultural life. They were associated with the control of the weather and the seasons. Dragon King temples were created for the people to make offerings to the dragons for a good harvest. Four Dragon Kings called Lóng Wáng rule over the four seas.

As well as bringing rain, Oriental weather dragons could apparently divert floodwaters away from towns. The deep pools left by intense storms also caused the growth of healing herbs such as the all-purpose Red Herb. This may be a form of the red Reishi herb, described in Chinese medicine for prolonging one's life span.

However, if angered by mortals, the dragons would gather all the waters in a basket creating drought. Dragons were even believed to cause an eclipse by swallowing the sun.

Mythical Chinese dragon types include Celestial dragons that live in the heavens and serve the gods, the male air and weather dragons that bring the winds and rain to ensure a good harvest, and their female earth counterparts who are responsible for preserving rivers and subterranean waters. There are also dragons who guard subterranean treasures. They are closest to the Westernized dragon and are believed to be responsible for volcanoes and earth tremors. Five thousand years ago, the dragons taught wisdom and the technique of writing to the legendary emperor Fu Hsi.

Dragons could, however, be bad-tempered. From Tongren City, Guizhou Province comes the legend of Nine-Dragon Cave. Once six yellow dragons lived happily on Liulong Hill (Six-Dragon Hill), which is behind Nine-Dragon Cave. They invited three black dragons living in Jinjiang River, which faces the Nine-Dragon Cave, to come to the cave for a celebration. When the nine dragons entered the cave, they realized what a wonderful home it would make. They all wanted to live in the cave, but there was not enough room, so they quarreled. Some believe they are still inside the cave, though they make themselves invisible when tourists come. The rumbling heard within earth is believed to their continuing bickering and jostling for space.

THE DRAGONS IN THE STARS

Draco is a northern circumpolar constellation, which means it is close to the North Pole. It is visible for much of the year in its own hemisphere, never sinks below the horizon, and really does resemble a dragon. Draco is historically important as the home of the former pole star Thuban (now Polaris), which was the main orientation for the building of the Egyptian pyramids of Khufu or Cheops at Giza around 2500 BCE. Draco was named by the Roman astronomer Ptolemy (90 BCE–168 CE) who lived in Romanized Egypt. In Greek myth, Draco is identified as Ladon, the hundred-headed dragon that guarded Hera's golden apples of the fabled garden of the Hesperides nymphs, akin to an Ancient Greek Garden of Eden. After Heracles the hero killed Ladon, Hera the Mother goddess and wife of Zeus, put the dragon in the skies as a reward for her loyalty.

Dragons were associated with meteors and comets in earlier times. For example, in the Anglo-Saxon Chronicle, dated 793 CE, lights and flames in the sky were interpreted as fire-breathing dragons, and as a warning of earthly disasters caused by bad human behavior.

THE MYSTICAL RED AND WHITE DRAGONS
OF THE CELTIC WORLD

The red dragon is associated with Celtic leaders, and partially according to myth and partially according to history, it symbolized their right to power. It is recorded by Geoffrey of Monmouth in a romanticized version of events around 1136 CE.[3] He states that while Uther, father of King Arthur, was leading his army into battle, a dragon (probably a dragon-shaped comet) flared across the sky. Arthur, in spite of the mediaeval courtly spin, was an ancient British king of Celtic origin who united large parts of Britain in the later fifth century against hostile forces after the collapse of the Roman Empire. (Geoffrey of Monmouth had written long after the supposed event.) Merlin the magician prophesied from the fiery dragon in the sky that Uther would win the battle and that the present king Aurelius, on whose behalf Uther was fighting, would die and Uther would take his place. The battle was won and Uther adopted the name Pendragon which means the head of the dragon. When Uther returned after the victory, he discovered that Aurelius had been poisoned. Uther was made king. Thereafter he had a golden dragon as his emblem.

That was not Merlin's first dragon prophecy. Merlin, or Myrddin, as a boy, according to Geoffrey of Monmouth, saved his own life by revealing subterranean dragons. At Dinas Emrys, near Beddgelert in Snowdonia Wales, Vortigen was trying to build a fortress, but the main stone tower fell down every night. Vortigen was told by his soothsayers that only the spilled blood of a fatherless child could stop the nightly earth tremors destroying the tower. Merlin came to his notice because he did not have a father. The young Merlin told Vortigen that the tower was being built upon a site where there were two warring dragons, a red one and a white one. When the builders dug deep, they found the pool, and on young Merlin's instructions the pool was drained. The dragons woke and fought each other to death. The red dragon died first, but mortally wounded the white one. Merlin then made a prophecy that the red dragon symbolized the Celts and the white dragon the invading Anglo-Saxons. He also predicted that first the white dragon would be victorious, but that in time the red dragon would take back what was rightly his. Subsequently Vortigen was killed in battle but Uther and later Arthur drove back the Saxons, fulfilling the prophecy. A version of this story may be found in Geoffrey of Monmouth's *Prophecies of Merlin*.[4]

The red dragon standard was actually adopted from the Roman battle standard during their occupation of Britain. After their departure it became the rallying symbol of the Celts, a number of whom had become Romanized, against the new invaders. The Anglo-Saxons had the white dragon as their battle flag, and this was last seen in 1066 at the Battle of Hastings when the Normans under William the Conqueror (actually Danish Vikings who had settled in northern France) defeated the Anglo-Saxon King Harold. The white dragon flag is shown on the Bayeux tapestry recording the battle. The tapestry can be seen in the cathedral of Bayeux, northern France.

CHRISTIANITY, DRAGON SLAYING, AND THE DRAGON SAINTS

Before considering the role of dragons in other cultures, it may be helpful to see how dragons were regarded as the enemies of the saints. Partly this is historical and comes from the Middle Eastern and Ancient Greek concept that dragons were forces of evil to be overcome by gods or heroes, though they were used as guardians of treasures.

In pre-Christian times and even during early Christian times in Europe, dragons were considered the guardians of burial places and sacred sites. This may explain why there is a dragon hill, attributed in myth to St George, opposite an ancient sacred chalk white horse etched in the hillside at Uffington in Oxfordshire. The horse is a symbol of Epona the Celtic and Roman Horse goddess. In the United Kingdom there are numerous Anglo-Saxon or even earlier burial mounds named after dragons. For example, Drake Howe on Cranimoor on the Yorkshire moors in northeast England. This burial mound was first recorded in 1332 as Drechhowe. Drake and Drech are old Norse names for dragon. The mound was also called Odin's grave. Because Odin was the powerful Father god of the Vikings, and Viking activity was common in the area, it may be that the dragon was once considered to guard the wealth of the grave goods of someone who must have been important enough to take the Father god's name. But nothing was found from the excavated grave and so the dragon's power was not effective.

But gradually during Christian times, as with serpents, dragons became regarded as a symbol of pure evil, and so a number of the Christian saints were credited with slaying dragons. Accounts of these appear in literature and art. The saints such as St George were described in mediaeval terms, although the accounts come from much earlier centuries. For example, the painter called Raphael, whose real name was Raffaelo Sanzio, painted *St George Fighting the Dragon* between 1504 and 1506. The oil painting on wood may be seen in the National Gallery of Art in Washington, D.C.

Why had this dragon hating become so strong? Saints needed some fairly spectacular deeds to impress a population resistant to the new religion that, unlike the Roman one, would not coexist with their indigenous gods. Therefore, St Patrick driving all the serpents into the sea (maybe beaten beforehand into one area of thick grass on a cliff top by his followers) was dramatic enough to demonstrate the power of the new Christian god. But tales of dragon slaying were even more dramatic.

St George is the most famous of the dragon-slaying saints. He is commemorated in Russia, where he is venerated in the Eastern Orthodox Church, as well as being on the coat of arms of Moscow. In both England and Canada, he is the patron saint. St George was born between 228 and 275, and was martyred on April 23, 303 CE. He came from a Christian family in Anatolia, now part of Turkey, and fought in the Roman army. Though there are no historical sources for his life, an anecdotal account of his dragon slaying, along with the lives of other saints, is given in the *Golden Legend*, written by Jacobus de Voragine and published by William Caxton in England in 1483.[5]

The episode of St George and the dragon was brought back to the West by the Crusaders and was absorbed into mediaeval courtly tales. Set in Cyrene, Libya, the story tells of a dragon that moved near the town's water supply and would give the townspeople water only if a young female was given in return to the dragon every day. When it was the turn of the princess to be sacrificed to the dragon, George turned up in time and killed the dragon. There are numerous dragon hills named after George's dragon-slaying prowess, even in countries where George did not venture (though he may possibly have come to the UK with the Roman army). For example, at Uffington Hill on the borders of Oxfordshire and Berkshire, central England, there is a Dragon Hill. It is said that St George killed a dragon, and so no grass will grow on the place where its blood fell. Opposite is the famous chalk-white horse etched in the downs, dated in 1996 by the Oxford University Archaeology Research Unit as being created between 1400 and 600 BCE. In myth, the Uffington White Horse has been described as portraying the horse of St George, which could not be true datewise.

Other male dragon-slaying saints include St Romain of Rouen, who destroyed the dragon called La Gargouille, which was threatening the area around the River Seine in northeastern France. He is said to have given his name to the hideous gargoyle figures that are seen on the outside of mediaeval cathedrals in Europe. The legend shows a justifiably harsh side of the saint, who during the eighth century CE lured the monster into a bonfire in Rouen on Ascension Day, using a condemned prisoner as decoy.

THE ARCHANGEL DRAGON SLAYER

The Archangel Michael, also known as St Michael, is typically portrayed dressed in armor crushing a dragon underfoot or piercing it with a lance. According to the Book of Revelation 12:7–9, Michael will defeat the slumbering dragon monster Leviathan at the last battle, Armageddon. Various stories from different lands attribute safety from dragons as part of his ongoing protective role because dragons were frequently depicted as living on or near former pagan sites. Churches of St Michael would be erected on those sites as protection. For example, in the Radnor Forest area of Wales, four local churches dedicated to St Michael encircle the forest to keep the slumbering dragon, the last in Wales, trapped in his lair so long as the churches stand. This may well be a reference to the pagan religion because of the link through the serpent in the Garden of Eden.

It is significant that the dragon-slaying legends, as told in the *Golden Legend* and other anecdotal books on the saints, became popular in the late 1400s and 1500s in Europe. Prejudice grew against women, and especially against those seen as dabbling in the old pagan ways that had coexisted with Christianity to some extent before then, albeit hidden. In December 1484, the *Bull of Pope Innocent VII* was published appointing two clerics, Heinrich Kramer and Jakob Sprenge, as chief inquisitors in a crusade against witchcraft.

In 1487 Heinrich Kramer and Jakob Sprenge described in lurid detail in their book *Malleus Maleficarum, or Häxhammaren, or The Witch Hammer*, the tortures that could and should morally be used to obtain confessions from suspected witches. They stated that it was better to kill an innocent person, who would be rewarded in heaven by God, than to allow a guilty person to remain unpunished.

> All witchcraft comes from carnal lust which is in women insatiable. Wherefore, for the sake of fulfilling their lusts they consort even with devils.
>
> Blessed be the Highest who has so far preserved the male sex from so great a crime:
>
> There was a defect in the formation of the first woman, since she was formed from a bent rib—she is an imperfect animal, she always deceives.
>
> From the *Malleus Maleficarum* (The Hammer of the Witches)[6]

Psychologically, dragons became linked with the temptress serpent of Eden, who was entwined with the idea of the experienced and slightly older woman tempting the man to sin. Slaying the dragon was then perhaps fraught with symbolism of overcoming all kinds of temptations. Pure young virgins were considered dragon fodder in the stories.

FEMALE DRAGON SLAYERS

Female saints were exempt from such female prejudice because they were either virgins dedicated to the church, like St Margaret of Antioch, or, like the motherly St Martha, respected followers of Jesus and icons of a women dedicated to service to a man. Therefore, they also could be dragon slayers.

The most fascinating female dragon slayer is St Martha, patron saint of housewives, cooks, and servants, who in the Gospel of St Luke is described as cooking and tending to Jesus's needs while her sister sat listening. St Martha's dragon-slaying role started, according to unsubstantiated claims, when she crossed the Mediterranean to go to France after the Crucifixion. St Martha defeated a dragoness at Tarascon by sprinkling it with Holy Water. The dragoness was called Tarasque and had lived near the River Rhone for twenty-one years, during which time various would-be heroes failed to kill her. Martha led the subdued dragoness back to the town, where she was killed by the local people, unfairly it seems if the dragoness had been converted by St Martha. The town was thereafter named Tarascon.

Another female dragon-slaying saint was St Margaret of Antioch (in modern Turkey), during the rule of the Roman Emperor Diocletian in the late third century CE. Olybrious, the Roman governor of Antioch, fell in love with St Margaret and wanted to marry her. But she refused because he was a pagan, and she wanted to devote her life to Christ, so Olybrious denounced Margaret as being a Christian, then illegal. She was thrown into prison and tortured. In prison Margaret wished to see her foe in his true form. At this, Satan appeared in the form of a dragon and swallowed her. But the cross around her neck became so large that it split the dragon in half, and she was released from the dragon's stomach unharmed. Later attempts were made to kill her by fire and water, but those attempts too failed, and the miracles she performed at this time resulted in the conversion of many bystanders. Just before her death, Margaret promised safe delivery of infants to all mothers who prayed to her because she was delivered unharmed from the dragon's stomach. She also promised that anyone who built a church dedicated to her or lit candles in her memory would be granted something of use that they had asked for.

MIDDLE EASTERN DRAGONS AS THE FORCES OF DARKNESS

The purely evil dragon has its origins in the Middle East, which influenced Christianity through Judaism. In the Middle East, dragons were regarded as demonic forces of darkness to be defeated in ongoing battles by various deities of light and sun. This pattern begins, according to the earliest recorded dragon myth, as early as 5000 BCE, the time the Sumerians settled in Mesopotamia, now modern Iraq.

Zu the dragon was said to be old when the world began. He stole the tablets of law that were necessary to maintain order in the universe from the Wind and Storm Father god Enlil. The Sun god Ninurta defeated the dragon and so prevented chaos from overwhelming the world. Zu is also known as Anzu.

In a later myth in Ancient Babylon, the Sun god Mithras constantly fought against the evil Ahriman, who threatened the heavens in his dragon-like form. Mithras was first worshipped in what is now Iran around 2000 CE. His worship spread throughout the Middle East and Mediterranean, and he became one of the main gods of the Roman Empire.

Another Middle Eastern dragon in a myth from the Caspian Sea region tells of Azhi Dahaki, a gigantic three-headed dragon whose body was filled with spiders, lizards, and snakes. In one account, he tried to destroy the sacred flame that warmed the world, which was guarded by Atar the Fire god. The dragon was eventually defeated by the god hero Thraetaona, who imprisoned Azhi Dahaki in Mount Demavend near the Caspian Sea. It is said when the world ends the dragon will emerge once more to kill a third of all creatures before he is finally overthrown.

A similar myth of the dragon versus the Sun god is found in Ancient Egypt. However, the huge Chaos dragon Apophis, or Apep, is more of a gigantic serpent. Apophis is described as wrapping its deadly coils round the sun boat of Ra as he sailed through the Duat, the underworld waters within the womb of the Sky Mother Nut. Bastet, the cat-headed goddess, was one of the deities who protected the solar boat each night by wounding the serpent Apep, whose blood colored the sky at sunrise and at sunset. But the principle in both myths is the same, and the battle in Ancient Egypt was a nightly one of the Sun god versus the dragon with no certain victory. It is said that at the end of the world Osiris, the rebirth god, and Ra, the Sun god, will survive in the form of serpents/dragons.

TIAMET, THE CREATING DRAGON OF BABYLON

Most intriguing is the story of Tiamet, the dragon who gave birth to the world, but was then destroyed by her sons. One description of Tiamet says she had four legs, the head and upper body of a lion, scales along her body, feathery wings, an eagle's talons at the back, and a forked tongue (shades of the serpent). Her skin could not be penetrated by any weapon known to man or to the gods. There are various versions of the myth of Tiamet's destruction.[7] In early versions she gave birth to the universe from her menstrual blood that flowed continuously for three years and three months. But in other myths, creation occurred after and because of her destruction. The war-like Babylonian myths may have evolved after the Anonite conquest around 1900 CE, which culminated in the rule of Hammurah (1792–1752 BCE). Anonite established the supremacy of the city of Babylon and adapted much of the earlier Sumerian culture.

It is told that the Babylonian supreme god, identified as Tiamet's eldest son Marduk, split open his mother in fury because she was treacherous, so bringing about creation and giving him the credit for the birth of the universe. Marduk killed Tiamat with an arrow through her open mouth as she tried to swallow and so reabsorb him. Half of her body became the dome of heaven, and the rest became the earth that held back the waters. Her eyes became the Tigris and Euphrates rivers that flow through Iraq, close to what remains of the Garden of Eden. Kingu's blood gave birth to humans.[8]

Tiamat contained within her body the potential for all life. In all the versions, first she conceived her sons, the gods. But Apsu, her consort, was jealous of the other gods because they were rebellious, and he demanded that Tiamat should kill them. Being a mother, she refused. When the gods, led by Marduk, learned of Aspu's plans to destroy them, they killed him. This outraged Tiamat, and she and her youngest son (or second husband, Kingu) battled against the gods. To do this she created eleven monsters (some say eleven dragons), which unleashed their evil upon the world. Other versions describe the monsters as a viper, a shark, a scorpion, the storm demon, a lion, a dragon (from which subsequent dragons were descended), a wild dog, and four creatures that are not specified except as terrible.

Ironically, Marduk himself had as his symbol the Mususssu dragon, which was important in the New Year festivals. Glazed terracotta bricks depicting the dragon of Marduk, part of the Gate of Ishtar once in Babylon, can be seen in the Detroit Institute of Arts. The bricks date from 604–562 BCE during the reign of King Nebuchadnezzar, who created the gate in honor of Ishtar the Fertility, Love, and War goddess. On the gate, the dragon bricks of Marduk alternated with tiers of bricks depicting bulls sacred to Ada the weather god. The gate formed the entrance for the procession on the most important day of the New Year festival.

ANCIENT GREEK GUARDIAN DRAGONS

Like serpents, dragons were viewed with great suspicion in Greek myth, though they played an essential role as guardians of what was precious. However, they are best remembered for being slain by heroes such as Jason and Heracles, and so their negative role is the one most emphasized.

The best-known dragon of Greek legend was the hundred-headed Ladon, who guarded the golden apples on the Tree of Life that gave immortal life in the magical garden tended by the beautiful Hesperides nymphs.[9] The garden belonged to Hera, the consort of Zeus, the Father god. The tree was given to Hera by the Earth Mother Gaia on her wedding day.

Heracles, or Hercules, killed the dragon as one of his twelve labors, efforts that were supported by Zeus. This may reflect again in story form the supremacy of the Father god culture over an earlier more matrilineal one. The Hellenic people, who invaded mainland Greece from the north between 2200 and 2100 BCE, imposed their deity Zeus as the main god in Greece, supplanting Hera, the indigenous Earth goddess. The invaders married Zeus to Hera, in effect legitimatizing themselves and their gods. Therefore, what could be more natural than the dragon of Hera being defeated by the hero of Zeus?

The parents of Ladon were Typhon, the serpentine god of the winds, and Echidna, half nymph–half serpent, who was the mother of Medusa and her sisters the Gorgons. They were credited with spawning most of the dragons in the Ancient Greek world. The Greek geographer Strabo located the garden on an island to the west of Spain. But the garden was also described vaguely and mysteriously as being at the edge of the oceans of the world.

Another dragon was overcome by Jason and the Argonauts in their quest for the magical Golden Fleece.[10] It is told that the hero Jason reached Colchis, which is described as being located in Georgia, near the Black Sea. Forced to complete three apparently impossible tasks to win the fleece, Jason was helped by the king's daughter Medea, who, assisted by the love arrows of Eros, fell in love with him. The third and final task was to overcome the dragon who never slept, who guarded the fleece. To induce sleep, Medea used drops of a sleep-inducing potion made from magical herbs.

DRAGONS IN SCANDINAVIAN AND
EUROPEAN TRADITIONS

Scandinavian dragons are the true fire and earth dragons, living in deep sub-terranean caves. Stemming from the Norse world, dragons have a strong tra-dition in Scandinavia, Germany, and other parts of Western Europe (where the Anglo-Saxons settled) as guardians of treasure, a quality they shared with Celtic dragons. Dragons were accorded a certain respect, and the Vikings had dragons on the prows of their ships to strike fear into enemies seeing them approaching the land. The Vikings would lower these figureheads when approaching home so as not to offend the land wights, or spirits, on the cliff tops. In the Norse as well as the Anglo-Saxon and Celtic traditions, dragons were thought to guard the wealth of chiefs, who were sometimes buried with fabulous treasures for their life in the next world. It was believed that deceased warriors might be transformed into dragons to protect the gold hoards of their chiefs from grave robbers—an apt deterrent that may partly explain the Fafnir and Beowulf legends in which the stolen treasure is cursed.

Norse and European myths describe dragons in great detail as possessing all or some of the following features: eagle's feet, batlike wings, the front legs of a lion, a reptile/dinosaur's head with a huge mouth and teeth from which smoke and fire pours, huge scales, the horns of an antelope, a soft underbelly, and a spade-like snake or lizard tail that may begin close to the head.

Smaller fire drakes found in the myths of France and Germany do not have wings, but they are also cave dwellers, red with fiery breath, where they live with their great hoards—the riches of the earth.

According to Bulgarian dragon lore, the male dragon was a fire dragon and a benign protector of humans and crops. Bulgarian dragons had three heads and three wings. Scandinavian and European dragons, already described in the section on dragon-slaying saints, were thought to grow to be up to sixty feet long. They laid eggs, although the incubation period of their eggs was much shorter than that of Chinese dragons.

THE GIGANTIC DRAGONS OF SCANDINAVIA

In Scandinavian myth, two gigantic dragons appear, similar to the Ancient Egyptian world serpent. The dragon Nioðgg, or Nidhogg, whose name means dread biter, lived in Nifleheim, the realm of ice and snow. He devoured the corpses of those who had been evil in life. The World Tree Yggdrasil contained the nine realms that made up the Norse universe, including Asgard, realm of the gods, near the top; Midgard, the realm of humans, in the center; and Nifleheim, the regions of cold and darkness, at the base of the tree, to which the dead descended who were not chosen to live with the gods.

One of the roots of the World Tree extended over Nifleheim. Nidhogg constantly gnawed at this root, when he was not devouring the corpses of criminals (or of other evildoers banished there). Nidhogg's movements were held responsible for earthquakes in the Viking world. Nidhogg, eating away at the roots of the World Tree, was one of the factors predicted to contribute to the literal fall of the world of the old gods and race of old human gods, when a great earthquake would shake the tree and cause it to be uprooted. This destruction would culminate in the battle of Ragnarok.

As with Ancient Egyptian dragons, there is some confusion with Scandinavian dragons over what is a serpent and what is a dragon. Jormungand, or Iormungandr, was described as the offspring of the trickster god Loki and his giantess wife Angurboda, whose name means *anguish boding.* Jormungand, known as the World Serpent, encircled the whole of the ocean surrounding Midgard, the world of mortals. Jormungand was so large that he had to bite his own tail. When he turned, tempests and tidal waves were said to be caused in the world.[11] At the last battle Jormungand would rise from the ocean onto the land, causing floods and tidal waves never before seen. It was foretold by the Norns, the three Norse goddesses of Fate, that Jormungand would fatally poison the Thunder god Thor, but that at the same time he would be killed by the dying god.

Fafnir was another significant Norse and German dragon. (The Anglo-Saxon culture shared many of the Viking myths.) Norse myth records that the dwarf Regin persuaded his godson Sigurd (called Sigfried in Germany) to seek and kill Fafnir, who had a fabulous hoard of treasure. However, Sigurd did not know that Fafnir was the brother of Regin. In one version of the myth, Fafnir had been rewarded with a hoard of gold and gems by the gods. He was so afraid of losing it that he hid in a cave with it, and over the years he turned into dragon form because of his obsession with the gold.

Of course the whole dragon-slaying idea was actually a plot by Regin to seize the hoard for himself. Sigurd rode with Regin to find the dragon. At Reign's suggestion they hid in a deep ditch, and when Fafnir came to drink at a nearby pool, Sigurd stabbed his soft underbelly with his magical sword. Regin cut out the heart of his brother and roasted it, but some of the hot fat dripped on Sigurd's finger. He licked the burn and immediately understood the language of the birds, who told him that Regin intended to kill him as well. Therefore Sigurd beheaded the dwarf and claimed the treasure and the wisdom of the birds for himself.

In another version, Fafnir killed his own father in order to take the treasure his father owned, and hid in a cave with it. Because of this evil deed, he was transformed into a dragon. This is very different from the Chinese concept described earlier in which becoming a dragon was a blessing. In a third version of the legend from the Volsungr Saga, Fafnir was changed into a dragon after stealing the cursed treasure of the dwarf Andvari.[12]

BEOWULF AND THE DRAGON

The most famous English dragon slayer after St George was Beowulf, who was also non-English. The epic poem *Beowulf* was written in England in the seventh or eighth century CE, or perhaps later during the twelfth century. The poem recounts events from the late fifth and early sixth centuries CE, and it originally comes from Swedish sources.[13] This was the time when the Anglo-Saxons, relatives of the Danish Vikings, were occupying England. The Anglo-Saxon epic poem was possibly recorded by a monk, and it is considered the first English literary work. In one of his many adventures, the hero Beowulf overcame a fire-breathing dragon. The epic poem tells that when Beowulf was a king and much older, one of his servants stole a golden cup from a dragon's den. The furious fire-breathing dragon came in pursuit. Though Beowulf led his warriors against the dragon, all ran away except for a young warrior Wiglaf. Though they defeated the dragon, Beowulf was fatally wounded and was buried in a high place overlooking the sea. The treasure was buried with him. The treasure was considered cursed because it was taken from a dragon guarding it. Though not intended to be, perhaps it can be read as a sound ecological message saying that humans should not excessively plunder the minerals of Earth.

REFERENCES

1. Latsch, M. L. *Traditional Chinese Festivals, Singapore.* Singapore: Graham Brash, 1985.
2. See note 1.
3. Geoffrey of Monmouth. *A History of the Kings of Britain.* Translated by L. Thorpe. London: Penguin Books, 1973.
4. Geoffrey of Monmouth. *Life of Merlin, Vita Merlini.* Cardiff: University of Wales, 1973; [Text in English and Latin] Goodrich N. L. *Merlin,* New York: Harper Perennial, 2004.
5. de Voragine, J. *Golden Legend.* Translated by W. G. Ryan. Princeton, NJ: Princeton University Press, 1995.

6. Peters, E. *Magic, the Witch and the Law*. Amherst, MA: University of Massachusetts Press, 1982.

7. Mackenzie, D. A. *Myths of Babylonia and Assyria*. Whitefish, MT: Kessinger Publishing, 2004.

8. See note 7.

9. Brommer, F., and S. J. S. Schwarz. *Heracles: The Twelve Labors in Ancient Art and Literature*. New York: Aristide D Caratzas, 1986.

10. Apollonius, R. *Argonautica, Book 111*. Cambridge: Cambridge University Press, 1989.

11. See note 10.

12. Guerber, H. A. *The Norsemen*. London: Senate Publishing, 1994.

13. Byock, J., trans. *The Saga of the Volsungs: The Norse Epic of Sigurd the Dragon Slayer*. Berkeley: University of California Press, 2002.

CHAPTER 4

Fabulous Birds and Other Winged Creatures

Birds have always been regarded with wonder because of their ability to fly. In myth they were considered messengers between humans and the deities. Deities took the form of birds to travel through the heavens and earth. Bees and butterflies also had connections with the deities and have been seen in many ages and societies as a symbol of rebirth and transformation.

Birds have been identified (and consequently feared) as being an emanation of departed souls. This belief stemmed from the Ancient Egyptian ba, or hawk-headed, part of the human spirit, which was said to fly from the mummy after death and could return as a swallow or hawk to the world of the living. For this reason birds such as swallows and owls entering a house or tapping at a window were taken as a bad omen, especially if a family member was sick. It was believed that the bird was the spirit of a deceased relative who had come to fetch the soul of the sick person or of a vulnerable child (of course a mere superstition).

THE BIRD GODDESSES

Because birds were seen flying upward, it is not surprising that early goddesses were perceived in bird form. One of the finest examples of the ancient Bird goddess has been called the goddess of Lespugue, with a birdlike head and fanlike feathers. Made of mammoth ivory, she was discovered on a hearth-stone in a shallow cave in the Pyrenees in southern France, The Lespugue Bird goddess is less than six inches tall. She dates back to about 23,000 BCE.

The Bird goddess is linked in myth with birth through the egg symbol. A Bird goddess with an egg-shaped body and a slender neck and beak made in terracotta and dating from round 6000 BCE was excavated in Sesklo in Thessaly, Greece.[1] The cosmic egg appears in various myths, some of which are described in this chapter. As early people saw birds hatching from eggs, this may have seemed one explanation of how the world might have been created.

More graceful and more humanlike is the River, or Nile, goddess with a strongly beaked face and wings like dancer's arms extended in an arch over her head. Statues of Nile goddesses are made of ancient Nile mud dating from about 4000 BCE. One of these figures may be seen in the Brooklyn Museum of Art in New York. The Nile goddess was excavated from a grave near Edfu in Egypt.

Over the centuries as Egyptian civilization developed, a number of goddesses were portrayed with wings. Four such goddess statues made of gold enclosed the shrine of Tutankhamen, who was buried around 1322 BCE. They were the Egyptian Mother goddess Isis; Nephthys her sister, goddess of twilight; Neith, goddess of fate; and Selkit, or Serqet, the Scorpion goddess. Isis was often shown on statues with her protective wings enfolding the pharaoh.

THE VULTURE MOTHERS

Isis was also portrayed as a vulture. Vulture goddesses, in some mythology, represent the death aspect, taking the deceased and stripping away the old outworn body so that the spirit might be freed or reborn in a new body. In the ancient ruins of Çatal Hüyük in Anatolia (modern Turkey) remains have been found of a room that has been called the Vulture Shrine. The Shrine dates from as early as 6000 BCE. Around the walls are images of seven huge vultures removing the heads of the deceased. This shrine may be linked to a Vulture goddess. In another painting at the same site, the vulture is portrayed with human legs. The vultures, painted red on a pink background, hover over the headless figures, whose arms are raised in seeming welcome to the vultures.

Some early cultures in the northern parts of Europe and Scandinavia placed human corpses on hilltops for carrion eaters to devour the flesh. Shamanic myths from Siberia talk of a Bird goddess who picked clean the bones of a potential shaman wanting to be reborn. This was of course entirely symbolic, but it may have been experienced in a trance during an initiation ritual. At a cave site near the Zab River, now in Kurdistan, graves were excavated that date from around 8870 BCE. They contained goat skulls and the wings of vultures and eagles. Of course it is hard to be certain of the significance of artifacts, but from myth we do know that vultures were viewed in a mythological way.

In Mongolian shamanism, Mother Earth is called Itugen and the name for a female shaman is derived from her name. Her daughter Umai is the Womb goddess and caretaker of the unborn human souls roosting in the World Tree. Umai is a surviving form of the very ancient Bird goddess, sometimes called the Bird of Prey goddess, who was believed to hatch the cosmic egg. When life was done, she pecked away the flesh of dead humans, vulturelike, so that the spirit might be freed and reborn. Umai or her mother, during a trance ritual, symbolically picks clean the bones of the Siberian shaman during his initiation so he can be reborn.[2]

In Ancient Egypt the main Vulture goddesses were Mut, Isis, and Nekhbet. Nekhbet, sister of Buto the Cobra goddess, was the protective deity of Upper Egypt, and her image was worn on the forehead of the pharaoh along with the cobra of the north. She is sometimes linked to Isis. The Vulture hieroglyph shown in Figure 4.1 represents the protection and power of Mother Isis, or Nekhbet and was used as an amulet of protection for the deceased, with the ankh for life engraved on each talon.

Nekhbet was said to give her maternal milk to the pharaoh. The symbol of the vulture is the hieroglyph for Mother, and her image was worn as a headdress by queen mothers of the pharaohs. Nekhbet was also a protective deity for ordinary women, especially for mothers who asked her for fertility and for protection of their children, and was the patroness of snake charmers. Her

Figure 4.1

image was that of a vulture with wings outspread for protection, or of a woman with a vulture head or with snakeskin on her headdress.

Mut, whose name means *mother*, is regarded as the archetypal Mother goddess, the feminine and nurturing counterpart of her creator husband Amun. With their son, the Moon god Khonsu, they were often portrayed as a family group or idealized family. The vulture was Mut's symbol. Worshipped with her husband at Thebes, she was also regarded as a mother of pharaohs. Mut wore a vulture headdress and above that the double crown of Egypt. She carried the scepter of Upper Egypt. Her dress was usually red or blue, patterned with feathers.[3]

CELTIC BIRD GODDESSES

Celtic birds reflected the indigenous birds of Western Europe, where the main carrion-eating species was the crow or raven.

There were three Raven goddess sisters, Morrigan, Macha or Nass, and Badbh or Nemhain, who appear primarily in old Irish myth. They were called the Morrigu. Macha flew over battlefields as a huge crow or raven, accompanied by a flock of ravens, protecting the tribes she favored, warning them of the enemy's approach, and encouraging them to victory.

Badbh, the Crone goddess, carried the souls of the slain to the otherworld for healing and rebirth. She had the power to choose who should live and who should die. Sister and prophetess of fate, Badbh, it was foretold, would herald the end of time when her otherworld cauldron overflowed. Ravens, like vultures, pick the flesh off corpses; this carrion-eating aspect had magical significance in the matriarchal Celtic world, with the Death Mother being Badbh's alter ego, the mother who birthed new life.

Nemhain, whose name means *frenzy*, was the wildest of the sisters. She was called the confounder of armies. Nemhain was the trickster of battle who could set armies fighting against allies by sending down a storm or mists, or who could appear out of the mist, luring warriors onto marshy or unsafe land.

The Roman chronicler Tacitus gave us a clue about the priestesses of Nemhain when he described the slaughter of many of the Druids, Druidesses, and their children in 61 CE.[4] He described the Druidesses screaming curses against the Romans as being ravenlike. My own theory is that these mysterious raven women were perhaps a separate order of oracular Druidesses who wore black, and who may have been dedicated to the prophetic Morrigu goddesses. Indeed the concept of the Morrigu may be much older than Celtic times, dating back to the age when the goddess was depicted with the head of a bird. Her priestesses may, as with modern shamans, have worn feathers on their robes. There are descriptions by Tacitus of Druidic cloaks made of feathers.

THE BIRD GODDESSES OF ANCIENT GREECE

THE HARPIES

In early Greek mythology, the three Harpies were not ugly or evil as were their later personae. With bird bodies, and heads and breasts of women, they were originally described as beautiful, long-haired, winged goddesses of the storm, with the ability to fly faster than the wind. Like the Valkyries, the swan maidens of Viking myth, the Harpies bore away the souls of the slain for healing. In time, however, they acquired the image of hideous old women with the bodies, wings, beaks, and claws of birds, who seized mortals or semideities and carried them off to the underworld, leaving in their wake a foul stench.

One of the most famous victims of the Harpies was the prophet Phineus, whom they tormented at the command of Zeus, either because he had revealed the secret hiding place of the sun's nightly resting place, or because he had allowed the blinding of his own children at the behest of his second wife. However, Phineus's real crime lay in challenging the authority of Zeus and proving a more accurate seer that Zeus. Thus it may have been Zeus himself who blinded Phineus, leaving the Harpies as celestial jailers.

But in an amazing about-face, the winged sons of Boreas (the North Wind) Calais, and Zetes, in league with the Argonauts, freed Phineus from his torment by the Harpies. He was given second sight under a pact with Helios the Sun god to compensate for his blinding, and the Harpies were driven to the Whirling Isles, where for most of the year they were trapped in a vortex. They were freed only when the islands came to rest for a short period. Indeed they were saved from total annihilation only by their gentler sister Iris, the messenger goddess of the Rainbow, who appears as Temperance in some Tarot card packs.[5]

BIRD CREATION MYTHS

THE EGG OF THE WORLD

After the time of the River or Nile goddess in Egypt, the primal egg concept developed, which says that the egg of the world was laid by a god in the form of a goose, rather than by a goddess. In the Hermopolitan Ancient Egyptian creation legend from around 3000 BCE, Geb the Earth god, in the form of a goose, laid the egg of the world from which Atum the first Creator god, or Ra the Sun god, emerged to bring light into the world as the first sunrise.

In the later Theban creation myth dating from sometime between 1546 and 1085 BCE, Amun the Creator god was the Great Goose, calling creation into being by his cry, and laying the egg of the sun. He, like Geb, was called the Great Cackler because of this sound.

According to the mythology of Finland, the world was created from an egg that broke into thousands of pieces to form the land, the trees, the hills, and all the creatures of the earth. The top of the shell formed the sky, supported by a column or World Tree at the North Pole, below the North Star. From Finland also comes the tale of Lintukoto, the land of birds, which lay at the edge of the world. This was the warm place to which all the birds migrated in winter. They traveled along the Milky Way, called Linnunrata, meaning the path of the birds, to this land.[6]

In India, according to one creation myth, a swan laid the golden cosmic egg from which Brahma, Hindu Creator of the Universe, emerged.

THE CREATOR BIRDS

Waters were the first matter of creation, so in a number of cultures the world was created when water fowl dived down, bringing up the seeds of new life. Inspiration for these myths may have come from natural observation of water birds that dived deep and came up carrying in their beaks mud or grasses, in which shrimps or other water creatures might be hiding.

Siberian myth tells us that the earth was once covered with water. Two water birds, the diving loon and the golden-eyed duck, continued to dive until they had brought up enough mud to form the first land.

In Japanese folk tradition, the wagtail assisted with the creation of the earth. The earth in its original form was a huge marsh. The creator sent wagtails to beat the land with their wings and tails until the hills formed so that the water could drain away, and humankind could cultivate the soil.

Magyar was the Hungarian Sun god whose parents were the original god and goddess. He is described as a youth with sunbeam hair, who transformed himself into a golden diving bird. He descended to the bottom of the ocean and brought up the seeds to create the first humans so that they would be his people.

The Tlingit people of Alaska credit the raven as creator of people, animals, the sun, the moon, and the stars. The raven appears in a number of Native North American myths as the one who brought light and fire into the world.

The raven and the sun story I have heard is actually Celtic, and there are a number of similarities between Celtic and Native North American spirituality. I heard this story when I was a teacher more than thirty years ago in Fife, a central region of Scotland. I was collecting stories from the older members of children's families, and this was told by a boy called James, who had heard the story from his great grandmother in Ireland.

The raven was once pure white, and the world was very dark and cold. Nothing would grow. High in the sky was a golden ball that was the sun. The raven decided to go and fetch it down into the world, but the other animals warned him that it was too dangerous. Raven did not listen, and he flew even higher than the eagle had ever been. He carried back the sun in his beak. It was so hot that it burned his feathers black, and in the struggle a flame from the sun fell to earth setting fire to a tree. This gave the cold humans their first fire, and soon the sun was shining brightly. Everyone was sorry for the raven, who was no longer beautiful. The raven also lost his singing voice, but he said it was better to have warmth and light than live in the dark and cold. The gods were very angry with the raven because they wanted to keep the sun and fire for themselves. So from that time, gods allowed the raven to eat only what nobody else wanted.

THE SOUL BIRD

In Finnish mythology it was believed that birds were the servants of Sielulintu, the soul bird. On his behalf they carried human souls into their bodies at birth, and took them back when the person died. For this reason in modern folk custom it is said a wooden bird should be placed at the bedside so that the soul will not fly off during sleep. I saw a wooden soul bird in the home of some elderly Finnish immigrants in Sweden. The old lady of the household said the custom was dying out in modern Finland.

MAGICAL BIRDS

The human imagination has run riot regarding the magical equivalents of powerful birds such as the eagle. If such creatures could exist in the everyday world, then their spiritual equivalents must be much more incredible. Descriptions of fabulous birds apparently sighted in far-off lands appear in the mediaeval bestiaries. Exotic birds may have inspired the chroniclers who likened them to the less spectacular species they had seen at home.

Some of these exotic birds were adopted as heraldic signs to signify, for example, the ability of the phoenix to come through anything and rise above suffering.

ALERION

The Alerion, popular in heraldry, is described by Prester John during his travels in the Far East as a kind of super eagle.[7] Prester John was a legendary Christian king who took the title of a descendant of one of the Three Magi, and who reigned over a nation identified variously as being in Ethiopia or India. These stories were popular in Europe from the twelfth through the seventeenth centuries. A letter written by Prester John to the Byzantine Emperor Manuel I Comnenus in the 1150s described various exotic bird species in his kingdom.

The Alerion was, according to Prester John, the same color as fire, with razor-sharp wings. It was much bigger than an eagle. There was only one pair of Alerion at a time, and every sixty years twin eggs hatched after the sixth day. Then the original birds would drown themselves, flying to the sea with a flock of all the other birds in the region, who then acted as surrogate parents to the chicks till they could fly.

BENU

The blue Benu bird was the original mythical phoenix in some versions of the Ancient Egyptian Heliopian creation legend. The Benu bird perched on the first mound as it rose from the primal waters at creation with the sun rising behind (representing the first sunrise). The Benu was considered the ba, or spirit, of the Sun god Ra, or of Osiris, the rebirth and vegetation god. The Benu was also considered, in the original Heliopian creation legend from around 3100 BCE, as an aspect of Atum, the creator and solar deity, whose identity was merged later with that of Ra.

The concept of the Benu bird may have come from the blue-grey herons who returned each year with the Nile flood. They were considered creatures of rebirth. Benu birds can be seen rising in flight from rocky outcrops in the waters at dawn. The Benu is said to be consumed by flames every five hundred years, after which the young bird rises, carrying the ashes of its parent, which it buries beneath the sacred mound at Heliopolis, now an obelisk located in modern Cairo.

Another version of the Benu myth that I heard in Egypt is that it still flies from old Arabia, carrying the egg of the young, and as the young bird is born, it burns up in the sunrise.

CINNAMOLOGUS OR CINNAMULGUS

This is another bird associated with old Arabia. It made its nest in the cinnamon tree. The Cinnamologus is described vividly in mediaeval bestiaries.[8] Legend tells that this particular cinnamon tree was specially prized as incense, and so in the ancient world the nests would be shot down because they could not be reached by climbing; the trees were too high, and the branches were too delicate. No doubt this myth was encouraged to ensure a high price for particularly fragrant cinnamon.

CALADRIUS OR CHARADRIUS

Known as a bird of prophecy that resembled a white heron, and because of its rarity, only kings could own a Caladrius. If there was illness in the household, the bird would look into the sick person's eyes and take out the illness, carrying it to the sun, where it was burned away. However, if the bird would not look at the sick person, it indicated that nothing could be done to save the sick person.

GARUDA

Garuda is the Hindu god king of the birds, who can fly faster than the winds. He acts as steed for the preserver god Vishnu, whom he carries on his back. Garuda is portrayed with the head, wings, talons, and beak of an eagle, and with the body and limbs of a man. His body is gold, and his face is pure white. When he was born his radiance was so brilliant that he was mistaken for Agni, the Hindu god of fire, and so is himself worshipped, though he was not born a deity.

Garuda flies constantly, it is told, to right the wrongs in the world and to attack the destructive naga serpents who threaten the world order. Garuda rescued his mother Vinlata, or Vinita, the serpent woman, who had been imprisoned by his father Kashyap's older wife Kadru in Patal, the realm of the naga serpents beneath the waves. The serpents demanded a cup of amrita (or ambrosia) the drink of the gods, for Vinlata's release. This Garuda obtained from the celestial mountain by overcoming three perils: a ring of flames, a spinning wheel of spikes, and two fire-breathing serpents guarding the amrita. God Indra pursued Garuda and took the amrita from the serpents, but they drank enough to make them immortal.

HERCINIA

The Hercinia is a brilliant bird from the Hercynian forest in Germany whose feathers are so bright and glowing that if plucked and thrown to the ground they offer a pathway through the forest for travelers (the original electric torches). The Hercina, also known as the Harz bird in the Harz Mountains of Germany, was described in mediaeval bestiaries.[9]

THE PHOENIX

The phoenix, of Arabian origin, can be found in the tales of many lands. In the Western tradition there was only one phoenix, a female. The bird is described as having brilliant gold, red, and purple feathers, and as being the size of a huge eagle. This symbolism stemmed from the ancient legend that the phoenix was made up of the elements of the cosmos. It burns itself on a funeral pyre every five hundred years. From the ashes, as they turned golden, a new phoenix would be born. In Christianity the phoenix came to represent the resurrection of Christ

According to the Greek poet Ovid, the phoenix ate frankincense and other exotic gums from trees to sustain itself. The Greek phoenix, unlike the Arabian/Egyptian one, was not consumed by fire. Rather, every five hundred years, it built a nest in the branches of an oak, or in the top of a palm tree, out of cinnamon, spikenard, and myrrh, and there it breathed its last. From its lifeless body emerged a young phoenix, who carried the nest to the city of Heliopolis in Egypt (part of modern Cairo) and offered it in the temple of the sun. This shows the influence of the Egyptian Benu myth on the Greek legend. Historically the Greek general Alexander the Great conquered Egypt in 332 BCE and was welcomed as the son of Amun.

The Roman chronicler Pliny claimed that an actual phoenix was on display in the Roman Forum during the reign of the Emperor Claudius, who ruled between 41 and 54 CE. The phoenix concept was adopted by mediaeval alchemists. The resurrected glorious phoenix was the symbol of alchemy's ultimate aim of turning base metal into gold.

In China and Japan, the appearance of a phoenix in a dream or vision fore-told the coming of a great emperor or sage. Images of the phoenix were car-ried or worn to ensure long life and health. In China the male phoenix, Feng Huang, the vermillion bird, made of flames, is the symbol of the positive yang energy associated with the sun. The female, the yin or receptive principle, is called Hou-ou, bird of the moon.

The phoenix in the Orient was either the enemy, or, more usually, the lover of the dragon. To the Japanese the phoenix symbolized the empress, and so it signified lasting fidelity. The dragon was the creature of the emperor. The Oriental phoenix has the head and comb of a cockerel, signifying the sun, the back of a swallow, signifying the crescent moon, and the tail of a peacock, rep-resenting nature. Its wings represent the winds, and its feet represent the earth. It was said to have had the most enchanting voice ever heard.[10]

QUETZALCOATL, THE FEATHERED SERPENT OF MESOAMERICA

There are four species of birds called Quetzals in the Central and South American rainforests. They were said to have been the companions of the feathered serpent Quetzalcoatl, though they do not fly very well. The males have very long tail feathers, hence perhaps the idea of a feathered serpent.

All the legends of Quetzalcoatl credit him with the creation of humanity, and he is either directly involved in the actual process or acts as humanity's protector and teacher, bringing the gifts of fire, domesticated animals, and maize. He gave the laws and the calendar, instructed the priesthood, and brought healing for eye problems and fertility.

The feathered serpent appeared in various forms throughout the myths and art of the Mayans, the Toltec, and also the Aztecs, who were culturally influ-enced by the first two. Even today in remote parts of Mexico, there is a belief that a feathered serpent lives in certain graves and must be left offerings to bring rain. He travels through water, land, and air. As Lord of the winds, Quetzalcoatl delivers the storm clouds at the beginning of the rainy season.

In the earlier Toltec myth that was absorbed by the Aztecs, at some point in its history Quetzalcoatl was forced, through trickery, to leave Mexico. As he flew away across the eastern seas, now called the Gulf of Mexico, he prom-ised to return in the form of a white-skinned, bearded man from the east to reclaim his heritage and bring in a new age.

According to the Florentine Codex that was written describing the Spanish invasion of Mexico, the Aztec Emperor Moctezuma II thought that the inva-sion of Hernán Cortés and his followers in 1519, was the promised return of

Quetzalcoatl (the Spanish leader matched the description in the prophecy), so they put up no resistance. That, of course, is the Spanish account, which was eager to portray the Aztecs as a primitive, superstitious people.

ROC

The Roc is a huge, white bird described in the Arabian Nights stories. The Roc was so huge and with such a great wing span that as it flew it obscured the sun. It was, according to myth, so strong that it could carry away up to three elephants in its claws. Its wings controlled the winds, and lightning flashed from its eyes as it flew. The Roc, according to Arabian legends, never came to earth, but landed only on Mount Qaf, the Axis Mundi (World Axis). Its gigantic egg shone so brilliantly that it became a symbol of the sun.

In the Arabian nights, the hero Sinbad described how the Roc carried him to safety after a shipwreck. Sinbad became stranded in the Roc's nest on top of Mount Qaf. He escaped by tying himself to the Roc's leg. The Roc flew so high that Sinbad lost sight of the earth.

Marco Polo describes rocs in Madagascar from the journals of his travels. Marco Polo, who lived between 1254 and 1324, journeyed through Asia for twenty-four years and traveled farther than any of his predecessors, beyond Mongolia to China.

In fact, Madagascar was the home of a gigantic bird called the elephant bird, which probably became extinct during the 1500s. Though it did not fly, this may have been what Marco Polo saw.

THUNDERBIRD

Thunderbirds, a magical form of the eagle, are associated mainly with the North American Indian tradition. For many Native North American nations, the thunderbird symbolizes the power of nature at its most dramatic and magnificent. It is the bringer of rain, which pours from a lake on its back as it flies. Its flashing eyes create lightning, and its vast, eaglelike wings cause the thunder. It appears in legends and on totem poles throughout North America and Canada. The thunderbird is often accompanied in flight by eagles or falcons, and it may be shrouded in clouds.

The Passamaquoddy people believe that the thunderbird regulates the weather. The thunderbird can tame the winds to bring calm, sunshine, and necessary fertilizing rain. It was among the first birds to appear at creation. The thunderbird is chief of all the birds of the upper world, who are in constant battle with the land animals and their leader, the trickster raven, who is not a bird of the upper realms. The thunderbird is the protector of all the Indian nations from enemies such as Waziya, the bitter North Wind. The symbol of the thunderbird is a red zigzag. As spring turns to summer, the thunderbird moves from the winter to the summer side of his house.

Among the Plains people he is called Wakinyan, which may be related to the word Wakan, which means sacred power. Some tribes say there are four thunderbirds, one for each of the cardinal directions, but the bird of the West is the most powerful.

Japan also has a thunderbird that resembles a giant rook. It is a bird of the sun, creating thunder and lightning and guarding the approaches to the heavens.

ACTUAL BIRDS WITH MAGICAL ASSOCIATIONS

ALBATROSS

A legendary weather prophet, forecasting winds and bad weather, the albatross is said to care for its eggs on a floating raft and sleep motionless on the wing. Killing an albatross was once believed to bring a curse. The English poet Coleridge based his "Rhyme of the Ancient Mariner" on the legend of a sailor who brought disaster to the ship by killing an albatross. The sailor was then condemned to carry the bird's corpse around his neck.[11] The albatross is a sacred bird in Japanese folklore. It is the servant of the chief god of the sea, and seeing one is a good omen. In New Zealand, ancestors were said to appear as giant cormorants, birds that had oracular properties similar to those of the albatross.

BIRD OF PARADISE

Real birds of paradise are now under conservation in New Guinea and its neighboring islands. The female birds are dull, but the males have brilliant plumage. It may have been these birds or a similarly rainbow-plumed creature that inspired stories of the legendary Bird of Paradise, who perched in the Tree of Life in various cultures, especially in the Far East. Also called the Bird of god, the mythical Bird of Paradise was said to have brilliantly-colored plumage. It did not have wings or feet. It used its slender tail feathers to hang from trees. According to Far Eastern legend, its eggs were dropped from the tree on to the ground, and as they broke, full-grown birds emerged.

In Ancient Persia, now Iran, the Bird of Paradise was called the Huma. It was said that the touch or even the sight of the shadow of Huma would bring good fortune. If Huma perched on the head of a person, that person would become a great leader or a king. Huma was believed to unite the male and female together in its form, representing each by a wing and a leg.

In Slavic folklore, Mater Slava (Mother Glory), or Mater Sava (Mother Owl), sometimes took the shape of a brilliantly colored bird. With each of her feathers shining a different hue, she would lead armies to victory or to glorious death.

BLACKBIRD

In Celtic myth, the magical blackbirds of the goddess Rhiannon sang on the tree at the entrance to the Celtic otherworld and acted as doorkeepers. So sweetly did they sing that none were afraid to enter. In the otherworld they shed their dark feathers and became like rainbow birds. The blackbird was one of the creatures that rescued Mabon, the divine child, from his imprisonment in the Celtic otherworld. Mabon took his rightful place as the Son of Light and fought the Dark god at the spring equinox around March 21, bringing light back to the world.

Blackbirds are the birds of the gentle Irish Saint Kevin, who died around 618 CE, and whose feast day is on June 6. When a blackbird laid its egg in his hand, Saint Kevin maintained the same position until it hatched.

COCKEREL OR ROOSTER

The cockerel was a sacrificial animal in many cultures, and it was buried under the foundations of ancient buildings as a guardian.

In Viking myth there are two cockerels. Vithafmir was the golden cockerel perched at the top of Yggdrasil, the World Tree, as a guardian against evil. Fralar, cockerel of the underworld, lived in Valhalla, abode of the slain warriors, to waken the heroes for the final battle.

In Christianity the cockerel crowed to announce the birth of Jesus. At the end of his life Jesus warned St Peter that after his death, before the cockerel crowed twice, Peter would betray him three times. The Church Fathers of early Christianity declared that the cockerel would signal the beginning of the final Judgment Day.

The rooster is one of the twelve Chinese astrological creatures, and years of the rooster are good for politics and money, for overcoming inertia and injustice, and for self-sufficiency.[12] Rooster people are honest, efficient, good organizers. Among the rooster people are the late Pope Paul VI and Prince Philip, the outspoken husband of Queen Elizabeth II of England. Years of the Rooster include 1933, 1945, 1957, 1969, 1981, 1993, 2005, 2017, and 2029.[13]

It is said that if a cock crows in the afternoon, an unexpected visitor will arrive, whereas crowing at sunset foretells a wet sunrise. For a girl to hear a cock crowing while she is thinking of her sweetheart is a good omen. But if a bride or groom on the way to the church hears a cockerel crowing, that indicates bickering.

CONDOR

The graceful condor, both the Andean and California species, has the largest wingspan of any bird in the world. The Andean condor lives in the South American Andes Mountains. The condor was named *Apu Kunter* by the Incas, which means the one who carries our prayers to the gods. They mate and raise a chick on a high mountain ledge only every two years, and male and female share the incubating and feeding process, always remaining together in the same family. The California condor can fly 300 km or more in a day in its search for food, and it is considered sacred to the indigenous peoples. Condors are compared with the mythical thunderbird and even thought of as a thunder deity.

It is said among the Indians that if the condors (both endangered species), but especially the California condor, die out, so will the human civilization of that area.

CRANE

A guardian of the Celtic otherworld, the crane represented great knowledge and was associated with longevity. Aoife, wife of Mannanann Mac Lir, god of the Sea, was turned into a crane for giving humans knowledge. Far from stopping her teaching, this change meant that she could fly over the whole world in crane form, spreading wisdom. Aoife lived for 300 years. A legendary crane on the island of Innis Kea, in County Mayo, was said to have existed since the beginning of the world.

Cranes carry out intricate mating dances. These were emulated by humans in Minoan Crete around 1800 BCE. Wall paintings and vases reveal male and female dancers whirling and forming arcs as part of ritual circle crane dances.

The crane is a sacred bird in Japan, where it is a symbol of health and long life. It is called the "Honorable Lord Crane," and according to both Japanese and Chinese myth, it lives for a thousand years and more. In China white cranes are considered sacred and are said to originate from the Islands of the Blest, the Chinese earthly paradise.

The Roman Pliny wrote that cranes post sentries while they sleep. The sentry holds a stone in its claw. Should it fall asleep, it will drop the stone, and the noise will alert the other birds.

CROW

Crows were sacred to Athena, Greek goddess of Wisdom, but she did not permit crows to perch on the Acropolis in Athens because that was regarded as a bad omen. Apollo, however, seems not to have been well disposed toward crows. Corvus, or Crow, was sent by Apollo to fetch a cup of water from a sacred spring. But Corvus wasted time eating figs on the way. When he realized how late he was, he caught Hydra, a water snake and claimed it had blocked the stream. In his fury Apollo cast the crow into the skies, along with Hydra and Crater the Cup. The constellation Corvus may be seen in the southern hemisphere close to Virgo. The crow cannot reach the water, and that is why he croaks.

In another myth, the crow was once white. Coronis, the daughter of Phlegyes, was pregnant by Apollo. Apollo left a white crow to watch over her at Delphos. Coronis, however, married the hero Ischys, and the crow told Apollo everything. After killing Coronis and Ischys, Apollo turned the crow black for being the bearer of bad news. The child was miraculously brought to life by Apollo, and he became Asclepius, the healer semideity.

The Crow people who today live on the Crow Reservation in southeastern Montana are called the Apsaalooke, the children of the large beak bird. They have a rich crow mythology.[14] However, the crow also features in many other Native North American mythologies, sometimes as the wise teacher of magic and sacred law, and at other times as a trickster and force for change. The role can depend partly on the perspective. For example, among the Sioux nation the white crow was once the guardian of the buffalo herds and would warn them of hunters approaching. However, the people became angry and threw him onto a fire, burning his feathers black and making his voice hoarse.

Crow divination, using the direction of its flight and interpreting its cawing, is still popular in modern India.

DOVE

The dove features in the Flood stories of the Babylonians, Hebrews, Chaldeans, and Greeks, as a symbol of peace and reconciliation. The dove bearing the olive branch back to Noah's Ark as a sign that there was land ahead has become an international sign of peace.

The dove is also a love symbol, emblem of the Roman Love goddess Venus (and Aphrodite, the Ancient Greek counterpart of Venus), representing faithful, committed love. The dove is, in addition, a sign of wisdom sacred to Athena, and the symbol of Sophia, saint and angel of Wisdom. Gnostic belief during the second century CE linked her with the concept of a female Holy Spirit. The cooing of sacred doves in the oracular groves dedicated to the Ancient Greek Sky god Zeus at Dodona was used for prophecy by the priestesses.

Popular legend describes how two black doves flew from Thebes, one of the main Ancient Egyptian oracular centers. The first dove settled in Dodona in the grove of oaks sacred to Zeus, the father of the Greek gods. The dove spoke in a human voice and declared it the place where an oracle would be established. The second dove flew to Libya to another site sacred to Zeus in the form of Amun, or Ammon, and established a second oracle. This story may in fact refer to priestesses taken back to Greece by Alexander the Great from the Egyptian Oracle that was already established at Thebes.

If a single white dove flies around a house or perches on the roof, a love match or marriage of a member of that household is expected in the near future. Only in Japan is the dove sacred to the War god Hachiman.

EAGLE

The Eagle is known as the king of birds in many cultures. It was the totem bird of powerful earthly rulers and of the sun. In Ancient Greece when Zeus the Father god was preparing for his battle with the Titans, the old giant order of gods, the eagle brought him thunderbolts. He was adopted as the emblem of Zeus and later of Zeus's Roman counterpart Jupiter. Because of its close connection with Jupiter, the eagle became a symbol of earthly power. In Ancient Rome it became the symbol of the Roman emperor and empire. In more recent times the white-headed American bald eagle with outstretched wings has been adopted as the emblem of the United States. It became the official bird in 1789 when George Washington became the first president. However, during the previous six years there had been fierce debate, and in 1784 Benjamin Franklin declared the turkey to be more suitable.

The eagle is also central to Native North American spirituality, and in several myths it was considered the messenger of the Great Spirit. Its feathers were believed to carry the prayers of the people to the Father sun. It was said that the eagle could fly closest to the sun without being burned and could look into the noonday sun without flinching.

In Ancient Egypt in a phoenix-type myth, the eagle flew into the fires of the underworld every ten years, soared upward aflame, and plunged into the Nile and so was reborn.

In the Christian Church the eagle is the symbol of St John the Evangelist and appears on church lecterns. A less orthodox legend suggests that Adam and Eve did not die, but were turned into eagles and flew to Ireland, which became the Blessed Isle.

DUCK

Ducks, like other diving birds, appear in many creation legends of how land was brought forth from the first waters that covered the earth. In Native North American Iroquois lore, ducks were among the first to be created, and, much larger than they are now, caught First Woman in their large wings as she fell from the stars. They carried her safely to Grandmother Turtle, on whose back she rode as she created the land and the plants.

In China a pair of mandarin ducks is often kept as a symbol of faithful, committed love. In modern Feng Shui, ceramic mandarin ducks are set facing each other to attract love, or side by side facing the same direction to indicate a lasting relationship. Afterward small ducks called K'un are added in the southwest side of the home, one for each child desired.

The migratory and breeding habits of ducks and geese were used in various Native North American moon calendars to indicate the progress of the year. For example, among the Megawanipis people, just south of the Arctic circle, the August full moon was called "when young ducks fly" to indicate that the young ducks were learning the skills necessary for them to fly south in the autumn.

HUMMINGBIRD

The hummingbird, though among the smallest of all birds, was one of those who helped to carry back fire to the North American Indians, according to the legends of the Wintu people. He always speaks the truth.

The hummingbird was created, according to Hopi myth, when a small boy made a bird from a sunflower stalk to amuse his sister, and the Creator goddess Grandmother Spider breathed life into it. Because the hummingbird is skilled in hovering and flying backward, his feathers are used as charms in modern folk custom for safe plane journeys (obtained ethically of course).

The hummingbird was another creature of the feathered serpent, Quetzalcoatl, who wore hummingbird feathers.

JAY

The jay was originally named after the ancient Greek Earth goddess Gaea. The blue-crested jay was one of the earliest creatures to be created in a number of North American Indian myths. It was believed to carry messages between the dimensions. It is a member of the crow family and, like the crow, it is a questioner/trickster. It can mimic other creatures, especially hawks. The jay is very secretive about its nest, and it often flies unseen, betrayed only by its raucous call. Jays store food, especially by burying acorns. In Europe the less brightly colored jays are said to be the souls of Celtic Druids forever planting their sacred trees, the oaks.

According to Texan folklore, the jay was once much larger and was on one occasion trapped by humans and harnessed to a plough. The jay at last broke free and asked the Great Spirit for a smaller but fiercer form so that it would never again be enslaved. It is said that the blue jay still bears the mark of the plough on its breast.

KINGFISHER

Many kingfishers are bright blue, except in America, where they have blue-grey feathers and are pure white underneath. Legends say that kingfishers used to be dull in color, but when they flew out of Noah's Ark, one of the pair flew straight for the sun and so absorbed the brilliant blue color of the sky. The other was not so brave and perched on the roof of the Ark, absorbing the softer light.

The kingfisher promises a tranquil period for fourteen days after it is seen. It is often called the "halcyon bird," and it gave rise to the phrase "halcyon days." The origin of these halcyon days comes from Greek myth. Alcyone, daughter of Aeolus, King of the Winds, threw herself into the sea, overshadowed by grief at the death of her husband. The gods transformed her into a kingfisher, and Aeolus said that henceforward the winds would not stir up the sea during the "halcyon days." These fourteen calm days, located around the Mid-Winter Solstice, about December 21, occur between the hatching of eggs and when the young birds are able to fly.

KOOKABURRA

In Australian Aboriginal lore the Keeper of the Sun created the kookaburra to awaken humans, animals, and birds with its laughter on the first dawn, and to bring joy into the world. It is said that so long as the kookaburra laughs to greet the morning, the sun will rise to herald a new day, and joy will be renewed. In another version the kookaburra sings just before dawn so that the Star people can light the fire to generate the sun's light for the day ahead.

The kookaburra's young remain part of the family and help to raise the next batch of chicks. Even if one parent dies, the siblings remain to help keep the family together.

MAGPIES

Black and white magpies are divinatory birds. Throughout the British Isles, seeing one magpie alone is traditionally considered a bad omen. Unless a second magpie follows rapidly, you should take off your hat, or if not wearing one, bow. Then you have to say, "Good morning (or afternoon or evening), Mr. Magpie, and how are you today?" This ensures that any news you receive that day will be good. In the Far East, the magpie's arrival is welcomed, for there the bird is a symbol of happiness and prosperity.

There are several versions of the children's rhyme referring to the prophetic nature of the magpie. Here are two:

> One for sorrow,
> Two for mirth,
> Three for a letter,
> Four for a birth,
> Five for silver,
> Six for gold,
> And seven for a secret never to be told.

Another version says,

> One's sorrow,
> Two's mirth,
> Three's a wedding,

Four's a birth,
Five's a christening,
Six a dearth,
Seven's heaven,
Eight is hell,
And nine the Devil's self as well.

OWL

There are more than 100 species of owl.

The Roman goddess of wisdom Minerva has the owl as her sacred creature, as does her ancient Greek counterpart, Athene. Athene was often depicted with an owl, which was considered a symbol of wisdom in both cultures. The best-known image of Athene's owl, the Little Owl, is seen on ancient Athenian coins dating from the fifth century BCE. To the Romans an owl feather placed near sleeping people would prompt them to speak in their sleep and reveal their secrets.

However, in Rome the owl was considered a harbinger of death if it perched on a roof or on a public building and hooted. The deaths of several Roman emperors, including the assassination of Julius Caesar, were signaled by an owl landing on the roof and hooting.

The owl is called Night Eagle in Amerindian lore, being the bird who is Lady of the night and moon as the eagle is Lord of the day and the sun.

The Owl goddess of the Celts is a bird of the Crone or Grandmother goddess associated with the waning moon and with winter and death. She is said in Celtic lore to be the oldest of creatures, except for the salmon which is described in Chapter 8. The Celtic Owl goddess was called Scathach, goddess of the Isle of Skye. Sometimes the owl was called the old white wife because of its links with the banshee, the protective family spirit whose owl-like wailing was said to herald death, especially if a white owl flew against the window while a person inside the house was sick.

The white owl was one of the forms taken by Gwynn app Nydd, Celtic god of the underworld, who guarded the entrance on top of Glastonbury Tor in Somerset, said to be the isle of Avalon in Arthurian legend. It ruled the souls of slain warriors. In Wales the owl is a symbol of fertility and easy childbirth.

In Japanese folklore, the omens varied according to the kind of owl. The eagle owl as messenger of the gods symbolized wisdom and favor from the gods. The screech owl was friend to the hunter. Only the call of the Horned Owl heralded misfortune.

In New Zealand, owls, especially white ones, are seen in Maori tradition as guardian spirits and noble ancestors.

PARROT

According to the Amahuaca of Eastern Peru, fire was stolen by a parrot from the giant Yowashiko, who had refused to share his gift with humankind. Though Yowashiko tried to drown the parrot with rain storms, larger birds shielded him with their wings and kept the gift safe.

The parrot is the news bringer and revealer of secrets in Afro-Caribbean lore. Among the Yanomami people of the Amazonian basin, parrot feathers are especially prized for their healing and protective properties, and tame parrots are kept in the villages as a source of feathers. The feathers are attached to arrows and sent into the skies to ask the deities for healing and to bring abundance to the village.

In Pueblo Indian myth, the parrot is a bird of the sun and a bringer of abundance. There are now more than 300 species of parrots in the wild, though a large number have been domesticated.

Kamadeva, Hindu god of love, who had a bow strung with humming bees, rode on a huge parrot as he flew through the skies shooting his arrows of love.

PEACOCK

The peacock was the bird of the Greek Hera and Juno, Roman Mother goddess, both of whom were goddess of joy and marriage. If a peacock spreads its tail feathers before your eyes, it is told that love, happiness, and prosperity will follow.

A Greco-Roman myth in Ovid's *Metamorphoses* tells how the eyes of the hero Argus were placed in the tail feathers of Hera/Juno's special peacock. Zeus, or Jupiter, seduced the nymph Io, and to hide her from his angry wife turned her into a cow. However, Hera/Juno saw through the deceit and made Argus, her servant, guard the cow. Her servant had a hundred eyes, only two of which closed in sleep. The messenger god Hermes/Mercury used his staff of snakes to bring sleep upon Argus and then decapitated him. Hera/Juno took the eyes, put them in the feathers of her beloved peacock, and filled the tail with jewels in his memory.

As the old pagan gods and goddesses became discredited with the spread of Christianity, the eyes on the tail feathers were unfairly regarded as the evil eye. For this reason, peacock feathers are rarely brought indoors.

RAVEN

In Norse myth, ravens were the birds of Odin, the Norse All-Father. His two ravens, Hugin and Mugin (Mind and Memory), sat on his shoulders and the Vikings carried Odin's raven Banners into battle. These banners could be made only by the virgin daughters of Viking hero-warriors, and the raven on the banner appeared to come to life during the battle, striking terror into enemies. Sometimes the banner was pure white, and the raven would appear on it. It was said that if the raven moved, victory was assured, but the person carrying the banner would not return. Such banners were also recorded as being carried by Danish Vikings invading Belgium and northern France in the ninth and tenth centuries.

The raven was likewise the sacred bird of Bran, the Celtic god-king. Ravens are still kept at the Tower of London because legend says that if they leave their sacred place (the Tower) London will be destroyed and England will be invaded. That is because, as Bran lay dying, he ordered that his head be cut off (warrior heads were greatly prized by the Celts as a source of strength) and buried beneath the White Mound, now beneath the White Tower in the Tower of London. His seven sacred ravens were set to guard the head.

In the Bible the raven was one of the birds sent out by Noah to find land, but he did not return.

ROBIN

Several European legends explain why the robin has a red breast. One says that he burned it in the fires of hell bringing water to lost souls. Others claim it was stained with the blood of Christ as the robin pulled the thorns from Christ's Crown. A third version says that the robin covered the dead with leaves, and as he was covering Christ, he was touched by his blood.

The robin is so beloved in England that he is protected by various prohibitions. One old rhyme says

> If a robin you dare kill,
> Your right hand will straightway lose its skill.

The robin, especially the first robin of spring, can grant wishes. For good luck in the twelve months ahead, you need to make your wishes before the robin flies away.

SEAGULL

Seagulls are said to be the souls of dead sailors and so should never be shot. Storm petrels, known as Mother Carey's chickens, are also especially protected by sailors. If a gull settles on any part of a ship in which a person is traveling, the voyage will be a happy one.

In Salt Lake City, Utah, in the United States, there is a monument to the California Gull in front of the State Capitol Building. Soon after the Mormons came to the area, a plague of millions of crickets appeared and were destroying the crops. The Mormons prayed for help, and thousands of California Gulls arrived and consumed the crickets.

SWALLOWS AND MARTINS

The swallow was sacred to Isis, the Ancient Egyptian Mother goddess, and also to Venus and Aphrodite, the Classical goddesses of Love. Like the stork in Swedish tradition, at the time of the crucifixion the swallow flew over the cross, calling "svala, svala," which means "console." The coming of the swallows has been regarded in many lands as a symbol of awakening after winter and of the renewal of life since early times.

The swallow, like the wren, was a bird associated with bringing fire from the heavens to humans. In American Indian lore, the swallow carried the fire from the sun on her tail feathers. She has red tail feathers and a forked tail because that was where she got burned.

A legend associated with alchemy that grew up in Europe in the Middle Ages tells us that the swallow carried the flowering herb celandine in her beak to restore the eyesight of those in need. In another version she had two gems in her stomach, one a red ruby, or garnet, to bring wealth, and the other a black jet, or pearl, to bring good fortune to those who found the stones on their doorstep. Seeing a swallow in early spring is a promise of a happy summer. If swallows build nests in the eaves of a house, success, happiness, and good fortune are promised to all who live there.

The Martin, the largest form of swallow, is considered especially blessed. It was called God's bow and arrow because of its forked tail. Martins are believed to be messengers of God as in pre-Christian times swallows were believed to be messengers of the goddesses they served.

SWAN

The Swan was a form taken by Celtic goddesses and, in later myths, by fairy maidens and enchanted princesses who were identifiable by the gold and silver chains around their necks. In the Celtic tradition, Swan goddesses/fairies were famed for their wonderful voices and healing powers and were identifiable from other swans by gold and silver chains around their necks.

Swans were also forms frequently adopted by fairy women and goddesses as did, for example, the Viking Valkyries, the beautiful Viking maidens who chose half of the noble slain to return with them to Valhalla. Valkyries could be forced to retain human form if a would-be lover stole their feathered cloak when they discarded it to dance by the lakeside.

The most famous of the many swan maiden tales is that of Angus Mac Og, god of Youth, son of the Irish Father god, the Dagda, who lived in a palace at New Grange. One night Angus dreamed of a lovely fairy woman and so desired her that his mother Boanna, after whom the River Boyne is named, searched all Ireland. After the search had continued for more than a year, the maiden was found on the Lake of the Dragon's Mouth in the form of a swan, with 149 other swan maidens, each chained in pairs with silver and gold, hung with bells. She was called Caer, fairy maiden of Connacht, Ireland, and she assumed her fairy form every other year. Her father said Angus could marry Caer only if he identified her from among the other swans. On Samhain, or Halloween, Angus found the Lake of the Dragon's Mouth and instantly recognized Caer. Angus called her and was also transformed into a swan, whereupon they flew away to his palace on the Boyne, creating such sweet music as they sang of their love that all who heard it slept for three days. Angus's palace was on the site of the megalith of Brugh na Boinne, where their singing can still be heard on moonlit nights. Because of the belief in fairy swan maidens, it was forbidden to kill a swan in Ireland for many years.

In India, a swan was said to carry Sarasvati, Hindu goddess of wisdom and music, the wife of Brahma, whenever she traveled. The Black swans of Australia are considered the manifestation of the Mother-Sister female counterpart of Balame, the Aboriginal All-Father deity. Swans are also considered to contain the souls of great poets, writers, and musicians because the Roman Sun god Apollo's soul took the form of a swan. Apollo was god of the creative and performing arts. For this reason, William Shakespeare is sometimes called the Swan of Avon, the river that runs through his birthplace Stratford-upon-Avon in central England. Many swans congregate outside the Royal Shakespeare Theatre.

TURKEY

Turkeys, known as the jeweled fowl, were sacrificial creatures in ancient Mesoamerican society. On the North American continent, turkeys were a symbol of self-sacrifice in the noblest sense and of the famous potlatch, or giveaway ceremony, among the Native North American nations when tribes presented gifts to other tribes.

To the Mayans, the turkey was a symbol of the sun, daylight, life, and fertility. To the Native North Americans it signified the Earth Mother, and, like the buffalo, it was considered a willing sacrifice of Mother Earth to feed her people.

The Navaho tell that when all living things climbed as high as possible to escape the Flood, the turkey let the other animals and birds go ahead of him. For that reason only a low branch was left, and his lovely, jewel-colored tail feathers trailed in the water and got wet. All the color washed out of them, and that is why turkeys have white tail feathers.

The turkey became the focus of Thanksgiving Day in the United States on the fourth Thursday in November. This festival commemorates the first harvest feast of the Pilgrim Fathers in 1621, when four wild turkeys were eaten.

BEE GODDESSES

Bee goddesses have already been discussed in Chapter 1. Bees predated humans and therefore have probably always fascinated humans with their ability to produce honey and sweet-smelling beeswax which was formed into candles. Thus Bee goddesses became associated with abundance as a food- and light-giver.

The first bee-keeping images appear on cave walls in Valencia, Spain, and date from around 7000 BCE.

Because of the complex social arrangement within the hive and the importance of the queen bee and her virgin workers, a bee colony may have seemed a reflection of how a Bee goddess might rule over her devotees.

BEES IN MYTHOLOGY

From early times, the bee was used as an image to represent the Mother goddess, and the hive was likened to the womb of the Great Mother. In Otzak, Thessaly an early image of the Bee goddess was found painted on a vase dating from around 6000 BCE.

The goddess was also depicted as a Queen Bee in Minoan culture. Here the bee represented the soul and rebirth because it was believed that bees were born from dead bulls, especially if the carcass was buried up to the horns in Mother Earth. This idea pervaded other European cultures and was still recorded in mediaeval times in England. Demotricus of Abdera, called the laughing philosopher, described how bees came from dead oxen.

THE MELISSAE

Over the millennia, bees have been adopted as the icon of Rhea, the Greek Earth Mother; Demeter, the Grain Mother; Cybele, originally an Anatolian Earth and Mountain goddess, whose worship spread throughout the Ancient Greek world and Roman Empire; Artemis; and her Roman counterpart Diana. Aphrodite, Greek goddess of love, was worshipped at a honeycomb-shaped shrine at Mount Eryx.

The bee priestesses of the various bee goddesses were called Melissae, Latin for bees. In the *Homeric Hymn to Hermes*, written in the eighth century BCE, three prophetic Melissae, or bee priestesses, who practiced divination beneath the cliffs at Parnassus and drank a kind of honey mead to induce prophecy, were given to the messenger god Hermes by Apollo.[15]

In Greece bees were considered to be the souls of dead priestesses and so could endow one with prophetic powers. Zeus the Father god was born in a cave of bees and nourished by them. It was believed that an infant touched by a bee soon after birth would be a great poet or philosopher. It was thought that this had happened to Plato, Sophocles, and Virgil.

BEES AND THE VIRGIN MARY

The importance of bees survived into Christian times. Bees became symbols of the Virgin Mary throughout the Western world and especially in Eastern Europe. In the Slavonic folk tradition, the bee is linked with the Immaculate Conception. July 26, the feast of St Anna, mother of Mary, whose birth resulted from an immaculate conception, is the time when beekeepers pray for the conception of new healthy bees.

In the Ukraine, bees are the *tears of our Lady*, and the Queen Bee of any hive is called *Queen Tsarina*, a name associated with Mary, Queen of Heaven. Throughout Eastern Europe, Mary is the protectress of bees and beekeepers, and consecrated honey is offered on altars on the Feast of the Assumption of the Virgin Mary on August 15, the date linked with her ascension into heaven.

BUTTERFLIES

THE BUTTERFLY GODDESSES

Insects have always been of fascination to humans for they are the most ancient of creatures. A caterpillar being reborn from the cocoon as a fabulous butterfly became a symbol of rebirth by Neolithic times. The caterpillar was described by the sixteenth-century mystic Teresa of Avila as the spirit emerging from the body after death.

Around 4000 BCE, the Minoan Crowned Butterfly goddess symbolized fertility and regeneration in ancient Crete, and, like the Bee goddess, it is seen rising from the horns of a bull.

The mortal Psyche, whose name is Greek for soul, married Eros, God of Love, but she was permitted to meet him only in darkness. She was transformed into a butterfly on her death, according to early Greek myth, a common form for the human soul to take between incarnations.

Hina, the Butterfly goddess of Hawaii and the South Pacific Islands is associated with the moon. Hina is called the one who eats the moon to explain its different phases. She is regarded as one of the creating goddesses of the world, and her spirit is said to be contained in every woman, for she was the first woman. Now Hina lives in the moon, having traveled there on a rainbow pathway. Every butterfly is a reminder to enjoy every moment of happiness.

THE HOPI INDIAN BUTTERFLY MAIDEN

Palhik Mana is the name given to the Native North American Hopi Butterfly Maiden. She is represented as a doll and dancer at the Katsina (or Kachina) Nature, Earth, and Weather spirit celebrations in August. Her headdress, or tablita, is adorned with corn and butterfly symbols to call forth a good harvest because butterflies are associated with the pollination of crops. Kachinas who come to the earth between December and July bring rain and good harvests, and they are invoked in dance and rituals.[16]

DRAGONFLY OR DAMSELFLY

The dragonfly is the national emblem of Japan, which is sometimes called the Island of the Dragonfly. A symbol of joy and reunion, the Japanese dragonfly of rebirth carries the spirits of the family back home on the August festival of Bon, the equivalent of Halloween. During the festival families celebrate the lives of deceased loved ones and light a fire outside the family home to welcome them.

Ix Chel, the Mayan goddess of creativity, who was described as holding the womb jar of the world upside down so life could continue, has the dragonfly as her special creature. This is because she fell in love with the sun, and her grandfather attacked her and almost killed her. But the dragonfly beat its tiny wings to revive her and sang magical songs to restore her to health.

In American Indian Navajo law, the dragonfly's name is *she who is spread out on water*. The dragonfly is welcomed ceremonially and its energies absorbed by the tribal holy man so that they can be used in healing ceremonies.

Among the Lakota Indians dragonflies, like butterflies and lizards, are believed to remain unharmed by hailstones or storms. From Japan to Africa dragonfly energies are linked to whirlwinds. Using dragonfly rituals, warriors transferred the powers and protection of the dragonfly to their shields and battle clothes to avoid harm when fighting and also to keep them safe in storms and whirlwinds.

A symbol of the summer, of the sun, of rainbows and light, the dragonfly is also considered in many lands a creature of the fairy realms. It is said that if you approach a settled dragonfly, your wishes will be granted.

BIBLIOGRAPHY

1. Gimbutas, M. *The Living Goddesses.* Edited and supplemented by R. D. Miriam. Berkeley/Los Angeles: University of California Press, 1999.
2. Ginzburg, C., J. Tedeschi, and A. C. Tedeschi. *Clues, Myths and Historical Methods.* Washington, DC: John Hopkins University Press, 1992.
3. Lesko, B. S. *Great Goddesses of Egypt.* Norman: University of Oklahoma Press, 1999.
4. Tacitus. *The Complete Works.* Berkshire, Maidenhead, England: McGraw Hill Higher Education Press.
5. Guerber, H. A. *The Myths of Greece and Rome (Anthropology and Folklore).* London: Dover Publications, 1993.
6. Virtanen, L., and T. DuBois. *Finnish Folklore [Studia Fennica Folkloristica].* Helsinki: Finnish Literature Society, 2002.
7. Pastoreau, M. *Heraldry: Its Origins and Meaning.* London: Thames and Hudson, 1997.
8. White, T. H. *The Book of Beasts: Being a Translation from a Latin Bestiary of Twelfth Century England.* London: Dover Publications, 1984.
9. See note 8.
10. Campbell, J. *The Masks of God: Volume 2, Oriental Mythology.* London: Penguin, 1991.
11. Coleridge, S. T. and W. Keach. *The Complete Poems of Samuel Taylor Coleridge.* London: Penguin, 1997.
12. See note 10.
13. Walters, D. *The Complete Guide to Chinese Astrology: The Most Comprehensive Study of the Subject Ever Published in the English Language.* London: Watkins, 2006.
14. Medicine Crow, J. *From the Heart of the Crow Country: The Crow Indians' Own Stories.* Lincoln: University of Nebraska Press/Bison Books, 2000.
15. Gaisser, J. H. *Homeric Hymn to Hermes.* Brynn Mawr Commentaries. Philadelphia: University of Philadelphia, 1983.
16. Day, J. S. *Traditional Hopi Kachinas: A New Generation of Carvers.* Flagstaff, AZ: Northland Publishing, 2000.

CHAPTER 5

Unicorns, Lost Animals of Legends, and the Magic of Animals

Mythology is filled with a wide variety of fabulous animals. Some were based on actual animals such as Pegasus, the winged horse of Greek legend, or the fairy cattle of Wales. Even relatively ordinary animals such as the dog and cat have a whole wealth of myths about their magical powers. These myths are based on characteristics such as the intense loyalty of the dog, seen in more mundane versions of the species.

However, a number of more exotic species are described in myth as having parts from different animals. One such creature was fabled Leucrota. Leucrota had the back of a stag, the chest and legs of a lion, and the head of a horse with a mouth that extended right across its face and a single bone for its teeth, but which nevertheless spoke with a human voice. Leucrota was said to run faster than any other creature. Like many fabulous creatures its home was said to be India, a land believed even in mediaeval times to extend across much of the Far East. These strange creatures were described by the author Physiologus, apparently from Alexandria, who may have been St Ambrose (340 CE–397 CE), Bishop of Milan, writing under a classical name to gain historical credibility.[1] Another source of information for these amazing creatures was Saint Isidore of Seville who lived between 560 and 636 CE. He was Bishop of Seville and wrote the *Etymologiae*, which included information on exotic animals.[2]

Indeed mediaeval chroniclers, like their classical predecessors, believed that before humans evolved there was a race of composite animals (that is, beasts made up of different animal and bird characteristics). These were destroyed by the deities once they had perfected making true animal forms, but a few escaped and lived for hundreds of years in remote places until they finally died out or were killed by would-be heroes in search of glory.

FABULOUS CREATURES OF MYTH AND LEGEND

This section focuses on the best-known exotic and entirely imaginary creatures about which much has already been written.

CENTAUR

The Ancient Greeks wrote of the half man–half horse centaurs that were human to the waist. They were more highly evolved intellectually than Pan's satyrs, the half-goats of discussed in Chapter 1. Chiron was the wisest and most perfect of all the centaurs. He was taught by Apollo, the god of prophecy and the performing arts, and by Apollo's twin sister Diana, the huntress and Moon goddess.

Chiron became famous for his skills in hunting, medicine, music, and the art of prophecy and taught many Greek heroes including Hercules. He reared the infant Aesculapius who became god of medicine and had the power to restore the dead to life.

Sagittarius, the Archer (23 November–21 December), the constellation, and star sign was named after a very active centaur named Crotus. Crotus was the son of Pan the Woodland god who, like his father, loved the forests and hunting. However, through the influence of his mother Eupheme, nurse to the Muses who were his playfellows, Crotus became a skilled artist and poet. He continuously shoots arrows toward the scorpion in the sky killed by Hercules, in case it ever attacks again.

There were less benign variations of the true centaur. A bucentaur, for example, had the head and upper body of a man and the lower body, legs, and tail of an ox. A centycore was a true composite, with horse's hooves, lion's legs, elephantine ears, a bear's muzzle, and an antler with ten points on its forehead. Though it spoke like a human, it was said to be totally vicious.

GRYPHON/GRIFFON/GRIFFIN

The griffon, a popular figure in mediaeval heraldry, is said to have the body of a lion, the head and wings of an eagle, a back covered with feathers, a hooked beak, and two huge talons or claws on its front two legs.

The griffon had a nest made of pure gold in which it laid agate or jeweled eggs. Sometimes female griffons are depicted without wings.

Its name in Persian means *lion eagle*, and so it combines the powers of the King of the Birds (the eagle) and the King of the Animals (the lion). In old Persia it was regarded as a guardian of the light and its statues guarded palaces and public buildings. The first griffon image dates from around 5000 BCE from the former city of Susa, now in Iran. In European heraldry, the griffon became the totem animal of families whose founding member was both warlike and noble to reflect qualities of the eagle and the lion combined. On crests and shields of Kings and nobles the griffon was shown rearing up, standing on one hind leg with the other leg and its claws raised as though springing.

The griffon is found in the mythology of many lands as a creature of the sun and often pulls the chariot of sun deities including the Greek Apollo and the wise goddess Athena. The griffon is also found painted or engraved on Egyptian tombs. One of its main homelands was believed to be the ancient kingdom of Scythia that extended from the modern Ukraine to central Asia. Griffons dug for gold from mines to create their nests and also instinctively knew where treasure has been lost or hidden. Scythia legends say they protected local gem and gold resources from plunderers. In Christianity, being a creature of the heavens and earth, the griffon was adopted as a symbol for Christ. Griffon was also a symbol of faithful marriage because it was said a griffon would have only one partner, and even after the death of one of them, the other would never seek another mate. Able to carry an ox or its mortal enemy the horse off in its talons, the griffon was nevertheless considered to be a healer of blindness, and its feathers could detect poison. The griffon was described by the Roman historian Pliny the Elder. Stone griffons may still be seen made on cathedrals or churches over entrances as protection.

HIPPOGRYPH, OR HIPPOGRIFF

Created by the mating of two traditional enemies, the griffon and the horse, the hippogryph was, even in myth, considered a rarity. However, it could be tamed enough by a wizard to use as a steed. Thomas Bulfinch, the

nineteenth-century collector of classical myths and curiosities,[3] described the
hippogriff as having the head, talons, and feathered wings of an eagle and the
rest of the body that of a horse.

MANTICORE

Another composite magical beast from India, the manticore, the size of a
horse, is described in bestiaries as having a red-colored lion's body; the face
of a man with gray eyes but with three rows of iron teeth, one inside the
other; and a tail like a scorpion, ending in spikes. It leaps great distances and
makes a sound like a hiss, or in other descriptions like the playing of a flute
or trumpet, and it eats humans.

PARANDER

A creature from Ethiopia, another suitably umbrella term—this time for
the regions south of the known Middle East area—is the parander. It is pictured as the size of an ox but leaves footprints like an ibis (popular in Ancient
Egypt as symbol of Thoth, god of wisdom). With color and fur like a bear,
the head of a stag, and huge branching antlers, its chief characteristic was the
ability to change shape when frightened. It took the form of the nearest
object, whether a tree or a large stone, and maintained that form till the danger has passed.

THE SPHINXES OF THE EGYPTIAN AND
CLASSICAL WORLD

While creatures like the parander and manticore were rare, the sphinx may
be found in statue form in Egypt. Sphinxes were more like protective statues.
In Ancient Egypt recumbent sphinxes acted as guards, protecting temples and forming the base of the king's throne. The lion's body was used
for the body of the sphinx, and in Egypt it usually had the face of a
pharaoh. For example, the colossal Great Sphinx was carved around 2500
BCE, the same time as the Great Pyramids were created in Giza near Cairo.
The Great Sphinx has the face of King Khafre (or Cheops) whose pyramid
it guards.[4]

The most famous predictive dream in Egyptian history was that of King Thutmoses IV, who ruled from 1400 to 1390 BC. This may offer clues to the magical powers seemingly possessed by the Great Sphinx. Thutmoses had his dream while he was still a prince and not directly in line to be the next king of Egypt. A record of his dream can still be seen on a stela, a commemorative tablet, between the front paws of the sphinx at Giza. The stela tells that during a hunting expedition near Giza, Thutmoses became tired and fell asleep, shaded by the sphinx that was half-buried in the sand. In his dream, the sphinx appeared and complained that his statue had been neglected and was rapidly disappearing into the sand. The sphinx promised the prince that he would become king if he restored the monument to its former glory. Though he was not heir to the throne, Thutmoses agreed and, when he was later made king, kept his promise to restore the statue to its former glory and erected the stela to record the experience.

The sphinx was also regarded as the solar guardian of the horizon. As a protective statue the sphinx ensured Apep the Chaos serpent could not follow the Sun god into the sky after their nighttime battle in the underworld.

The Criosphinxes, guardians of Amun's temple at Karnak, formed an avenue of ram-headed sphinxes with lions' bodies, representing the Creator god. They would let pass only those who were pure of heart, as the Temple of Amun symbolized the heavens. Amun was often pictured with the horns of a ram or as a ram.

The Greek sphinx was less benign and was famed for its great knowledge and ability to create riddles. It lived outside the city of Thebes and had the body of a lion and the upper part of a woman. It lay crouched on the top of a rock, and stopped all travelers who came that way, proposing to them a riddle, with the condition that those who could solve it should pass safely, but those who failed should be killed. The hero Oedipus was the only one to answer her riddle correctly. It is told that the sphinx was so mortified at the solving of her riddle that she cast herself down from the rock and perished.[5]

UNICORN

A pure white horse with a spiral horn or spiral grooved in the center of its forehead, the unicorn was first described in 398 BCE by the Greek Cresias. Cresias traveled throughout Persia and the Far East and told of a creature he encountered that seems remarkably similar to the fabled unicorn. Cresias said that the dust from its horn had healing properties, a power that was also mentioned in stories from many other lands. Powdered unicorn horn was also recommended in medieval literature as an aphrodisiac and to reverse the effects of poison.

In China the unicorn was thought to see the evil in human hearts and to kill the wicked with a single thrust of its horn, hence its association with holiness and purity.

The unicorn of myth could run faster than light and walk across grass without disturbing it. Though the unicorn is fierce, and so fast that no hunter can catch it, it will stop and approach a pure maiden and will sleep with its head against her breast or in her lap. The unicorn is another symbol of Christ and like the griffon was used as a heraldic symbol and family emblem by powerful families in the Middle Ages.[6]

The German mystic Hildegard von Bingen, who lived between 1098 and 1179 CE and wrote various treatises on nature, considered that a ground unicorn liver mashed with egg yolk could make a lotion to cure leprosy.

The beautiful unicorn tapestries, created around 1500 may still be viewed at the Cloisters, a branch of New York's Metropolitan Museum of Art.[7] In these seven tapestries, the unicorn is shown as a Christian symbol. The tapestries were thought to have been designed in France and woven in Brussels. One theory about the creator of the tapestries says that she was Anne, queen of Brittany, who was also queen of France.

DOMESTICATED CREATURES THAT ARE REAL, BUT GIVEN MAGICAL ASSOCIATIONS

THE MAGICAL HORSE

Because the horse was an important means of transport, both in battle and domestically, and such an intelligent devoted creature, it seems quite natural that the steeds of deities and heroes should be considered magical and have extraordinary powers. White horses are considered especially magical.

Epona, the white horse goddess, became one of the most influential goddesses, not only in Gaul and Britain but throughout the Roman Empire. She is often depicted as a white horse accompanied by a foal or, in Roman images, as a beautiful woman riding sidesaddle accompanied by mares and foals as symbols of her fertility. The huge chalk figures of horses etched on hillsides throughout England recall her worship.[8]

A survivor of the Celtic magical horse tradition is the Grant Horse of English folklore who is said to walk on his hind legs. The Grant Horse, which is found almost entirely in oral folk tradition, acts as guardian to villages and warns of approaching danger. As recently as the Second World War in the area around London, the Midlands, and the east coast as far north as Yorkshire, there were anecdotes about the Grant Horse warning inhabitants of air raids by appearing as a small black horse that reared up, driving dogs and other horses into a frenzy. After giving the warning, it disappeared.

In Norse myth, Odin had a magical gray steed called Sleipnir who had runes, magical symbols, engraved on his teeth. Odin rode Sleipnir into battle. This eight-legged horse of Odin, the swiftest of all horses, could travel throughout the nine worlds of the gods, giants, elves, men, and the underworld, and across land and sea. It is told that once he even jumped in a single leap the gates of Hel's realm leading to the regions of Nifleheim, the land of the dead, when Hermod the messenger tried to rescue the slain Sun god Baldur. He carried slain warriors on his back to Valhalla. Because Sleipnir carried Odin through the skies around Christmas in the Wild Hunt when Odin left gifts for the faithful beneath pine trees, it has been suggested that the eight-legged Sleipnir may have given rise to the concept of Santa Claus's eight reindeer.

Horse fairs and horse cults were sacred to Freyr the fertility god in the Viking world.

MAGICAL HORSES IN ANCIENT GREECE AND ROME

According to classical myth, Poseidon (Neptune in Roman myth) created the first horse Arion (meaning *warlike*) by striking the earth with his trident. Its right feet were those of a man. It had a human voice and ran as fast as the wind. At first it was given to Adrastus, King of Argos, who led the seven heroes against Thebes. The horse eventually passed to Hercules.

The symbol of the winged horse appears on coins as early as 430 BCE and became a symbol of magical flight. Pegasus was the winged horse of Greco-Roman legend that was created from the blood of the head of the monster Medusa that the hero Perseus slew. As Medusa's blood sank into the earth, the winged white horse sprang up from the sea. Pegasus was caught by Minerva, the Roman goddess of wisdom, and tamed so that the father god Jupiter could use the steed to carry thunder and lightning and deliver messages between the deities. Pegasus lived on Mount Helicon, the mountain where the semidivine Muses, inspirers of poetry, had their home. Here he struck the ground with his hoof and the fountain of Hippocrene sprang up, which had the ability to endow those who drank from it with poetic or musical abilities.

Pegasus was, with the help of Minerva, captured by the mortal warrior Bellerophon, using a magical golden bridle given by Minerva. On seeing the golden bridle, Pegasus allowed himself to be saddled and rose into the air with the young Bellerophon on his back. Pegasus and Bellerophon became a devoted team and defeated the Chimera, a fire-breathing monster. Bellerophon and Pegasus went on to win many quests, and as a reward Bellerophon was given King Ioabtes' daughter as his bride and was named the successor to the throne. But Bellerophon became too ambitious and tried to ride Pegasus to Mount Olympus and the realm of the gods. Jupiter became angry and sent a gadfly to sting Pegasus, who threw and injured Bellerophon. Bellerophon fell to the earth. But Pegasus became a constellation in the sky as a reward for his devoted service.[9]

THE MAGICAL COW

Cows, because of their ability to give milk, were associated with nourishment and mothering. Hathor, the Ancient Egyptian mother goddess, was depicted with cow horns or as an actual cow nourishing the pharaoh. Statues of cows were often placed in tombs to ensure nourishment of the deceased in the afterlife, so Hathor also became a family goddess whose image was set on domestic altars.

In Norse myth, bovine nourishment was available from the beginning of creation, because in the Viking world the cow was regarded as a source of wealth and could be taken on the longboats to other lands: it could give milk on the journey and start a herd in the new land. There is even a rune, a mag-ical Norse symbol *fehu*, meaning wealth that refers to cattle as a source of wealth.[10] Therefore, it would seem sensible to myth weavers that the cow would be among the first creatures created.

Audhumla, the primal cow in Viking myth, was formed from the melting ice that, with fire, was considered a material of creation. Four rivers of milk flowing from her udder sustained the giant Ymir. She licked hoar frost and salt from the melting ice to nourish herself. As she licked, the first god Buri emerged. He was the ancestor of the later gods, including Odin the Father god.

The Aurochs, the huge wild cattle that roamed the plains of Scandinavia and Germany until the 1600s, were the name given to another rune, *Uruz*, which symbolized primal strength. Their horns were probably the ones worn on Viking helmets to offer magical strength in battle.

In Celtic tradition, the cow was sacred to the goddess Brighid and from the later fifth century to St Bridget, or Brigit of Ireland. The saint was often pictured with a cow, and she was credited with various milk miracles, including her ability to turn water into milk whenever she offered a stranger a drink.

Cattle were, in Celtic myth, believed to be gifts from the deities. It is told that in Ireland the first cattle came from the sea: one red, one white, and one black. White cows were sacred and associated with Boanna, goddess of the rivers, who gave her name to the River Boyne and whose name means *Woman of the White Cows*.

Small fairy cattle were, according to fairy stories from the Celtic world, much prized as dowries from fairy brides. Small, perfectly formed women were said to marry humans, especially in Wales, where small, brown, sturdy cattle have thrived in mountainous conditions. In Ireland, until the mid-1900s and still in remote places, a cow's milk is first squirted on the ground as a gift for the little people.

The *Gruagach* is a Celtic female fairy (in pre-Christian times a goddess) who guarded the cattle at night in Scotland and ensured that bad fairies did not sour the milk. On Scottish islands such as Skye can still be seen hollow "gruagach stones" at farm entrances where milk was left for her. Because it was said if she was not given milk, the best cow of the herd might mysteriously die during the night.[11] The most fascinating of the fairy cow legends is that of the huge Dun cow of Dunsmore Heath in central England. Originally belonging to a giant, the Dun cow provided milk to all who asked and apparently grazed happily over a period of many years, on Mitchell Fold in Shropshire. However, one day the cow became very angry because an old woman demanded that the cow filled her sieve as well as a pail with milk. The Dun cow went on the rampage and was finally killed by Guy, Earl of Warwick, on Dunsmore Heath. Her horns may be seen today in Warwick Castle on the castle wall in central England, though skeptics insist they resemble a pair of elephant tusks.

THE HINDU MILK MIRACLE

The cow is a sacred creature to Hindus. The cow, called Guias, symbolizes the earth and is considered a gift from the deities to humankind, created from the churning of the cosmic ocean.

Milk is the sacred fluid in the Hindu religion, much as holy water is regarded in Christianity. The ritual offering of milk, fruit, sweets, and money to the gods is an established practice in the Hindu faith. Milk is poured over Shiva, the Hindu god, and Ganesha, his elephant-headed son, during festivals.

The most universal simultaneous event that has occurred in modern times is probably what was called in the popular press of the time the Milk Miracle. The Milk Miracle was a phenomenon that was witnessed on Thursday, September 21, 1995, by people all over the world. I was able to interview witnesses of the event in London.

The Milk Miracle was foretold in the Punjab. Pandit Chaman Prakash, Head of the Khampur Shiv Mandir Temple in Chandigargh, was approached by a young woman before sunrise on Thursday, September 21, 1995. She told him that her sister had dreamed that Ganesha would come to earth to drink milk at 4 A.M. The priest reluctantly opened the temple, and at exactly 4 A.M., the statue accepted milk from a spoon.

News spread throughout India and to Hindu communities all around the world. In India, during Thursday morning many of the statues of Ganesha were reported to be drinking milk. Within hours, millions of Hindus world-wide flocked to their nearest temple where statues of Ganesha were also witnessed accepting milk. By Thursday evening the phenomenon was being reported in Kolkata, Chennai, Singapore, Hong Kong, Indonesia, Bangladesh, Nepal, Dubai, Kenya, Germany, Bangkok, Brisbane, Toronto, New York, and Jersey City in the United States and throughout the UK. Other idols—Shiva, Krishna, and Brahma—were also accepting milk on that day.

In the UK, ten thousand people visited the Vishwa Hindu Temple in Southall, West London, where the white marble statue of Nandi, Shiva's sacred mount, was also said to be accepting milk. A few hundred meters away in the home of Asha and Anil, a Hindu couple who came to England from Uganda, a small clay statue also began to drink milk. Before long devotees were crowding the small suburban living room of Asha, waiting patiently to offer milk to the small painted statue of Ganesha that stood in the fireplace.

Asha explained, when I interviewed her on the telephone soon after the event, "My statue is made of clay, but when I felt inside, it was completely dry and no milk had seeped through. This continued for about a week and then the statue would accept no more." From India, confirmation came by Friday, September 22, 1995, that Ganesha and the other deities had ceased to accept milk.

The phenomenon was regarded by Hindus as a sign that the problems of the world would be overcome through faith. The fundamentalist World Hindu Council declared the milk-drinking a manifestation of Divine Blessing. Scientists have put forward many theories to explain away the Milk Miracle, such as capillary action and natural absorption by marble. But the fact that the statues did not before and have not since absorbed milk suggests that this is not the entire story. As some statues were tiny or made of solid metal, there seems no adequate explanation for the absorption of such relatively large amounts of liquid.

In India the cow is strongly associated with the cult of Krishna, a divine being who was considered the avatar of earthly manifestation of Vishnu the preserver god. On earth Krishna took the form of a cowherd in his youth.[12]

MAGICAL PETS

As humans value relations with dogs and cats as close companions, it was thought that the deities and heroes must be accompanied by animals who displayed a super version of the qualities shown by more ordinary pets. In Chapter 9, the possibility is explored, and some experiments are described that may suggest pets have intuitive links with their owners. The myth weavers may have felt a strong instinctive bond with their pets that inspired the stories of magical pets.

THE LOYALTY OF THE DOG

Our pets came originally from wild animals, perhaps individuals of the species that came close to settlements and were naturally responsive to people. Indeed the findings of three research teams, reported in November 2002 in a UK *Science* magazine, suggested that 95 percent of all dogs evolved from three founding female wolves, tamed by humans living in or near China less than 15,000 years ago. Even dogs in the New World have their origins in Eastern Asia. According to Carles Vila of Uppsala University, Sweden, one of the teams studying the New World dogs, the dogs traveled with the colonists to America and Canada. Their use as hunting animals and to protect vulnerable humans began the mutual dependence that we see today even in the most pampered urbanized dogs.

The dog, known as a human's best friend, has a dual function in myth: the domesticated faithful friend and fearsome wilder creature of the otherworldly hunting pack as with, for example, the Norse Odin's Wild Winter hunt when he rose with huge baying black hounds through the skies. Fierce dogs also guarded the entrance to the otherworld in Celtic and classical myths. So-called demon dogs and guardian dogs of the underworld are also discussed in Chapter 6.

In Irish lore, many of the famous dogs were humans who had shape-shifted or changed to protect their clan. Irish heroes, kings, and chiefs were given the prefixed title of dog or hound to indicate their courage in protecting the land

and the people. For example, the hero Chulainn became known as Cu Chu-lainn, which meant Hound of Ulster (see also Chapter 7).[13]

In Wales, where there is a strong mythical tradition, there is a story about the Prince of Wales, Llewellyn, and his faithful dog Gelert. Cynics say that the legend was created to bring tourists to the area of Bedgellert in North Wales, but the story has been dated to 1120, when it is said that Prince John of England presented Llewellyn with the specially bred wolfhound Gelert. Sometimes stories to illustrate a moral point have a seed of fact that is elaborated with the telling.

One day the prince left his faithful wolfhound Gelert to guard his sleeping infant son in his royal tent while out hunting or, some versions say, on a battle campaign. When Llewellyn returned, the cradle was empty and the dog covered in blood, sitting outside the tent. The tent was also bloodstained. Llewellyn thought the worst of the dog and killed Gelert in fury, but then saw his son lying safely within the tent and the body of a huge wolf that had tried to attack beside the infant. Llewellyn buried Gelert with great ceremony and the place where the camp was held became known as Bedd Gelert, which means the grave of Gelert. A town grew up there.

One of the most famous dogs in Greek legend was Odysseus's faithful hound, Argos, described in Homer's *Odyssey*.[14] Argos waited faithfully for his master to return and was the only one to recognize his heavily disguised master after many years of absence, but the joy was too much for his old heart and he died. Homer, the Greek poet, wrote the *Odyssey* sometime during the late ninth century BCE.

The everyday world also creates animal heroes that will become the myths of tomorrow. Perhaps the most dramatic and uplifting story of animal devotion comes from the aftermath of the World Trade Center disaster on September 11, 2001. There were many heroic rescue dogs that assisted hour after hour in choking conditions in the attempts to save survivors. But most remarkable was the story of Dorado, the guide dog who was at work with his blind owner, Omar Eduardo Rivera, a computer technician. Omar became trapped on the 71st floor of the World Trade Center's north tower when the first hijacked airliner crashed into the building. Fearing there was no way he himself could escape; Omar unleashed Dorado, patted him, and told him to go. But the four-year-old Labrador retriever refused to leave his master in spite of the heat, flying glass, and crowds who were panicking and rushing past. Dorado was actually carried away by the rush of people but fought against the tide and returned to guide his owner.

Another legendarily loyal dog in an attested true case is Greyfriars Bobby, a Skye terrier who, after his master John Grey's death in Edinburgh, Scotland, on February 15, 1858, sat at the graveside in Greyfriars churchyard in all weathers for fourteen years. Locals built the dog a shelter in the church grounds and made sure he was fed. After Bobby died in 1872, Baroness Burdett Coutts had a statue of the loyal dog placed in the churchyard.

THE MAGICAL CAT

Even the most devoted domesticated cat keeps its natural independence, so the folklore of the cat is shrouded in mystery and magic.

Bastet, discussed in Chapter 1, was the Egyptian cat-headed goddess. She was called Bast when she took the form of a cat, her sacred animal, and was frequently depicted as a mother cat caring for her kittens. In her fiercest form Bastet protected the solar boat each night by driving off the serpent Apep as his tentacles grasped the boat. She was the mistress of love, fertility, and joy and protectress of women and children.

In northern Europe and Scandinavia, the wild cat was the power creature of Freyja, the goddess of beauty, magic, and fertility; two of them pulled her chariot through the skies. Snorri Sturluson writes of her cats in his *Prose Edda*.[15] Sturluson was an Icelandic Christian historian and statesman who lived between 1179 and 1241. He wanted to preserve the ancient oral traditions. When Christianity came to Scandinavia in the eleventh century CE, because the cats were black, Freyja became demonized as a witch who lived on mountain tops. The black cat became associated with evil witches and a symbol of good or bad luck depending on the country in which you live. In America, the black cat is considered unlucky if it crosses your path. In the UK it is considered as lucky.[16]

THE TEMPLE CATS OF BURMA

There is a belief that the sacred Birman temple cats are, in fact, reincarnated priests. There are a number of versions of the legend, of which the following is a composite. The legend tells of a temple built by the Kymer people on Mount Lugh in Burma, where there was a golden image of the goddess Tsun Kyan-Kse, who had sapphire eyes. The holy Kittah, or head monk, was called Mun-Ha. It was believed that after the monks died they would be transformed into temple cats for a lifetime, before being released into Nirvana, or heavenly bliss (the heaven beyond illusion).

There were 100 cats belonging to the temple. Mun-Ha was usually accompanied in his meditation by the most beautiful one, Sinh, a pure white cat, except for his yellow eyes, golden ears, brown nose, and tail and paws brown like the earth. One moonlit night, Mun-Ha was sitting on his golden chair meditating deeply into the eyes of the goddess. Mun-Ha could not hear anything as Siamese invaders rushed in and killed him. The white cat leaped onto the chair to protect his dead master's body and touched his robes with his paws. Instantly the cat's fur became golden, its eyes blue like the goddess's eyes, its tail, ears, and face a rich brown, and its paws pure white.

The invaders were terrified, and the other monks came rushing into the temple room to ask what they should do and saw their master dead. But staring into the eyes of the goddess was the beautiful golden-colored cat. Instantly the monks stopped panicking and drove the invaders back beyond the temple walls. Sinh stayed sitting on the golden chair looking into the eyes of the goddess by his dead master's side for seven days. Then he too died, it was said, carrying his master's soul to heaven.

However, a fierce dispute broke out over the succession. Instantly all the temple cats entered in complete silence and were likewise transformed into a golden color with blue eyes and so the Birman cat breed came into being. The cats surrounded the youngest of the monks, indicating he should succeed Mun-Ha. The reincarnated Kittah monks in the form of the cats had cast their vote, and the new leader proved wise and just. It was thereafter believed that whenever one of the temple monks died, he would be reincarnated as a Birman cat before attaining Nirvana.

MAGICAL ANIMALS IN THE WILD

Wild animals were also seen as creatures sacred to various deities. Sometimes they represented a fierce, or occasionally gentle, animal form that their protective deity would take. They tended to be animals that were hunted and so it may be that the associations go back to pre-agrarian times when a successful hunt was vital to survival and the Mistress of the Animals and Lords of the Hunt were important deities to appease.

THE MAGICAL WILD BOAR

The boar was a sacred animal to the Celts; it appeared as an emblem on their banners, their shields, and even their helmets. It represented the pugnacious courage and the willingness to fight to the death that Celtic warriors themselves displayed when fighting for a worthwhile cause. A cast iron and bronze boar, Celtic emblem of war, was one of the earliest purely Celtic animal figurines created. The figurine was found in Hounslow in Middlesex near London, England, dating from 150–100 BCE. The Celts blew long upright horns, on the top of which was a bronze boar, and the sound is believed to have been so fearsome it struck terror into the enemy.

Folk custom describes the Boar Stone, engraved with a boar, being used by Scottish kings to stand on, or if upright as some are, to touch, while oaths of loyalty were sworn. The Boar Stone was found in the Grampian region of Scotland. It is told that if you touch or stand on a Boar Stone, then you will be filled with the courage of the boar. One such upright stone called the Knocknagel stone, near Inverness in the Highlands, has Pictish symbols as well as the image of a boar. However, the figure of the boar is much older than the engravings and may date back to about 200 BCE.

Cerridwen was called the white sow goddess of the Celts because the sow was a symbol of divine fertility and she was a symbol of rebirth. She was seen as a domesticated pig as well as a wild boar, but even a farmyard pig can be a killing machine if angered. In her goddess form Cerridwen had a cauldron of transformation.[17] Henwen, another name for Cerridwen the Sow goddess, ate the beech nuts of wisdom while in the form of a white sow. Henwen gave birth to a wolf cub, an eagle, a bee, a wild cat kitten (all sacred animals to the Celts), and a grain of wheat to symbolize the future harvest.

Ardwinna was another Gallic/Celtic sow goddess but was associated with hunting wild boar. She was given offerings at the beginning of the annual boar hunt. She was pictured riding on a wild boar and sometimes as having tusks.

Sows were associated with rebirth because they sometimes ate sickly piglets. Thus it was thought sows gave birth to them again in stronger form. There were, in addition, various legends of pigs in the Celtic otherworld who were constantly reborn after slaughter or of otherworldly cauldrons that were never empty of pork. Sows were sometimes buried in Celtic times with the bodies of the Great to feed them in the afterlife. They were also ritually interred as, for example, at the pre-Christian Druidic center at Chartres in central France, the site of the medieval cathedral as thanksgiving to sow deities such as Ardwinna.

To the Vikings, Gullenbursti, the golden boar of the fertility god Freyr, could be seen riding across the sky with Freyr on its back restoring light to the world at the Midwinter Solstice around December 21.

Because of the cold climate in Scandinavia, fatty meats like pork were considered important. It was imagined that in Asgard, the realm of the Aesir gods, there would be a limitless supply of boar for hunting and eating. Wild boar is a popular meat in Sweden, where there is still a great deal of hunting for meat even among city dwellers. Andhrimnir, the cook of the Aesir, slaughtered the cosmic boar every evening and cooked it. The boar was then returned to life that night to be hunted, killed, and cooked again the following day.

On earth, called the realm of Midgard, to commemorate this heavenly feast, a cooked boar, crowned with laurel and rosemary in honor of Thor, lord of the winter, formed the midwinter feast (around December 21), the beginning of a twelve-day feast. According to popular folklore in Sweden, the father of the family would put his hand on the boar's head, called the Boar of Atonement, and swear he would be faithful to family and fulfill clan obligations.

THE MAGICAL BEAR

The Bear is popularly thought to be connected to the earliest forms of known worship, and archaeology seems to support this. Bear shrines and bear skulls and bones have been discovered, buried with human remains of Neanderthal Man. Stone altars and buried hoards of bear bones and skulls in Drachenloch caves in Switzerland date back 43,000 years. Drachenloch caves (the name means dragon's hoard) were inhabited by Neanderthal man. In addition to more than 30,000 bear bones buried in the cave, there was found a stone-constructed chest containing seven bear skulls, their muzzles facing the cave entrance, perhaps as protective gesture to guard the cave entrance with seven bear spirits.[18] Dr Emil Bachler excavated the caves between 1917 and 1923. An even more intriguing bear skull was found in the cave with a leg bone forced behind its cheek.

Bern, the capital of Switzerland, is named after the first animal, a bear, killed after the founding of the city in 1191. The Helvetian Swiss people, akin to the Celts, worshiped Artio or Dea Artio, the Bear goddess, during Roman times, and there is a Roman statue of Artio, dating from about 200 CE, in the Historisches Museum in Bern. The statue shows the sitting goddess facing a bear, offering it fruit. It was excavated in 1832 and identifies the goddess as Artio in the Roman inscription.

In Ancient Greece and Rome, female bears were sacred to the Moon goddesses Artemis and Diana. In the cult of Artemis, maidens in yellow robes imitated bears at the festival of Brauronia.[19]

THE BEAR IN THE STARS

Roman myth tells that Callisto was one of the maiden priestesses of the huntress and Moon goddess Diana. The supreme god Jupiter wanted her and so took the form of Diana to lure her to him. Instantly he turned back into his own shape and raped her. As a result of the rape, Arcas (whose name means *little bear*) was born. Juno, Jupiter's wife, was furious and made Callisto walk the earth as a bear. One day after Arcas grew up, he was about to shoot a bear, who was in fact, his mother. Jupiter, in a rare fit of conscience, stopped him and turned Arcas into a bear also, placing mother and son in the heavens where they might be together.

In Celtic tradition the male bear was symbol of the Sun and Sun king and associated with King Arthur, whose name means *bear*. However, as with Artio the bear deities may be older ones. A sixth-century BCE statue dedicated to the Gallic (the French form of Celts) bear god Artaois, or Ardehe, was discovered in France in the town of St Pe de Ardehe near Lourdes in the Vallé de l'Ourse, which means *valley of the bear.*

THE MAGICAL WOLF

Wolves roamed the European forest until comparatively recently and can still be found in remote forests in eastern and northern Europe, as well as extensively in the wilds of America and Canada.

So ancient and revered was the wolf's lineage that a number of Celtic Irish clans claimed their origins in these fierce and loyal pack animals. Indeed, it is said that the ancient Irish King Cormac was reared by wolves and in adulthood had them as his hunting pack instead of hounds. These beliefs are discussed extensively in Chapter 7.

Legends abound of mother wolves suckling human children (and one or two reported actual cases in Asia). Lupa was the Roman she-wolf goddess who suckled Romulus and Remus, founders of Rome. According to myth, they were the sons of the god of war, Mars, and Rhea Silvia, one of the vestal Virgins, who was killed because she was falsely accused of breaking her vows of chastity. After her sons were left in the wilderness to die, the infants were found and suckled by Lupa.

The English Victorian poet and author Rudyard Kipling recounts in the *Jungle Book* his tale of Mowgli, the little human boy who was protected by a she-wolf. Kipling commented that the female wolf is the fiercest of all creatures in defense of her young and her pack, from whom even a tiger will run away.[20]

No doubt myths such as these were based on actual case studies, for throughout the ages there have been accounts, whether true or anecdotal, of the adoption of humans by animals. The classic source is Lucien Malson's *Les Enfants Sauvages*, translated into English by E. Fawcett and others in 1972. He listed fifty-three wild children in different countries since 1344. Several more cases have been discovered since the book's original publication in Paris in 1964. A recently written and more objective book by A. S. Benzaguen is a good follow-up if the subject interests you.[21] By far the majority of wild children reported on were apparently suckled or protected by wolves. A popular explanation is that they might have occurred when a woman working in the fields left the babies at the edge of the fields when it was not safe or practical to carry them. If a mother wolf had lost her own cubs, she might be tempted to carry an infant off and suckle it.

One of the most famous cases was from Midnapore, India. In 1920 the Reverend A. Singh became intrigued after locals described two malevolent *manush-baghas*, small ghostly creatures with blazing eyes, that haunted villagers from the forests near Denganalia. Manush-baghas were always accompanied by a female wolf. Their lair was located in an abandoned ant heap. The Reverend Singh decided after two fleeting glimpses that the ghosts were human children running on all four legs.

He arranged for local tribesmen to seek the lair out, and on October 17, 1920, the ant beaters and diggers surrounded the heap. Two wolves ran out as soon as the digging started and broke through the cordon. A third wolf, a female, appeared, and, according to Singh's journal, instead of running away, made for the Lodha diggers, scattering them to all sides before diving back into the hole. The female wolf made a second charge at the diggers, but this time the bowmen were standing by at close range. Before the Reverend Singh could stop them, they loosed their arrows and killed the mother.

The ant heap was opened, and the two children were found huddled in a ball with two wolf cubs. After a fierce struggle they were separated. The two wolf cubs were sold, and the two children were taken to Midnapore Orphanage. The youngest, age three at the time of her discovery, died within a year. The second, Kamala, a girl who was about five, lived for nine years, eventually learning to stand upright, eat by hand, and speak about thirty words of English.

Similar cases involving wild dogs have been reported very recently. In November 1996, a newborn baby abandoned in subzero temperatures in Bucharest, the Romanian capital, was saved by a pack of wild dogs. Two dogs stood guard over the tiny bundle while the barking of two others attracted patrolling police officers. The boy was found covered in fallen leaves and with the remains of his umbilical cord and placenta attached. It was thought that a dog had licked the baby's body clean. The child was adopted by one of the policemen.

GENTLER MAGICAL ANIMALS

THE FAIRY DEER OF THE CELTS

In the north of Scotland and the Scottish isles especially there is a long tradition of deer goddesses/fairies. After the coming of Christianity among the Celts from the late fifth century, a number of Celtic goddesses were downgraded into fairies, but the deer stories remained essentially the same.

Cailleach, the Celtic hag goddess discussed in Chapter 1, was known in pre-Christian times as the Mistress of Wild Things and took the form of a deer as one of her animal guises. Fairy women, it was said, would assume the form of a deer to escape pursuit or if enchanted by a powerful hunter-magician who sought to possess them. In the tale of Saba, the fairy mother of the Gaelic bard Oisin (little fawn) gave birth to her son as a deer after she had been enchanted by the Dark Man of the Sidhe, to whom she refused to give her love.

Fionn Mac Cumhal, the great leader of the Fianna, the semidivine Celtic warriors who have been likened to King Arthur's knights, came upon Saba in her form as a white hind while he was hunting. His magical hounds, one of whom, Tyren, had herself been enchanted into dog form, would not harm the deer. Fionn took Saba home, where in the night she was transformed into her true beauty. Saba told Fionn that she could marry him and stay as a fairy woman as long as she remained within the protection of Fionn's enclosure. Saba became pregnant, but Fionn had to leave her for seven days to defend the land against the Vikings. While he was away, the Dark One tricked Saba into leaving the enclosure by pretending to be the victorious Fionn returning from war, and he turned her once more into a white deer. Fionn hunted for seven years for his bride without success, but at last found in a cave a golden-haired boy who told Fionn that he had been reared by his mother, a white deer. Fionn realized it was his son and named him Little Fawn. Oisin returned to his mother's fairy land when he was an adult, having fallen in love with Niamh of the Golden Hair, a fairy princess.[22]

In North America among the Lakota nation is a legend that, when the animals were first created, the Great Spirit gave the deer speed so she might outrun pursuers. But when a hunter came in pursuit of the doe and her newborn fawn, the Great Spirit realized that he had forgotten to endow the baby fawn with protection, for its legs were too shaky to run alongside its mother. Therefore, he covered the back of the tiny deer with spots so it might be safely hidden among the bushes until its legs were strong enough for flight.

BIBLIOGRAPHY

1. Grant, R. M. *Early Christians and Animals*. London: Routledge, 2001.
2. Barney, Stephen A., W. J. Lewis, J. A. Beach, and O. Berghof. *The Etymologies of Isidore of Seville*. Cambridge: Cambridge University Press, 2006.
3. Bulfinch, T. *Bulfinch's Mythology: Age of Chivalry and Legends of Charlemagne*. London and New York: Penguin New American Library, 1962.
4. Oakes, L. and L. Gahlin. *Ancient Egypt: An Illustrated Reference to the Myths, Religion, Pyramids and Temples of the Land of the Pharaohs*. New York: Hermes House Anness Publishing, 2002.
5. Sophocles. *The Oedipus Trilogy: Oedipus Rex, Oedipus at Colognus and Antigone*. Translated by D. Fitts and R. Fitzgerald. Fort Washington, PA: Harvest Books (Harcourt Brace imprint), 2002.
6. Beer, R. R. *Unicorn: Myth and Reality*. Translated by C. M. Stern. New York: Van Nostrand Reinhold Co, 1972.
7. Cavallo, A. S. *Medieval Tapestries in the Metropolitan Museum of Art*. New York: Metropolitan Museum of Art, 1993.
8. Newman, P. *Lost Gods of Albion*. England, Gloucestershire, Stroud: Sutton Publishing, 1997.
9. Hamilton, E. *Mythology, Timeless Tales of Gods and Heroes*. New York: Warner Books, 1999.
10. Thorsson, E. *Northern Magick: Mysteries of the Norse, Germans and English*. St. Paul: Llewellyn, 1998.
11. Evans-Wenz, W. Y. *The Fairy Faith in Celtic Countries, a Facsimile of the 1911 Edition*. England, Buckinghamshire, Gerrards Cross: Colin Smythe Publishers, 1977.
12. Danielou, A. *The Myths and Gods of India: The Classic Work on Hindu Polytheism from the Princeton Bollingen Series*. Rochester, VT: Inner Traditions, 1991.
13. Mackillup, J. A. *Dictionary of Celtic Mythology*. Oxford: Oxford University Press, 2004.
14. Homer. *The Odyssey*. Edited by H. Rieu. Translated by E. V. Rieu. London and New York: Penguin Classics, 2003.
15. Sturluson, S. *The Prose Edda: Norse Mythology*. London and New York: Penguin Books, 2005.
16. Oldfield Howey, M. *The Cat in Magic and Myth*. Mineola, NY: Dover Publications, 2003.

17. See note 13.
18. Coles, J. M., and E. S. Higgs. *The Archaeology of Early Man*. New York: Frederick A Praeger Press, 1960.
19. Ashe, G. *Dawn Behind the Dawn: A Search for the Earthly Paradise*. New York: Henry Holt, 1991.
20. Kipling, R. *The Jungle Book*. New York and London: Penguin Books, New Edition, 1996.
21. Benzaguen, A. S. *Encounters with Wild Children: Temptation and Disappointment*. Montreal: McGill-Queens University Press, 2006.
22. Eason, C. *Complete Guide to Faeries and Magical Beings*. Boston, MA/York Beach, ME: Red Wheel/Weiser, 2004.

CHAPTER 6

Monsters and Weird Creatures

Humans are fascinated by beasts that represent their hidden fears of death and evil. This is probably the reason why more is written about frightening mythical and semi-mythical creatures than gentler ones. Encountering these fearsome animals in stories, films, and urban myths about devil dogs and werewolves is a relatively safe way of distancing fears about personal mortality and evil within others and ourselves. Bruno Bettelheim, a psychotherapist, in the mid-1960s and 1970s wrote about the deeper meaning of fairy stories. He theorized that the wolf in the traditional Little Red Riding Hood/Little Red Cap stories represents "all the asocial, animalistic tendencies within ourselves as well as an external all-devouring force that signifies the primitive human fear of being eaten alive and totally absorbed by another entity."[1]

A healthy skepticism can be very useful in studying the realm of monsters. However, new species are still being discovered in remote areas of rainforests, and it may be that some weird creatures are based on real creatures in an unusual setting. The characteristics of a real animal may have been exaggerated or misinterpreted by an active imagination if the creature was seen in the dark or in misty conditions. Many years ago, I took my three-year-old son, Jack, camping. He came rushing into the tent where I was feeding the baby to tell me there was a giant panda bear outside. (A month or so earlier, we had been to London Zoo, and Jack was fascinated by the giant pandas.) As I idly questioned him, I realized this was no ordinary escaped giant panda. With gestures and his relatively limited vocabulary, Jack said the panda had huge curved horns on its head, a string tail, and bones sticking out of its legs. It looked like a horse, but was fat with a tummy that touched the floor and had bells on the end of the tummy. Of course when I peered through the tent flap, wondering whether to take bell, book, and candle, or to call a cryptozoologist or the local newspaper, there stood a very large black-and-white, long-horned cow (which Jack had not seen before), complete with hooves and very much in need of milking.

DEMON DOGS

These devil, or demon, dogs, as they are popularly called, are the alter ego of the protective domesticated dog. They were the fierce spirit guard dogs set, according to local folklore in rural England, by some supernatural force to protect certain crossroads and highways. Crossroads themselves have supernatural associations, being places where witches and suicide victims were buried long ago. Crossroads were also linked in classical tradition to the underworld goddess Hecate, who was the mistress of Cerberus the dog. Cerberus guarded Hades, or the underworld. Hecate was accompanied by a pack of wolves, so there may be a link with the idea of these wolflike dogs and crossroads.

The majority of demon dogs are black. They are described as giant Labradors or mastiffs with flamelike red eyes and are almost always said to foretell doom when seen. Some of these black dogs are said to be souls of evil-doers.

Black Shuck, the most dramatic of the huge black demon dogs, has been apparently sighted for several hundred years in the countryside of East Anglia on the east side of England, in the north of England especially on the east coast, and on the Isle of Man. Black Shuck is as big as a calf with saucer-sized eyes that glow yellow or red. The phenomenon of howling devil dogs like Shuck has inspired many books, films, and plays, including Arthur Conan Doyle's *Hound of the Baskervilles*.[2] The two most fearsome Shuck incidents reportedly occurred on the same day—August 4, 1577. According to a pamphlet printed in 1577 by a local man, Abraham Fleming, the first instance took place in St Mary's Church at Bungay, Suffolk, an area on the east coast of England. There was a dreadful storm that day—"darkness, hail, thunder and lightning as was never seen before." The congregation was praying for relief from the storm, when Shuck, with its huge teeth and claws, attacked the people. A man and a boy in the belfry were apparently killed and the rest were burned as the church spire crashed through the roof, breaking the font. The tower bells fell, and the clock shattered as the dog ran snarling from the church. It is not clear which injuries were inflicted by the dog and which injuries were caused by the fire and storm. In modern Bungay, Shuck is still part of the town's coat of arms.

Of course a large, live black dog may have run into the church during the service (it may have been tied outside the church by a parishioner) and with the lightning strike occurring at the same moment, the storm and dog became linked in people's minds with the local demon dog of legend. The church would have been quite dark inside because of the storm, and everyone would have been terrified even before the dog arrived. The terror and uproar caused on seeing an apparent demon dog might have panicked even a relatively docile living dog into attacking.

Then the dog traveled at great speed the twelve miles to another church, in Blythburgh. The fiery hound attacked this congregation as well, killing two people and leaving another injured—"shriveled like a drawn purse" was the phrase given locally. Shuck is said to have left deep scorch marks on the door at Blythburgh. In 1933, when the door was cleaned, burn marks—local legends say they are the devil's own fingerprints—could be seen and remain there even today.

The fact Shuck attacked people in a church was seen as confirmation he was a servant of the devil. The Shuck stories probably derive from legends brought by Viking invaders of Odin's black hounds and Thor's dog, Shukr. Of course the dog and the hounds became demonized in Christianity. East Anglia is a very flat area, often shrouded in mists from the sea, and was settled by the Anglo-Saxons, who are related to the Danish Vikings from the sixth century as well as being subject to Viking raids in the tenth century.[3]

Sightings of a huge black dog have been reported in Norfolk as recently as the 1970s.

In America a demon dog is supposed to haunt Rose Hill in Maryland's Port Tobacco. He is said to resemble a huge mastiff that glows. His fur is blue-gray. Local lore explains this as a ghost dog, belonging to a soldier peddler. The soldier was murdered in the area for his gold in the period before the Civil War (in the early 1860s). The gold is said to be buried at the spot protected for all time by the dog, who was clubbed to death trying to protect his master.

THE WILD HUNT

Following the Wild Hunt are packs of apparently supernatural hounds that are either black or white. According to myth, they roam through the forests of the skies with various pre-Christian deity huntsmen and -women, looking for souls of living sinners. In Celtic myth the Cwn Annwyn are white hounds with red eyes. They are the size of calves and ride out with Gwynn ap Nudd, the White Lord of the otherworld on the magical Glastonbury Tor, or hill, in Somerset in southwest England. Glastonbury Tor is reputed in legend to be the Isle of Avalon, associated with King Arthur. According to ancient Welsh tradition, the Cwn Annwyn were believed to be an omen of death or severe disaster. The howling of the hounds was said to diminish as they approached their chosen prey, and the howling stopped when they struck—followed by a terrible triumphant baying. It was feared that living mortals who encountered the hunt while traveling might be taken to the land of the dead, leaving not even their bodies. It was even thought that sleeping people who left the window open might be taken and found in the morning lifeless. This explanation might be used to account for a sudden death on a wild, windy night—perhaps from natural causes or something sinister but definitely earthly.

The Wild Hunt is most often associated with Odin, the Norse Father god, particularly in the Scandinavian countries, and in eastern and northern England and Scotland. In Germany he was called Wotan. In Scotland the Wild Hunt hounds were called the Slaugh or Host and were considered to be the unblessed dead. Their appearance was likened to a huge dark cloud passing overhead on the night wind, and they were blamed for murders and kidnappings in the mortal world. They kidnapped less desirable humans to swell their numbers. Many disappearances of minor criminals and vagrants may have been attributed to them rather than mortal elimination processes.

On the European mainland, the Hunt was sometimes led by Odin and at other times by a goddess who is called by different names in different regions of the Germanic countries: Berchta, Perchta, Holda, Frau Wode, or Fra Gode. The Wild Hunt comprises various spirits of the dead—humans, horses, dogs, and occasionally other animals. It sweeps through the countryside during late fall and around the Yule/Christmas season, flying through the air, but occasionally galloping through forests to the sound of a wild horn and baying of dogs. Though considered very dangerous to humans, in early times the Wild Hunt was believed to bring with it fertility of the land, and renewal of the spiritual powers of the land. One of its more positive functions in earlier times was to gather up any lost souls of the dead to take them home to the otherworld. Anecdotal evidence of the Wild Hunt has been given from ancient times up to the present day. The hounds are called Gabriel in the United Kingdom—not after the Archangel Gabriel, as is popularly thought, but from an old word that means corpse, because it was believed they hunted for lost souls who had not gone to heaven.

The Cherokee Indians consider the Milky Way the trail the dog belonging to the Great Spirit ran, while some Scandinavian legends tell how the

Milky Way was formed by a dog dropping stars from the bag he stole from the gods.

There are of course all kinds of explanations for the sound of the baying of hounds overhead, including a flock of wild geese flying at night and a gale howling through trees. Since travelers were supposed to fling themselves facedown to avoid attracting the attention of the hounds overhead, it may not be surprising that the identity of the spectral creatures remained a mystery. In an area called Clun Forest in the west of England, Edric the Wild and the Wild Hunt are believed to appear before a potential invasion of England and Edric leads the Hunt to repel the enemy.

The medieval chronicler Gervase of Tilbury around 1212 CE called the Wild Hunt *familia Arturi*, the household of Arthur. In France it was called by the same name. It may be that the demonic aspect of ghostly riders and hounds seeking the souls of living sinners was emphasized by the monks who recorded the old legends. This not only fueled fear of the old gods but also served as an explanation for the disappearance without trace of people in wild country places. It is not so many years since wild animals roamed freely in Europe, Scandinavia, and North America. Even in Victorian times, bands of brigands preyed on travelers in lonely places and vampires and werewolves were still accepted as reality.

When Odin was demonized (he can still be seen in his devilish persona as Black Peter or Black Rupert in St Nicholas Day processions in Europe), Odin's huntsmen and hounds became the ungodly dead who, unable to gain admission to heaven, were released from hell to hunt for—what else but souls?

A Saxon version of the Wild Hunt mythology in England identifies the leader as Herne the Hunter, another form of the ancient horned god Cernunnos, mentioned in Chapter 1. Herne led his hunt in the forests of the southern counties of England, especially around Maidenhead in Berkshire, about forty miles from London. The Christianized twelfth-century Anglo-Saxon chronicles describe the black hunters and hounds, the hunters mounted on black horses and goats, blowing their horns of doom.[4]

There is an urban legend from the 1950s concerning Herne and his ghostly hounds that is difficult to substantiate or date accurately, which is told in local hostelries near Windsor Great Park, another Herne the Hunter Wild Hunt site. It is close to Windsor Castle, where Queen Elizabeth II often stays. Herne is believed to appear more frequently whenever the United Kingdom is under threat of invasion as a reassurance that all will be well. Three boys were damaging trees when one saw a hunting horn and picked it up and blew it. Immediately, baying hounds were heard close at hands, plus the obligatory huge dark shadows. It is told that two of the boys ran to a conveniently nearby church. But the third boy, the one with the horn, fell. The hounds were very close, an arrow was heard being shot from a bow, and the boy died, though there was no arrow and no injury that could be seen. Such stories show that even in the most rational, technological times, in the deep forest humans can feel afraid and try to express these fears in story form.

There are also folktales in the United Kingdon and western Europe saying that after a storm a black dog might appear in someone's home and that it must be kept for a year and a day. Black stray dogs must have greatly benefited from this superstition.

Significantly, the Wild Hunt is associated with autumn and winter everywhere, when wild winds and storms are more frequent. For example, in Scandinavia, the old festival of Winternights, which was celebrated around the old start of winter in mid-October, when travel and trade finally ended, was the time Odin's Wild Hunt took to the skies and the slain warriors chosen from battle rode with him.

On Walpurgisnacht, April 30, the Wild Hunt ended and the dead and nature spirits roamed freely for the last time after the long winter as light prevailed.

Ancient Greece and Rome also had their Wild Hunt in which the Moon goddess Diana was pictured riding across the skies on a huge white hound on the night of the full moon. In Northern Italy the shamanic *Benandanti*, followers of Diana and members of a fertility cult called the *good walkers*, or good doers, traditionally left their bodies on the four Ember days, religious days at the beginning of the four seasons, associated with prayer and fasting, that were originally pagan celebrations of nature. It is told how in their astral forms they fought sky battles against the Malandanti (evil witches, demons, and spirits) to ensure the safety of the harvest and their villages. They rode on cats, goats, and horses to ensure the crops would be safe. They were armed with fennel stalks, and sometimes appeared in the form of animals themselves. During the Wild Hunt, the Benandanti also kept the paths of the dead from this world to the next secure. Although they fought on the side of the angels, the Benandanti were regarded by sixteenth-century inquisitors as evil. However, in spite of persecution, the tradition continued and some believe may still do so symbolically as a secret society.

THE HELL HOUNDS OF THE ANCIENT WORLD

Since dogs are guardians of the home, it would seem natural that the different underworlds of ancient mythologies would be likewise guarded by fierce hounds, both to keep deceased souls from wandering and to prevent those who have no right there from entering.

CERBERUS, OR KERBEROS

In classical and Scandinavian myth the Hell Hounds were no ordinary creatures but the children of deities or semideities who had coupled with giants or monsters. Cerberus is the Latin name of the Hell Hound. He was the offspring of Echidna, the half-serpent goddess and her mate, the monster Typhon, god of the fierce storm winds.

Cerberus or Kerberos is the Greek name of the Hell Hound. Cerberus had three heads (or in some versions fifty or one hundred heads) and guarded the entrance to Hades, on the banks of the River Styx. Hades was the underworld, according to both Greek and Roman mythology. Cerberus was sometimes portrayed with a dragon's tail that contained a small, fiery dragon and snakes coiling from his back. One of the most famous images of the Hell Hound is shown on the Perseus Vase that is on display in the Louvre Museum in Paris. Dating from 530 BCE, the main panel shows Herakles (the Greek name of Hercules) holding the three-headed Kerberos on a red leash. Herakles was sent to capture the dog as his twelfth heroic labor, or task, and, using only his bare hands, was the only hero to physically defeat Kerberos. The dog's body and one of its heads are black. The other two heads are red.[5]

Cerberus's main tasks were to ensure that the living could not enter Hades and to prevent spirits from leaving. His saliva was poisonous, and he was so hideous that any mortal who looked into his eyes would be turned to stone.

However, according to myth, a few mortals and deities did manage to enter and leave safely, but through trickery rather than strength. Cerberus was placated by the dead with honey cakes. The nymph Psyche used this method to tame the fierce dog which allowed her to fetch a box from Persephone, goddess of the underworld, in order to complete the tasks necessary for her lover Eros to be restored to her. For this reason, honey cakes were placed in the coffins of the deceased, so Cerberus would not attack their spirits or prevent them from entering the underworld. According to Roman mythology, the Sybil, or prophetess, of Cumae used honey cakes soaked in drugged wine to send Cerberus to sleep in order to permit Aeneas to enter the underworld to talk to his dead father, Anchises.[6] The musician and poet Orpheus, son of Apollo, wanted to enter Hades and bring back to life his lost bride, the nymph Eurydice, who had been stung by a viper. He played his wonderful lyre music to send the dog to sleep. However, because Orpheus looked back to make sure Eurydice was following him, she was not allowed to return with him.

FENRIS WOLF

Scandinavian mythology mentions both an underworld guardian dog and a fierce wolf. Fenris was called the wolf of the swamp and was the son of Loki, the trickster god, and the giantess Angrboda. He was stopped from wreaking destruction among the Aesir gods and goddesses by a magical fetter created by the dwarves. However, capturing the wolf was not without sacrifice. The brave Tyr, god of war and justice, lost his sword arm in the process. It was foretold that at the final battle Fenris would escape and devour Odin and the sun at the end of time but he would himself be killed by Víðarr, or Vidar, called the silent god. Vidar avenged his father Odin's death by killing Fenris. In one version of the story, Vidar thrust a sword in Fenris's heart. In other versions, Vidar tore his jaws apart and crushed them by treading on the wolf's upper jaw with his thick shoe, which was made from all the leather discarded by shoemakers after trimming the toes and heels of the shoes they made. Vidar survived to found the new world.

A Hell Hound guarded Niflheimr, the land of the dead, ruled by the goddess Hel. He was called Garmr which means growler. The beginning of Ragnarok, the final battle, was heralded by Garmr breaking the chain by which he was tethered outside Helheim, the fortress of the goddess Hel. Garmr ran free throughout the world and killed the god Tyr. Because perpetual cold was the worst suffering imaginable to those living in Northern Scandinavia, with its long icy winters, this was how they imagined hell.

BEAR MEN AND WOLF MEN

This is an area where myth, fiction, and historical events merge in an attempt to express a primitive human fear of being eaten alive, or in psychological terms, of being totally taken over emotionally and abused sexually by a powerful, evil person. Werewolf and were-bear legends and reports of attacks on humans persisted, especially in Germany and Eastern Europe, from earliest times until the end of the 1800s.

THE BERSERKERS, OR BERSERKRS

These fearsome warriors, briefly mentioned in the introduction, wore a bear- or wolfskin in battle. They wore the pelt of a wolf or bear on their heads. They went into battle without armor and showed no fear or pain even when wounded. In the heat of battle, as they roared or screamed wild animal cries, the enemy might have easily believed they had changed physically or shape-shifted into bears or wolves. There is speculation that the bear warriors induced an ecstatic hypnotic state in themselves in the way indigenous shamans do, perhaps by chanting war cries before battle. They may have taken some hallucinogenic substance such as agaric mushroom or an alcoholic brew. It was believed in Viking myth that Odin, the All Father, endowed the bear men with a state of *wode*, or divine madness, with a draught of the magical mead of inspiration. This may have been an actual drink laced with fermented honey consumed before battle, which contained dangerous but powerful herbs such as mandrake root and hemlock that removed all fear and restraint.

Some early Scandinavian Christians believed that these bear men, or berserkers, were not good enough to enter heaven but were very courageous. It was thought that if they were killed in battle they became a bear with special qualities. There are various fairy tales that reflect this belief, for example, Grimm's *Snow White and Rose Red*, where the talking bear is an enchanted prince.

To the pre-Christian Norse people, the idea that warriors could change into animals was not surprising because they believed that the deities did it. Odin, for example, sometimes took the form of an eagle or a wolf. It may be that, more generally, young men in western Europe during the Dark Ages (from the fifth to twelfth centuries CE) formed mercenary or fringe warrior troops and wore wolf- or bearskins as a way of psychologically terrifying the enemy.[7]

A fascinating account of the seemingly magical powers of some warriors to transform into bears is recounted in the anonymous fifteenth-century medieval Icelandic saga of King Hrolf. The tale refers to pre-Viking Denmark and Norway in the sixth century CE. It tells of Hrolf's battles against King Alidis of Sweden and his own treacherous brother-in-law, King Hjorvard. Hrolf's grandson, and son of Bjorn, which means bear, was one of his twelve champions. His name was Bodvar Bjarki, and he was called the man bear. According to literature, Bodvar had the ability to change into a bear, and on one occasion he led his grandfather's army against King Hjorvard, killing many men with his forepaws and teeth and bringing down men and horses. In his bear form he was completely resistant to any weapon.

However, no one could see Bodvar Bjarki in the battle, only the bear. One of the other champions of the king, Hjalti, hurried back to the castle where Bodvar was sitting motionless, apparently asleep or in a trance. Hjalti reproached Bodvar fiercely for his cowardice, and at that moment the trance and the power of the bear was broken, and the battle turned against Hrolf.[8] The bear was Bodvar's *fylgiar*, or inner self. It derives from the Icelandic concept of the spirit in the form of an animal, also called the fetch. The spirit sometimes remained on earth after death if a person was killed unjustly and wanted revenge on the murderer.

WEREWOLVES, OR LYCANTHROPES

Werewolves are creatures that have fascinated as well as terrified humans throughout the ages in many lands. The werewolf is said to be driven by the craving for flesh, sometimes human, as lurid accounts of werewolf activity from many parts of the world recount, but more usually it is cattle and sheep that are attacked (probably by actual wolves). The werewolf can be male or female. It appears throughout the literature of northern Europe, with Germany being a particularly rich source of werewolf legends.

The most common method of deliberately becoming a werewolf involved tying around the body a strip of leather made from wolfskin that still had its hair. A more spontaneous change to lupine appearance was triggered by the full moon. Some legends say that a person is born a werewolf; in others a person becomes a werewolf after being bitten by a werewolf. Until the early nineteenth century the most popular explanation was that the person had made a pact with the devil.[9]

A popular protective device against werewolf attack, reportedly used by the farmers around Hesse in Germany even around 1854, was to throw a knife or a piece of shiny steel over the werewolf's head to land on the ground behind it. The werewolf would instantly be transformed into his true human form and stand there completely naked. If successful, the werewolf's pelt burst crosswise at its forehead, and the naked human emerged from this opening.

The most famous werewolf case is perhaps that of Stubbe Peter, described at his June 1590 trial as "a most wicked Sorcerer, who in the likeness of a Wolf committed many murders, continuing this devilish practice 25 years, killing and devouring men, women, and children." He lived near Cologne in what was then called High Germany and was said to have confessed, rather than being tortured, to have made a pact with the devil. After his execution, which began with his body being laid on a wheel and the use of red-hot burning pincers to pull the flesh from his bones, the imprint of a wolf was apparently found on the wheel. The real perpetrators of the crimes may have been actual wolves who killed travelers or carried off small children as their parents slept. Or, as suggested in the Introduction, the murders may have been committed to look like paranormal events. Stubbe Peter may have been a scapegoat who wrongly imagined he would escape suffering if he confessed, or he may have committed actual violent murders and tried to blame the local werewolf.

AN AMERICAN WEREWOLF

From America come accounts of the Louisiana and New Orleans werewolf called the rougarou, or loup garou, which means the man who becomes an animal. The legend dates back to the time when the Acadian French settled in the already culturally French area (though owned by Spain) after they were expelled from Nova Scotia by the British in the 1760s. The werewolf was believed to inhabit the swamplands around Arcadiana, the official French name for French Louisiana and New Orleans, and also local forest and farmland. The werewolf is described as having the head of a wolf and the body of a human. The werewolf myth may predate the arrival of the French who may have heard the legend from original Native North American Ojibwa or Chippewa settlers on the land, or it may have come from the French Canadian trappers in Nova Scotia.

The beast seems to have been used over the subsequent centuries as a deterrent for naughty children and to stop them from wandering in the dangerous swamplands. However, others say that the loup garou story is just a variation of the French Catholic belief that Catholics who did not observe Lent for seven years were forced to become a werewolf on every subsequent Lent because they had given in to their animal nature.

Other versions of the Louisiana werewolf say that a person becomes a loup garou for 101 days after being bitten by a loup garou. During the daytime, the bitten person is pale and takes to bed, but at night returns to health and goes out seeking victims to pass the curse to and thus be relieved of it (shades of vampire legends). It was said that everyone was too afraid of public censure to admit he or she had been bitten even after the curse had been passed on, but others became suspicious if a person became suddenly sickly after going to the swamplands. Even three drops of blood was enough to pass on the curse. Of course, there are living creatures in swamps that can cause bites or serious injury and death, not least the alligator, and that could account for the loss of a pet, or even a child or adult, who wandered too far into the swampland.

DO WEREWOLVES EXIST?

One possible explanation for werewolves could be certain medical conditions that give a strange appearance, which in earlier times encouraged superstitious people to victimize those who had a wolf-like appearance. Probably the most famous case is of Fedor Jeffichew. He was born in 1868 in St. Petersburg, Russia, with hypertrichosis, a medical condition that causes excess hair all over the body. Like other sufferers in less-enlightened times, Fedor and his father, who also suffered from the condition, ended up traveling throughout Europe and the United States with P. T. Barnum's circus. He was called the dog-faced boy. He and his father had supposedly been captured in a cave in Russia. Fedor would bark and snarl as part of the act. He died in 1904.

A more fanciful explanation for werewolves, at least in western Europe, was given in an Irish book written by Kongs Skuggsjo in the Old Norse language in 1250. It was called *Speculum Regale*. The Vikings colonized Ireland from the mid-ninth century CE and founded the city of Dublin. Skuggsjo collected oral tales of old Ireland. One tale concerns the sixth-century St Patrick who, while converting the pagans, encountered resistance from a tribe that howled like wolves to drown out the saint's prayers. St Patrick's response was to curse the tribe, so that their descendants would also be punished for the ancestral disobedience by becoming werewolves and howling to the moon when it was full. Some members of the tribe had the curse for seven years and the more fortunate became werewolves every seventh year.[10]

THE WEIRD CREATURES OF CRYPTOZOOLOGY

Nowhere has media hype become more frenzied than around the supposedly supernatural or alien creatures that periodically terrorize people in a particular area. Mothman, described in the Introduction, is a good example.

Some researchers, expert and amateur, say these strange creatures are relics of a bygone age and have survived in dark forests or in deep lakes in remote areas for thousands of years. Others believe that they are creatures from other dimensions who periodically wander into our world or that they may be hybrids, in this case the offspring of earthly animal species and creatures belonging to extraterrestrial beings, escaped from alien spacecraft.

Some accounts may be hoaxes or cases of mistaken identity, publicized perhaps in a week when there is little other news.

Another possibility put forward by those eager to prove the validity of these otherworldly beings is that some may not be physical beings at all, but apparitions that have assumed a collective identity as local legends have grown up around them, rooted in a factual and explicable, but far less dramatic, incident that took place centuries earlier. People may genuinely believe they see the creatures of legends, for example the werewolf in a dense, dark forest, because the mind will often interpret a hazy visual perception in terms of what is expected. If someone is feeling very scared and alone in an area renowned for werewolf sightings, then one may mistake a large but quite ordinary wolf standing on its hind legs to reach a tall tree as a werewolf.

However, it has been argued that some of the more plausible weird creatures, such as the American Bigfoot ape-man or the corresponding Himalayan Yeti, could have survived for thousands of years in inaccessible regions such as dense forests and mountain passes. Further, these creatures are not modern phenomena, as indigenous people have, for example, reported both Bigfoot and Yetis over hundreds of years. For example, in 1840 Reverend Elkanah Walker, a missionary, collected numerous accounts of hairy giants among the North American Indians in Spokane, Washington. They spoke of the distinctive strong smell that came to categorize Bigfoot. With new technologies and modes of transport it may be possible in the future not only to locate, but also to photograph clearly and monitor such creatures if indeed they do exist, or to find the more ordinary creature that has been talked and written about to monster proportions.

Strange creatures can be made scapegoats when livestock are mutilated and people attacked, perhaps as a way of removing the responsibility from humans or earthly predators. A spate of attacks on animals by mentally unstable people (who have watched one too many horror movies) may lead to apparent sightings of a bloodsucking monster in the area of the earthly, but horrific, attacks.

BIGFOOT

Bigfoot is the most enduring of the weird creatures of semi-myth. In different parts of the world and even regions of the same country it is given different names, for example Sasquatch in Canada.[11] Bigfoot is described as a cross between a man and an ape, between six and eight feet tall, with thick, long dark brown or reddish fur of consistent length even on the head, a pointed head, sloping forehead and a distinctive musty, pungent aroma. Bigfoot has been reported in remote forests in fifty American states, most frequently in California, Oregon, Washington, and Alaska, with some sightings also reported in Florida and Pennsylvania. It has also been sighted in every Canadian province, most notably in British Columbia. Some sightings have also been reported in South America.

Bigfoot acquired its name because of the huge footprints it left, fifteen to twenty inches long, with five toe prints. Strictly speaking, the term Bigfoot is used only for ape-men reported in the Pacific Northwest of America and western Canada, but in practice is applied to all large, hairy ape-men.

Though the Bigfoots are not friendly to humans, there are few accounts of actual attacks, apart from rock throwing when people enter their territory or when humans have attacked them, and the occasional unsubstantiated kidnapping. They seem to live in family groups, and they do not use tools. They use a variety of sounds to call one another, but do not speak. They wander from place to place, living on plants, frogs, and occasionally meat left by predators. All this information has been collected by people who study Bigfoot as though it were an ordinary, living species.

Further anecdotal evidence suggests that Bigfoots can read minds and anticipate the movements of those who encounter the creatures, usually while the animals are hunting for food. However, even if this were true, it could be an evolved animal instinct. Explanations vary from the more down-to-earth, such as that Bigfoot is a rare and intelligent cold-climate ape, to the more dramatic, such as its having escaped from alien spaceships or even that it is the result of genetic experiments crossing human and extraterrestrial DNA.

Occasionally, it seems that a Bigfoot can obtain a distinct personality and distinguishing features. Old Yellow Top has been classed as a Sasquatch, but it has very fair hair on top of its head. Reports of Yellow Top come from the area surrounding Cobalt, a town in Ontario. They date back to around 1906 and were last recorded in the 1970s, when it was speculated Yellow Top might have died, though no remains were found.

DOES BIGFOOT EXIST?

All the evidence is anecdotal, apart from casts or photographs of the footprints. Even then, there can be controversy about the authenticity. For example, in 2002, after the death of Ray Wallace of Centralia, Washington, his family claimed that he had admitted that he created giant footprints using specially constructed wooden shoes near a logging site as a practical joke that had started a local spate of Bigfoot sightings in 1958. What is more, no bones of a creature resembling Bigfoot have ever been found.

However, sightings continue. In December 2006, Shaylane Beatty, who lives in the Dechambault Lake region of Saskatchewan, Canada, reported seeing a Sasquatch beside the highway at Torch River while driving to Prince Albert. Men from the village, who were alerted, went to the spot and followed giant footprints through the snow but did not see the creature. However, they did find some brown fur (which could have been from any animal) and photographed the prints.[12]

The Hopi elders and the Iroquois Indians believe that Bigfoot's increasing appearances in recent years are a warning from the Creator to take better care of the planet and live in peace. Skeptics would say that the current fascination and increased sightings reflect the increasing hunger for the weird and wonderful, which might in itself express, as the Indians are saying in a different way, the lack of meaning in modern living.

YETI

Yeti, or Abominable Snowmen, are more like large bears than apes and apparently inhabit the Himalayan Mountains of Tibet and Nepal. Like the Bigfoot, Yeti are described as more than six feet tall, covered with white fur, having a musty aroma and also reportedly telepathic abilities, but seeming more aggressive toward humans.

One highly speculative theory for similarities between Bigfoot and Yeti is that the North American Bigfoot crossed the Bering Straits landbridge thousands of years ago when the continents of Asia and America were joined.

There seem to be different kinds of Yeti, though the most popular image is of the white, furry giant with long, shaggy hair, more giant gorilla than bear, called *meh-teh* in Tibet. The top of meh-teh's head is pointed. The really huge Yeti are called *dzu-the*, and they can walk upright as well as on all fours. They are a cross between a bear and an ape, but with the characteristic white fur and claws. In Bangladesh in Southeast Asia, a huge twenty-foot tall hairy giant called Nyalmo has been reported. It is similar to the Yeti.

Yeti are thought to be valley dwellers because of the need for food, but are mainly seen in narrow mountain passes as they travel, rather than in dense forests where there is more camouflage. Locally, Yeti are said to have supernatural powers and are sometimes considered sacred demons or guardians of the mountains, intended to scare away humans scaling mountains and disturbing the deities. However, in mist and thick snow it might be possible, especially at high altitudes where the brain suffers oxygen deprivation, to hallucinate and mistake bears or even rocks for Yeti.[13]

EL CHUPACABRAS, OR GOATSUCKER

At this point, fact and fiction seem almost indistinguishable. Such creatures as Goatsucker are called cryptids because they bear no resemblance to creatures known to science.

In March 1995, the Puerto Rican towns of Orocovis and Morovis were under attack from what appeared to be a vampire; carcasses of goats, chickens, and other small farm animals were found all the blood drained out through a single neat puncture wound. The first sightings of the creature were reported around September of that year. The perpetrator was identified as Goatsucker, a cross between a kangaroo, a gargoyle, and the extraterrestrial creatures called *grays* described as smaller than the average adult, with grayish skin pigmentation, huge oval heads, staring almond eyes, and spindly limbs. The Goatsucker is described by apparent eyewitnesses as about four feet tall, with a large, round head, a mouth with no lips, sharp fangs, huge lidless red eyes, a small body with thin, clawed arms and webbed bat wings, and muscular hind legs. The creature also reportedly had spikes from the top of its head down to its backbone. Sightings and slain livestock continued to be reported in various parts of Puerto Rico throughout the autumn of 1995, especially in Canovanas, where more than 150 animal bloodsucking incidents were reported. Sightings also occurred in Mexico and the United States, although cynics would say this coincided with increased media exposure of the creature.

Goatsucker, or El Chupacabras, has been linked with an earlier Puerto Rican monster known as the Moca Vampire, whose appearance coincided with reports of UFO activity in 1975. A number of farmers discovered animals massacred after strange lights appeared in the sky and again the animals, which included ducks, goats, geese, and cows, had been completely drained of blood through a puncture wound.[14]

One of the problems with investigating or trying to analyze what this creature might be is that there is very little consistency in description. For example, it is variously described as hairy, hairless, or scaly in parts, changing color to blend with surroundings, having red feathers or wings, and being able to jump over buildings.

However, since sightings no longer occur, it is hard to unravel the truth about this creature; many of the incidents may have been human attacks on animals, attacks that got tied up with media hype.

OWLMAN

Owlman is another creature that stretches credulity; it has been suggested Owlman might have been a huge Eurasian eagle owl (*Bubo bubo*) escaped from a bird sanctuary, or more likely, kept illegally as a pet and released when it became too large. Skeptics say Owlman was invented in England in response to the U.S. Mothman.

Owlman was described as resembling an owl, with silvery gray feathers (or in some accounts, dark feathers), wings, and a beak. He was said to be of human size with fiery red eyes and huge black claws but able to fly, making a hissing sound as he flew. Owlman was witnessed in Cornwall in southwest England around Mawnan Woods and the cemetery of Mawnan Old Church, mainly being seen by young girls in the mid-1970s. For example, on July 3, 1975, fourteen-year-old Sally Chapman, while standing outside her tent on a camping trip, heard a hissing and saw an owl as big as a man. It had red eyes and flew into the air, revealing black pincerlike claws. The creature was also seen the following day, and two years later in June and August 1978, again around the churchyard.[15] On one occasion he attacked the witnesses, two young boys, but no one was injured. The most recent sighting was by a female student from Chicago, in 1995, in the same area of Cornwall. She reported the incident to the local newspaper in the nearby town of Truro.

Japanese legends have told of a similar creature, regarded as a malevolent nature spirit, birdlike, but with four limbs that appeared human, and wings. It has been suggested that four-limbed birds could be mutations.

One problem with these truly strange creatures is that nothing quite fits. For example, the normal explanations for the Owlman, such as a huge eagle owl, do not quite explain the sightings. In the case of Goatsucker, could every eyewitness account have been a hoax or hallucination? Finding the balance between believing in little green men and dismissing strange phenomena as totally impossible or fantastic because we cannot categorize or explain them in our current frames of reference is important. An open mind is essential in trying to understand the significance of these creatures whether as modern myths or something more.

BIBLIOGRAPHY

1. Bettelheim, B. *The Uses of Enchantment: The Meaning and Importance of Fairy Tales.* New York: Vintage Books, 1975.
2. Doyle, A. C. *The Hound of the Baskervilles.* New York: Modern Library Classics, 2002.
3. McEwen, G. J. *Mystery Animals of Britain and Ireland.* London: Robert Hale, 1986.
4. Fitch, E. *In Search of Herne the Hunter.* Milverton, Somerset, England: Capall Bann Publishing, 1994.
5. Bloomfield, M. *Cerberus the Dog of Hades.* Whitefish, MT: Kessinger Publishing, 2003.
6. Virgil. *The Aeneid.* Translated by Robert Fitzgerald. New York: Vintage Books, 1990.
7. Larrington, C. *The Poetic Edda.* Oxford: Oxford Paperbacks, 1999.
8. Anonymous. *The Saga of King Hrolf Kraki.* Translated by Jesse L. Byock. New York and London: Penguin Classics, 1998.

 9. Hall, J. *Half Human, Half Animal: Tales of Werewolves and Related Creatures.* Bloomington, IN: Authorhouse, 2003.
10. Summers, M. *The Werewolf in Lore and Legend.* New York: Dove Publications, 2003.
11. Krantz, G. S. *Big Footprints: A Scientific Inquiry into the Reality of Sasquatch.* Boulder, CO: Johnson Books, 1992.
12. Byrne, P. *The Search for Bigfoot: Monster, Man or Myth.* Camarillo, CA: Acropolis Books, 1975.
13. Messner, R. *My Quest for the Yeti: Confronting the Himalayas' Greatest Mystery.* New York: St. Martin's Griffin, 2001.
14. Corrales, S. *Chupacabras: and Other Mysteries.* Pensacola, FL: Greenleaf Publications, 1997.
15. Downes, J., and G. Davis. *Owlman and Others.* Corby, Northamptonshire, England: Domra Publications, 1998.

CHAPTER 7

Clan Animals

Individuals and groups of people have a particular animal or bird they admire or with whom they identify, and whose idealized qualities they try to emulate: the courage of a lion or the loyalty and protectiveness of a dog toward its owner, for example. This practice is very old. Deities that assumed an animal or bird persona were discussed in Chapter 1, such as the falcon (or falcon-headed) Egyptian god Horus, who symbolized both the power of the pharaoh on earth and the freed spirit, or ba, of the individual after death.

The connection of a clan with a particular animal, bird, or plant is called totemism, which comes originally from an Ojibwa Indian word. In today's world, totemism is primarily found in societies where shamanism is the predominant spirituality, though traces remain in the names of old Scottish and Irish clans. In the modern urban world, there is an increasing trend toward turning to individual power animal helpers, either collectively as part of neo-pagan, nature-based religions or as individuals through alternative New Age spiritual practices.

THE SIGNIFICANCE OF TOTEM ANIMALS AND BIRDS

Why should animals and birds be so important to humans as icons of power when they lack our brain power and ability to rationalize and analyze? Native North Americans and Australian Aborigines believed that because animal life was created before human, it was purer. So the strengths of the creature were shared and refined by humanity, in an undiluted, unpolluted, and so more powerful form.

People who live close to nature may adopt particular animals or birds to symbolize not only personal values, but those they would wish to pass down through the generations, perhaps focusing on a legend from the family past of a particular creature who was associated with a heroic family member, such as a loyal dog or even a heraldic animal such as the unicorn.

If you read back over the earlier chapters, or look ahead at Chapter 8, you will see the symbolic strengths attached to different creatures.

CLAN KINSHIP WITH ANIMALS

In childhood you may have been fascinated by, although maybe a little afraid of, for example, tigers because of their fierceness and independence. In earlier ages you might have called yourself Joanna of the Tigers in acknowledgment of the emotional connection, or William McDeer if you identified with the swift, silent deer. Then, when surnames were still relatively fluid during medieval times, you might have passed on Tiger or McDeer as a family name in the hope that all your descendants inherited the same qualities. A number of Scottish clans, including the McBain and the Pictish tribe the Kati of the far northwest took the wild cat as their totem. Like Irish warriors, they often wore cat skins in battle. Of course, when you read that a Scottish clan is descended from otters, for example, you are not expected to believe that they literally mated with otters, although there are legends of men marrying what are described as fairies or nature spirits, such as the story of Saba the deer woman in related in Chapter 5. More likely otters in a local lake inspired the early ancestors of the clan with their ability to live on land and water, at a time perhaps when there were struggles to survive and the clan had to relocate and so identified strongly with the otter lifestyle.

Animal kinship is common to many cultures. In old Mongolia, Genghis Khan, who lived in the late twelfth century, claimed ancestry from a blue-grey wolf that came from the heavens (another example of a warrior claiming animal strength, as did the Norse berserkers), so high-born Mongolian warriors would refer to themselves as sons of the blue wolf.

Knut II the Great, the Viking king better known as King Canute, who lived from 995 to 1035 CE and was King of Denmark, England, Norway, and parts of Sweden, claimed descent from bears. As in Sweden, where Bjorn (bear) is still a very common forename, the royal line may have been founded by a man who had many bearlike qualities and wore bearskins.

In Siberia, a word for a female shaman is the same as the word for bear. In some Altaic (Siberian) languages *utagan* or *utygen* means bear, and in others the same word signifies ancestral spirit.

According to the Siberian Buryat myths, an eagle was sent by the deities to endow shamanic power to the first person he met, so that disease and suffering might be healed. The eagle encountered a young woman who was asleep at the foot of a tree. The eagle made love to her, and the shamanic heritage was founded as a result of this combination of the sky power of the eagle, who sat at the top of the mythical World Tree forming the axis of the world, and the symbolic female earth power at the roots. Thus began an unbroken line of hereditary shamans, male and female, from the original eagle ancestry.[1]

TOTEM POLES

The clan animals system is manifest most clearly in the Native North American totem pole. Indeed, a totem pole has on it the carved and painted images of animals and birds sacred to a tribal chief's family and those of individual important members as well as those creatures belonging to the collective clan. Individual families may also have their own poles as the tradition of carving them continues to revive in North America.

The carved painted faces on these tall poles represent the mythical animal ancestors who offered power and protection and their own special qualities and symbolic wisdom to the people. Though making totem poles is a pre–white settler tradition, from the 1800s onward the huge, magnificently carved poles were made from cedar trees that might be up to forty feet high. This tradition started when the indigenous people acquired the knowledge of and traded for more elaborate wood-carving tools the settlers brought with them.

Totem poles are not found everywhere in Native North America, because of the need for suitable trees, but there is a strong tradition of them among the Indian nations of the forested Pacific northwest coast, in Washington and British Columbia. For example, among the northwest Indians the Tlingit tribes had ravens, frogs, geese, sea lion, owls, salmon, beavers, codfish, skate, wolves, eagles, bears, killer whales, sharks, auks, gulls, sparrow hawks, and thunderbirds on their totem poles. (The auk, a Northern Hemisphere penguin-like bird with a dark brown head and black grooved beak, is now extinct.) There might be a range of different poles within the same community if it was thriving; however, many were stolen or bought cheaply by settlers and may be seen in museums around the world. Fortunately, the art is now being revived and new poles are being created. In addition, some of the old beautiful artifacts are being returned to national parks in the areas from which they came.

ANIMAL CRESTS

The significance of these totem animals, called crest animals when engraved on totem poles or regalia, comes from old stories of encounters between animals and ancestors. One story explaining Bear as a clan totem is told by the Haida and Tlingit peoples. An Indian princess, out berry-picking, stepped in a bear's feces and swore at the beast. Later she met and married a young man who turned out to be a bear. She gave birth to Bear people. Thus, Bear became the supporting spirit and animal crest for the clan. In Finland, a similar story is told about a woman who married a bear and how their children became the Skolt Sami clan.

Indigenous artists represented specific animals and birds on the North American crests with recognizable features such as eyes, beaks and feathers carved in standard abstract forms. They might use teeth for Beaver, beaks for Raven, Eagle, and Hawk, and a dorsal fin for Killer Whale. Each crest represents an ancestor of people with the right to use that particular image.[2] Many designs appear not just on totem poles but over the entire surface of chests and boxes that may be painted or carved. In London's British Museum, in the new Sainsbury galleries, which celebrate indigenous world cultures, is an exhibition of the regalia of Alver Tait, Chief Gadeelip, who was born in 1943 and is senior hereditary chief of the Eagle Beaver House of Chief Luuya. Each piece is decorated with a crest associated with the original owner's ancestors. The Eagle came from Alaska. The Beaver was adopted after a beaver with supernatural powers was apparently encountered during a hunt. Most of the regalia were made by Alver and his wife, Lillian. They were worn at tribal feasts and other ceremonial occasions.

The eagle-beaver totem pole on display in the museum dates from about 1860 and is made of red cedar. It comes from the Nisgala people, who lived in British Columbia on the northwest coast of North America during the nineteenth century. The pole is a memorial to Chief Luuya. The pole (ptsaian) was carved with a series of crests of Luuya's family. Each represents an ancient encounter between a helping animal and the ancestors. At the top is a monstrous figure of a sharp-nosed bird with a human face. Below it on the pole is the eagle, or thunderbird. Below the eagle is a mother and baby beaver. The beaver is the subsidiary crest. At the bottom is a man and at the base is a sea monster shown catching a whale.

ANIMAL AND BIRD FAMILIARS

A familiar spirit is considered a specific animal or bird spirit that resides within an actual living creature, usually a domesticated one such as a horse, dog, cat, or bird. This was considered a helpful, protective spirit for its owner. This belief was prevalent in indigenous societies, notably among the Native North Americans, where a warrior might take the name of an animal with whom he had a meaningful encounter during a personal spiritual journey, such as Running Horse or Sitting Bull.

Legend tells how Sitting Bull, the wise man of the Lakota Sioux tribe, was killed on December 15, 1890 in a conflict involving his followers when the federal government came to arrest him at Standing Rock Agency Reservation in North Dakota. As Sitting Bull fell from his white horse and lay dying, the horse (that had performed with him in Buffalo Bill Cody's Wild West Show) began dancing on its hind legs and circled its master as though performing in the circus ring even though the bullets were still flying. The horse continued to dance round its dead master even after the conflict was over, until it fell exhausted.[3] Some of the followers of Sitting Bull insisted the animal was dancing the Ghost Dance that had been revived by his people and was believed to invoke the power of the ancestors to give them protection against the white man's bullets.

The Inuit people of northern Canada and the United States have a similar vision of power or totem animals. They believe that every natural form, including the animals and the sea itself, has an *innua*, or living spirit. Such forces sometimes assume the role of *torngak*, guardians of individual Inuit hunters. Bears possess especially strong *innua*, and if the spirit of a bear becomes an Inuit's *torngak* he accepts that his fate may be to be eaten by a polar bear in order to be reincarnated as a shaman on the icy tundra.

The polar bear, the largest carnivore that lives on the icy tundra, is itself a symbol of the Good Spirit Torngasak and is thus a much desired torngak. The polar bear is called the Wise Teacher by the Inuit and the people of northern coastal Siberia because she teaches them how to survive. They also call her the spirit within the fur. Naturally they will still hunt her as part of the natural food chain, but they bury her bones in the tundra or return them to the sea with reverence. Similarly among the indigenous hunting people in Finland and Estonia, after special bear feasts, the skull of the bear is put high on a pine tree so that the bear spirits will continue to reincarnate. It was thought the first bear had come from the skies.

FAMILIAR SPIRITS IN THE WESTERNIZED TRADITION

Belief in familiar spirits pervaded Western urban life until the 1700s. Even some royalty subscribed to this belief. For example, Prince Rupert, who lived between 1619 and 1682 and fought for his uncle, King Charles I, in the English Civil War, had a dog called Boy. Prince Rupert was spectacularly successful in the early battles and seemed to have a charmed life, though he was not known as a good tactician or inspiring leader. Many soldiers who fought with him believed that this dog was possessed by a familiar spirit. This spirit brought Prince Rupert victory in battle, and the dog stayed close to the prince's side, even during the fiercest conflict. Rupert's first major defeat occurred on June 1, 1644, at Marston Moor after the dog was killed. Defeat was not caused by the dog's death, but the dog had acted as a lucky charm for the army and perhaps had given them the confidence to be more daring and to believe in their leader.

Interpreted psychologically a so-called animal familiar does not contain a discarnate spirit at all, but is simply very tuned in emotionally to the owner so that the creature fills the owner with a sense of being deeply loved and protected emotionally, especially if the familiar is a very intelligent species such as a dog or horse.

Few are as closely allied with an animal as the Irish semi-mythical hero Cú Chulainn, or Cuchullain, who was called the Hound of Ulster. Cuchullain also features in Scottish and Manx (Isle of Man) folklore, both of which share similar roots. His father was in some versions of the myth said to be the son of the Sun god, Lugh the Long Armed, and this made him semidivine.[4] He was given the name Cú Chulainn, which means *Culann's hound*, because he killed the fierce wolfhound of Culann the blacksmith when it attacked him. He was only a young child at the time and did not realize his own strength. Therefore he offered to act as the blacksmith's guard until a new puppy grew up and could be trained. For this reason his totem animal became the dog, and he fought fiercely and defended the vulnerable. After Cú Chulainn fought many heroic battles, the Raven goddess Medb conspired with warriors, whose fathers Cuchullain had killed in battle, to lure him to his death by taking away his strength so he could be easily defeated. In common with other heroes, Cuchullain had certain *geasa*, or sacred requirements, linked to his houndlike fierceness: first, he always had to eat the food he was given, and second, he could never eat the flesh of his totem animal the dog. His enemies served him a meal of dog meat, so he lost the protection of the dog spirit. Cuchullain is depicted as a defender of Ireland on statues and plaques by both factions involved in the recent Irish troubles.[5]

FAMILIARS AND WITCHCRAFT

Rational explanations for the emotional and quite natural closeness between animals, including birds, and their owners did not stop the hysteria of the witch-persecution years between the 1480s and 1712 in western Europe, or the events in Salem, Massachusetts between 1692 and 1693. During the mass hysteria in Salem, 141 people from the town and immediate area were arrested. Many of the accused were model citizens and devout church-goers who knew nothing of witchcraft. Nineteen were hanged, including a dog thought to contain the spirit of the Devil.

In western Europe, any old lady who had a cat was likely to be accused of being a witch and her animal a familiar and dangerous spirit belonging to the Devil. However, even if a toad was seen sitting near her doorstep at the height of the witchcraft frenzy, it would be considered a familiar. If any toad was seen near a neighbor's sick cow, people concluded that the witch had sent her familiar spirit to do harm.[6]

The most notorious witch trial in England involving a familiar was in 1566 at Chelmsford in Essex, a county near London. It concerned a black cat, owned by three women in turn: Agnes Waterhouse, the main person accused in the trial; Joan, her daughter; and Elizabeth Francis, a neighbor. It was claimed at the trial that each of the women had for a time owned the cat, which was quite true, and that its name was Satan, a name probably extracted from the three women by the inquisitors under torture. This was a very unlikely name to be given a cat by ordinary church-going people, which they all were. During the trial the cat was said to be responsible for a number of evil happenings, all of which would have been laughable had not the women's lives been in danger from the prejudice. First, Satan was said to have obtained a husband for Elizabeth, having previously caused the death of a man who had rejected her. The cat then was given to Agnes and Joan (maybe Elizabeth's new husband did not like cats). Satan then began a cycle of destruction, drowning cows, souring milk, and causing a man who had quarreled with the women to commit suicide. It was claimed that Satan could talk and transform himself into other creatures, including a toad and a dog. Though Joan was released, Agnes was hanged and Elizabeth, after being imprisoned for a year, was hanged in 1579.[7]

Black cats were especially mistrusted after Pope Gregory IX declared they were the spawn of Satan in 1233. As a result, many cats were destroyed, often cruelly. Mice, bats, toads, and frogs were also feared, not only as familiar spirits but as witches themselves who had shapeshifted into rodents or small reptiles to do harm to neighbors.

Animals were regularly burned or hanged alongside their owners during the witchcraft persecutions, and it was often claimed that hideous black demons were seen leaving the creatures that were in reality much-loved pets to the people accused of witchcraft.

SPIRIT FAMILIARS IN THE AMAZON BASIN

There is a belief, common to regions where shamanism is still practiced, that all living animals, birds, and fish have spirit counterparts that frequent water, rapids, mountains, and caves, creatures whose spirit origins link with life in the distant past but play a vital role in every form of existence.

In the Amazon region it was believed a shaman, under the influence of strong natural hallucinogenic substances from plants and other trance-inducing methods such as drumming or chanting, could be possessed by the spirit of a supernatural jaguar and thereby assume the power of this feared nocturnal predator as he traveled through the spirit realms.

Among the Paliu of northeast Amazon and the Upper Xingu in Southern Amazon, shaman stools, on which the shaman sits to make these spiritual trance journeys, are carved with powerful predators and raptorial birds. The spirit doubles of the carvings, it was said, would carry the shaman in trance. As the shaman mounted the stool, the jaguar or black panther would act as steed as well as protector against harmful spirits lurking in other realms. The Tukano shamans in the early twentieth century would wear necklaces of jaguar teeth to signal their capacity to metamorphose into their feline alter ego.[8]

AUSTRALIAN ABORIGINAL TOTEMISM

The Aborigines have lived in Australia for at least 40,000 years, and before European settlers arrived 200 years ago, probably no more than 300,000 Aborigines inhabited Australia's 2,967,909 square miles, nine-tenths of which is flat.

To the Aborigines, magic was indivisible from this natural world and life was a continuing ritual. Their tradition is oral, carried through myth, song, and ritual and depicted on cave walls and in natural rock formations. The rock engravings especially illustrate the Aboriginal belief in the Dreamtime, when their hero gods made human beings from plants, animals, and natural features. The original source species of each tribe of people became totem or guardian spirits to those people. For example, the Wanungamulangwa people who live on Groote Eylandt, an island off the north coast of Australia, say that their original ancestors were dolphins. The dolphins were called the Injebena, who lived in the sea and had their families there. The first humans came to the island after Dinginjabana, the leader of the dolphins, was killed by sharks as a result of his excessive boldness and transformed into a man. His grieving wife Ganadja cast herself on to the shore and became the first woman. People who live close to the sea and dive for food can become almost fishlike in their swimming abilities, so such concepts are understandable.[9]

THE STORY OF THE DREAMTIME

In Aboriginal lore, the Dreamtime of creation is not separate from the material world but coexists to be accessed in sleep and meditation as a source of inspiration and wisdom, direct from the first hero Creator gods. Because new animals, birds, and humans are constantly being born, the creative process is considered ongoing. It is the archetype of dreams and waking experienced by Australian Aborigines through contact with the sacred earth of which they are part. Central to Aboriginal spirituality is this interconnectedness of all life, such that if a tree is cut down, the man or woman who cuts it or witnesses the act shares its pain.

Because of their intimacy with natural forces, even something as seemingly insignificant as the blooming of a particular flower became for the Aboriginal people a sign that certain animals were entering their territory. When yellow flowers bloomed on the wattle tree, it indicated that the magpie geese would be flying along their annual route from swamp to swamp and could be trapped, and this close awareness of natural patterns may explain the belief in their connection with natural totems.

Most Aborigines were forced inland to the semi-arid or desert interior lands when European settlements were established, and their unique connection with nature was broken when their children were taken away and educated with European values, albeit for what were considered good motives. It is only in recent years that the people are returning to their lands and reclaiming the natural connection. Hopefully the practices and ceremonies of this way of life, reported by the early missionaries in the late 1800s, will become the reality again for the indigenous people.

The Aboriginal lifestyle is bound to specific regions where tribal ancestors had established sacred places during the Dreamtime. Members of each group believe that the spirits of infants exist in that territory until they are incarnated and that after death the spirits return to the same territory.[10] Even after humans were created, the Aborigines believe that they were still rooted in the matter from which they had been formed: animal, vegetable, or mineral. Therefore the totem affirms what the Aborigine was and still is at the time of the Dreaming. Because all members of a tribe were said to be descendants of a particular kind of plant, animal, bird, or fish, totemic ceremonies were held at the time of the year when the totem species bore fruit or gave birth to its young. These secret rituals were believed to ensure the continuity of the totem species through the individual. The secrets of these rites and the myths of the Dreamtime were passed on by the tribal elders to the younger generations at totem initiation rites. Although a totem is usually an animal or plant, it can also be a natural phenomenon such as water, the sun, cloud, or wind.

LUCK-BRINGING ANIMALS

Superstitions concerning the black cat were discussed in Chapter 5. During the time of witchcraft persecution black cats were considered demonic. However, it is said in eastern and northern England that if you have a black cat, you would never lack lovers. Any black cat entering your home unexpectedly is said to bring good luck with it, but you do have to wait for it to leave of its own accord, as shooing one away can apparently take the good luck with it.[11] A sneezing black cat indicates money coming.

Certain other animals are considered particularly lucky in a number of societies, and models or charms of them are sometimes kept in the home or carried (just in case) even by people who would not consider themselves remotely superstitious.[12]

Today in the West, the Far East, and Africa, an image of an elephant is considered to attract prosperity to the home. A ceramic or metal elephant is traditionally placed just inside each external door in the house facing inward. This ensures, so the superstition says, that bad luck remains outside and good fortune attaches itself to family members. A small elephant is also set at the foot of the stairs and a larger one at the top. This will, it is believed, ensure that your fortunes continue to rise and that you will get any desired promotion. Some people even go so far as to choose only model elephants with the trunks extended upward, though those with the trunks down are considered protective and are sometimes placed outdoors.

The Greek philosopher Aristotle credited the elephant with great wisdom and intelligence, a trait echoed in Hinduism, where the elephant-headed Ganesha is god of wisdom and is always invoked at the beginning of any journey or before any important enterprise. The Roman historian Pliny believed that the elephant had religious feelings and worshipped the ancient deities of the moon and stars.

Pigs are symbols of good fortune and prosperity in many cultures. In Chile and Peru, the three-legged lucky pig corresponds with the Chinese three-legged toad and is made of a lemon with pin legs, sprinkled with salt and burned to release good fortune. A similar charm was described in Italy by the American Charles Geoffrey Leland in 1886 in *Aradia, Gospel of the Witches*, a book based on the teachings of Maddalena, who claimed to be an Etruscan hereditary witch whose traditions went back to the early nature traditions.[13]

LUCKY FROGS AND TOADS

Frogs and toads are amphibious, having a dual life, the early part entirely in the water as a tadpole and later, as a frog, on land and water. In Ancient Egypt, the seemingly miraculous cycle of transformation from egg through tadpole to frog gave these creatures strong associations with rebirth.

Heqet, or Heket, was the Egyptian frog goddess, wife of the potter god, Khnum, who fashioned people from the Nile clay. In life her amulet brought fertility to women and in death promised resurrection. The hieroglyph of the frog was often found engraved on a blue faience or a green stone such as malachite (which was very popular in Egypt) or carried as a green crystal frog charm. Heket's frog hieroglyph, shown in Figure 7.1, was also used as a lucky charm and money bringer. Ancient Egyptians believed that, because many frogs appeared at the time of the Nile flooding, apparently from nowhere, they were made of mud and water and were a sign of prosperity and multiplying resources.[14]

Fig. 7.1

The Romans used frog-shaped oil lamps that, when lit, might attract abundance. In American Indian lore, the frog is the rain bringer and linked with the moon. In the lower Amazon, frog amulets are carried for fertility, and there too the croaking of frogs symbolizes the coming of rain. According to Romany legend, Mary, mother of Christ, was comforted by a mother frog after the crucifixion. Mary blessed the frog and said that wherever a frog was found, the water would always be pure enough for humans.

A three-legged Chinese toad is the power creature of Liu Hai, the god of prosperity. Most Chinese lucky toads have golden coins in their mouths. According to Chinese myth, a three-legged toad lives in the moon, its legs representing the three main lunar phases or the toad in the moon was believed to swallow the moon, causing an eclipse. The toad in parts of Africa is credited with obtaining the Moon King's daughter as a bride for an unspecified tribal chief by bringing her down on a spider's thread. In some versions he takes her place in the moon. In alchemy, toads were linked with the extraction of the material for the elusive Philosopher's Stone, which could turn ordinary metals into gold, from the watery *prima materia*, or first matter, from which all life was believed to come. Toads are also linked with male potency. The Toadstone is a rock formation in the shape of a giant toad, measuring seventeen feet by seventeen feet and overlooking the mountain hamlet of Alcala de la Selva in eastern Spain's Teruel province. Legend promises men great potency and virility as lovers if they touch the creature three times under a full moon. An annual ceremony is held on the first full moon in September, during which up to 1,000 people come to touch the stone.

THE LUCKY RABBIT OR HARE'S FOOT

Though the rabbit or hare's foot is seen less than it used to be thirty years ago as a lucky talisman, it is still popular in rural and hunting societies. It signifies the swiftness of the rabbit or hare to run from danger (with the exception of the rabbit whose foot forms the charm) and is thus protective. It also represents the ability to run toward opportunity.

The rabbit, like the hare, is linked to the moon and is a lucky sign in Chinese astrology. Rabbit years are calm, happy, and good for diplomacy, international relations, and pleasure. The same is true of rabbit people, though they can succumb to over-indulgence and putting off until tomorrow what needs to be done today. Rabbit people include Albert Einstein and Queen Victoria. Rabbit years are 1927, 1939, 1951, 1963, 1975, 1987, 1999, 2011, 2023, and 2035 (keep adding 12).

Brer Rabbit featured as the ingenious survivor in African folk myth and passed into the American folk tradition as the challenger and victor over Brer Fox.

The Lakota tribe in Native North America and a number of other tribes believed that rabbit fur on a bow or as an armband would transfer the swiftness of the rabbit to the journey or hunt. In American Indian Menominee myth, Rabbit created both day and night but gave nighttime to the Owl to rule over creatures who love the darkness. Among the northeastern American Algonquin people the hare was one of the first creators of the world.

A white rabbit indicated that the entrance to the Celtic otherworld was nearby, and for this reason white rabbits are considered lucky. In England, *white rabbit* is considered a lucky thing to say at the beginning of a new month. In the industrial Midlands area of England, there was sometimes a competition to be the first person in the family to say *white rabbit* and so secure the best luck.

The hare is especially associated with spring. She was the sacred animal of Ostara, Viking goddess who opens the Gateway of Spring at the spring equinox around March 21. She is called Oestre, Anglo-Saxon goddess of spring, whose name gives us *Easter* and *estrogen*. The hare is also sacred to the Celtic Andraste, the battle goddess, who was worshiped by Queen Boadicea. Boadicea challenged the Roman invasion of Britain. A story told to children in parts of Sweden says that while the snow still lay on the ground, Ostara the goddess, or in modern times the spirit of Spring, found a frozen white dove lying in the snow. She tried to revive it but could not, and she knew that even if she did, it might not survive till the snows melted. Therefore she turned the dead bird into a beautiful snow white hare and said that in future whenever anyone saw a hare running they would know spring was coming and that she would soon open the doors of springtime.

The Hare in the Moon myths probably began in India, where the "Man in the Moon" is said to be Chandra, Hindu god of the moon. He is depicted carrying a hare, or *sasa*. In India, the Moon is called *sasin*, or *sasanka*, which in Sanskrit means *having the marks of the hare*.

One of several similar Buddhist myths recounts that Buddha became lost in a wood and after several days was weak through lack of food. A hare took pity and offered itself as nourishment to Buddha. It told him to light a fire then hopped in among the flames. Buddha, overcome by the hare's nobility, revealed his divinity and plucked the hare from the fire unharmed. He then placed the hare in the moon as an eternal symbol of sacrifice where he remains to this day.

Modern ecologists often use a ceramic or tiny silver rabbit charm to bring the same luck as the original rabbit's foot.

GOLDFISH

The goldfish has strong connections with the Chinese principle of Feng Shui, the advantageous arrangement of artifacts and symbols to ensure the best flow of Qi, or the life force, through the home and workplace. The four celestial animals and Feng Shui are described in the Introduction. It is recommended that either pictures of goldfish and carp or a fish tank containing eight gold and one black fish be put in the wealth (southeast) corner of a living room or office to increase wealth as you feed them and they grow (that is the theory). The black fish is intended to absorb the negativity, so feed it well. In China and Japan the gift of goldfish promises continued abundance to both giver and recipient in the months ahead. Goldfish also attract good luck.

BIBLIOGRAPHY

1. Vitebsky, P. *Reindeer People: Living with Animals and Spirits in Siberia*. San Francisco: Harper Perennial, 2005.
2. Zimmerman, L. J. *American Indians: The First Nations, Native North American Life, Myth and Art*. London: Duncan Baird Publishers, 2003.
3. Crummet, M. *Tatanka Tyotanka: A Biography of Sitting Bull*. Tucson, AZ: Western National Parks Association, 2002.
4. Kinsella, T., trans. *The Tain*. New York: Oxford University Press, 2007.
5. Gregory, L. *Cuchulain of Muirthemne*. Mineola, NY: Dover Publications, 2001.
6. Wilby, E. *Cunning Folk and Familiar Spirits: Shamanistic Visionary Traditions in Early Modern Witchcraft and Magic*. Eastbourne, East Sussex, England: Sussex Academic Press, 2005.
7. Gibson, M. *Reading Witchcraft: Stories of Early English Witches*. London: Routledge, 1999.
8. Matteson Langdon, E. J. *Portals of Power: Shamanism in South America*. Edited by G. Bauer. Albuquerque: University of New Mexico Press, 1992.
9. Allen, L. A. *Time Before Meaning: Art and Myth of the Australian Aborigines*. New York: Ty Crowell, 1976.
10. Morphy, H. *Myth, Totemism and the Creation of Clans*. Sydney: Oceania (University of Sydney), 1990.
11. Leland, C. G. *Aradia, Gospel of the Witches*. Blaine, WA: Phoenix Publishing, 1990.
12. Gibson, F. *Superstitions about Animals*. Whitefish, MT: Kessinger Publishing, 2003.
13. Vyse, S. A. *Believing in Magic: The Psychology of Superstitions*. New York: Oxford University Press, 2000.
14. Budge, E. A. W. *Amulets and Superstitions*. Mineola, NY: Dover Publications, 1977.

CHAPTER 8

Creatures of the Waters

Many different water creatures feature in myths throughout the world. Sea-faring people naturally connect with what they regard as the spirits of the sea, which is a way of expressing the different sensations of the sea they experience, from soft lapping waters to fierce tidal waves.

Melanesian peoples, who live on the Solomon Islands, believe that humans possess a dual soul. After death, one of the souls passes into the Afterlife, a beautiful island across the waves in the west, the direction of the setting sun. The second soul assumes another life-form to be reborn. Because the sea is so central to existence among the islanders, one of the more desired forms of reincarnation by those who aspire to greatness is as a fierce shark which is both feared and revered.

It is believed that during their lifetime humans find kinship with the species that their soul will become in the next life. If a person shows affinity with sea rather than land creatures, the person's body will be placed in a hollow wooden shark after death and floated out to sea, in order that their chosen water life-form will come to them.[1]

THE SEA MOTHERS

The first ocean deities were called sea mothers, for the sea was considered the womb from which all life came, a fact confirmed by modern biologists. As mistress of all sea creatures, she was thought to release shoals of fish and seals to fishermen and -women and to hunters and so had to be appeased with offerings. Some of the indigenous sea mothers may date back thousands of years, since most are found in oral folklore.

The first fish of a catch is still thrown back as an offering to the sea as a folk custom in a number of societies, even where the ancient sea mythology has become obscured by time. Ceremonies of casting beer and loaves of bread onto the waters as tribute occur around Halloween in the northern isles of Scotland, especially those with Viking connections. For example, on the Isle of Lewis on the Hebrides, as recently as the eighteenth century, beer made with malt from the parishioners was brewed in the church. On All Hallows' Eve, the Christian Halloween on October 31, a cupful of the church beer was poured into the waves as a tribute to Shony, god of the sea, asking for blessings on the fish catch in the year ahead.[2]

Sedna of the Inuit, the Old Woman who lived under the Sea, is given different names throughout the Arctic, including Nerivik in Alaska and Arnarquagssag in Greenland. All sea animals and fish were, according to Inuit myth, formed from her fingers and knuckles when her father Angusta sacrificed her to the sea as a young girl to save himself from Kokksaut, the bird phantom who wanted the beautiful maiden as his bride. When people cannot catch enough seals or other sea creatures, the shaman or tribal magic man or woman dives during trance in astral or spirit form to the bottom of the sea to entreat Sedna to set the sea animals loose. In return, the shaman will comb her tangled hair that she cannot manage herself because of her injured hands.

Mama Cocha, or Mother Sea, is the Peruvian Whale goddess who was originally worshiped by the Incas. She has been revered through the ages by the people living along the South American Pacific coast, though feared by inland dwellers. The whale was worshiped as a manifestation of Mama Cocha's power with ceremonies held in her honor. Particular fish species are sacred totem creatures to her in different areas and may not be eaten. The archetypal lords or clan leaders of all the different sea mammals and fish are the servants of Mama Cocha. They live in the Upper Heavens, and each offers its own fish species to humans that Mama Cocha releases at her will.[3]

STELLA MARIS

The name Mari has been used for sea goddesses in different lands, all of whom are described in a similar way: in a blue robe and pearl necklace, fringed with pearly foam. For many centuries, a number of goddesses took the title of Stella Maris, or *star of the sea*, because of the importance of the stars in navigation.

The first Stella Maris was Isis, the ancient Egyptian mother goddess. She was given this name when her worship spread to Rome, though in Egypt she remained associated with Sirius the Dog Star, whose annual rising heralded the fertilizing Nile flood. With the coming of Christianity, the Virgin Mary became Stella Maris. Images of the Virgin crowned in stars are found in many Mediterranean coastal towns and villages and as far west as the Atlantic coast of Brittany. The Goddess Venus in her evening star form was also called Stella Maris in Italy. Even today, on Ascension Day, in an annual ceremony, symbolizing the sacred marriage between the sea and the people, the doge of Venice casts a golden wedding ring into the waters. This ceremony was originally performed in honor of Venus and is common in seafaring communities.

THE JAPANESE SEA TRADITIONS

Benten, or Benzai-ten, is the Japanese sea goddess. She is described as being very beautiful and rides a dragon while playing a harplike instrument, for she is also the goddess of music and dancing. Alternatively, she swims through the water either as a white snake or accompanied by her retinue of white sea snakes. The sea snake is an important sea spirit form in Japanese folklore. Benten is pictured with eight arms in her humanlike form. Six of her hands clasp a sword, a jewel, a bow, an arrow, a wheel, and a key. The other two are clasped in prayer. Legend tells us she came to earth to save the children from an evil dragon. The island of Enoshima rose from the sea so that she could walk across it on her journey. She is called one of the seven fortunate or lucky deities, for she brings prosperity to her devotees, who come to her waterside shrines to make offerings. Her worship originated in India and traveled with the spread of Buddhism to Japan in the sixth century. Her symbol is a white sea serpent, and snake skins are carried in wallets or purses to attract prosperity even today.

In Japanese myth, there are numerous stories of snake and water snake women. One of the most famous is of a snake woman who lived in a palace under the sea. A common folktale in Japan tells of a young boy who catches a rainbow-colored turtle while fishing and takes it home. The next morning the turtle has become a beautiful woman who is really a sea snake/serpent woman, and she takes him to her palace beneath the waves. After three years, the boy asks the snake woman if he can return home and she agrees, giving him a beautiful box that she says he must never open if ever he wishes to return to her. However when he goes home he realizes that 300 years have passed. He decides to open the box, but as he does so he becomes instantly old, his skin wrinkles, and his body dissolves into dust.[4]

THE POWER OF THE WATER SPIRITS

In Africa, masks or elaborate costumes made of wood and vegetable fiber are worn at seasonal celebrations to represent crocodiles, sharks, and sword-fish. The Abua or Expetia Igbo, people in the Niger Delta, dress as water spirits in these guises to bring the water creature spirits into the village to interact with humans. They are considered dangerous, unpredictable creatures of the swamp and rivers but are invited into the villages ritually to bring abundance and fertility to land, animals, and people.[5]

MYTHICAL WATER CREATURES

LAKE MONSTERS

Many lands have their tales of huge lake monsters, living in huge, very deep, murky lakes that either connect to the sea or formerly connected to the sea. There are reports of such creatures throughout Europe and Scandinavia, including Ireland, Denmark, Finland, Italy, Norway, and Wales. They are also reported from North and South America and Canada. More than 250 lakes around the world are believed to be inhabited by monsters.

Descriptions of lake monsters are remarkably consistent in different lands: a large creature with a long neck, a head resembling a horse, a humped back, and scales. Several lake monsters around the world seem to resemble plesiosaurs, including the Loch Ness Monster in Scotland, Nahuelito in Argentina, Ogopogo from British Columbia, and Storsjoodjuret, or Storsjödjuret, from Sweden. Plesiosaurs were large aquatic reptiles that lived from the Jurassic to the Cretaceous period (180 million BCE to 63 million BCE). They varied in length from eight to over forty feet long, and have been apparently extinct since the age of the dinosaurs ended some 65 million years ago.[6] Other researchers consider these sea-like monsters a primitive and now extinct kind of whale called a Zeuglodon.

The Loch Ness Monster, or Nessie, reputedly lives in Loch Ness, which is about twenty-four miles long, fairly narrow and up to 1,000 feet deep in parts. The loch joins to the North Sea by a wide channel, called the Caledonian Canal, that is linked to other lochs.[7] It has been speculated that this might allow any Nessie-like creature to migrate in and out of the sea. The water is very dark owing to the high concentration of peat. The Loch is rich in fish. Nessie is described as having a long neck and a wide body with fins, and is about forty feet in length.

The first recorded sightings were in the sixth century, when Nessie was described by the Celtic St Columba. Descriptions of Nessie suggest a prehistoric plesiosaur reptile or Archaeoceti whale living in the Loch. There is much photographic evidence, some probably faked, but modern scientific probes of the Loch have yet to either explain or find Nessie. Till then, her existence cannot be conclusively proved or disproved.

Though many people have reported seeing Nessie, misty conditions may have made it easy for the mind to interpret ambiguous physical perceptions in terms of what is expected. One explanation is that lake monsters like Nessie are not physical entities at all but, like mermaids, may be classed as nature essences, a way for the human mind to give form to the energies and feelings at certain places. If, for example, you stand by Loch Ness early in the morning with only the gentle lapping of water through the mists that obscure the mountains around, or cross the lake on a windy day in a small motorboat lurching from side to side, it is not hard to imagine the head and coils of the monster looming out of the grayness and stirring the waters.

Sweden, a land with about 100,000 lakes and a population of only 9 million, has a large number of water monsters: at least twenty-two known lake or sea monsters. They include Saltie, or Saltjobadsodjuret, sighted in the Baltic Sea off Stockholm in the 1920s, and Gryttie, described as a gigantic sea cow, at Lake Gryttjen in central Sweden (between Hudiksvali and Ljusdal) during the 1980s. The Storsjoodjuret is found in Sweden's fifth largest lake, Lake Storsjön in Jamtland County. It has been reported since Viking times and was recorded on rune stones. There are many hundreds of witnesses who have described a fast-swimming humped monster with a long neck, large eyes, and a large mouth. The sound it makes has been likened to two pieces of wood being banged together. In July 1996, Storsjoodjuret was recorded on video by GunBritt Widmark while he was boating on the lake off Ostersund. It is said to be about thirty-three to thirty-nine feet long, but subsequent explorations produced nothing. Some researchers have dismissed the video as inconclusive.

Other lake monsters are described more like huge seals, for example, the monsters in Lake Simcoe and Muskrat Lake in Ontario, Canada.

NORTH AMERICAN LAKE MONSTERS

One of the best known lake monsters in North America is called Champ because it supposedly inhabits the waters of Lake Champlain, a lake that is a hundred miles long and thirteen miles wide in places. The lake is located on the border between New York and Vermont. Champ has a long history, for long before the Europeans came, the Iroquois people told stories of a horned lake serpent. An early account, reported in the *New York Times* in 1873, told how railway track workmen in Dresden, New York, saw the head of an enormous serpent with bright silver scales rear up from the lake.

There is recent photographic evidence from 1977, when Sandra Mansi took a good-quality picture of what seems to be a long-necked creature rising from the water, but authentication has been difficult because the negative was lost. Most other photographic evidence is blurred. Sandra, her husband Anthony, and their children stopped along Lake Champlain's edge near the Canadian border in Vermont when Sandra became aware of turbulence in the water and saw what she subsequently described as a huge prehistoric-looking serpent with a small head eight feet above the surface of the water, a long neck, and a humped back. Anthony saw the monster, too, and fetched the children out of the water where they were playing. The monster suddenly sank after about six minutes, disturbed by an approaching boat.

In the 1980s, a New York social studies teacher, Joseph Zarzynski, founder of the Lake Champlain Phenomena Investigation, showed the photograph to various experts, including optical science expert Paul LeBlond from the University of British Columbia. He estimated from the surrounding wave sizes that the creature must have been between twenty-four and seventy-eight feet in length.

Another lake creature Ogopogo, which supposedly inhabits Okanagan Lake in British Colombia, is mentioned in Native North American folklore as Natiaka (the *Lake Monster*). This monster was frequently seen during the 1920s, most notably in November 1926, when it was sighted by about sixty people who were attending a lakeside baptism ceremony.

Manipogo, another monster, has been photographed in Lake Manitoba in Canada in 1962. Richard Vincent and John Konefell were fishing on their motorboat. A huge water serpent came within about sixty yards of the boat and they photographed the creature. The picture unfortunately was not very clear, though it does seem to confirm independent eyewitness accounts.

SEA SERPENTS AND MONSTERS

Reports of sea serpents are also quite numerous. They have been reported from every era of history and every ocean in the world, ranging from the totally mythical creatures of Greek and Roman legend such as the many-headed Hydra to actual reported sightings in modern times. It may be that the old myth tellers based their strange creatures on sightings of creatures less dramatic such as whales or gigantic crocodiles, reported in medieval bestiaries as being over thirty feet long.

Another creature implicated in sea and lake monster sightings (in lakes once joined to the sea) is the gigantic elephant seal, which that can be over twenty-five feet long. Some can live in fresh water, but because they lie in the sun when not swimming, they are less likely to be detected in lakes.

Of course, there are natural, rarely seen real sea monsters that may rear up and be seen in rough or misty conditions. For example, on October 18, 1997, three rare giant squids were caught by fishermen off the coast of Tasmania near Australia. The squids measured about 49.5 feet from head to tentacle tip.

A typical example of a huge whale or giant squid giving rise to legends of a sea serpent is the Bakonawa of the Philippines. In folklore, the Bakonawa is said to rise from the sea and cause the moon or the sun to disappear during an eclipse. The local people in times past would bang metal objects and make loud noises to scare the monster back into the sea and make him spit out the moon. This apparently worked because the moon or sun returned.

Sea serpents, like lake monsters, are described as undulating, with humps showing above the water, and are gray, black, brown, and green. They measure between twenty feet and several hundred feet in length.[8] Some have been reported with a row of fins along the head and neck.

Sea serpents may be given names local to their own region. For example, Cadborosaurus, or Caddy, is supposedly a kind of sea serpent similar to the freshwater Ogopogo. Caddy has been reported around coastal waters near the northwestern part of the North American continent, mainly Oregon, Washington, and British Columbia, and as recently as the late 1990s, around Vancouver Island. The Cadborosaurus has been extensively studied by Ed Bousfield, a research associate with the Royal Ontario Museum, who recorded 300 sightings during the twentieth century and even provided a 1937 photograph of a dead beast. However, sightings have dramatically decreased, which Bousfield links with an accompanying decline in sea-run salmon that are common to the places where it and the related Ogopogo have been reported. These nine lakes in British Columbia where the Ogopogo has been sighted were once joined to the ocean. Bousfield states that the Cadborosaurus do not resemble whales, seals, or otters.

OTHER MYTHICAL WATER CREATURES

People have described the energies in certain places—around fast-flowing rivers or deep lakes, for example—where there was potential danger to people from nature spirits or essences. The creatures often considered dangerous symbolized the danger to humans of drowning if they fell in. The creatures were a deterrent for children through many centuries and stopped them from playing too near deep water.

THE EUROPEAN AND SCANDINAVIAN TRADITION

KELPIES, OR WATER HORSES

Kelpies are Scottish water spirits who inhabit rivers, deep pools, areas near rapids, and fast-flowing streams, and take the shape of a horse. In Sweden, they are called Bäckahästen, or the brook horses. In Norway, they are known as Nacken or Water Nixes, another type of water spirit that often assumes the form of a horse. However, if anyone tried to mount the horse, it would instantly dive into the deepest part of the water and drown them. If the mortal throws an ordinary bridle over the kelpie, it could compel the horse to work for him or her. The fairy horse is as strong as ten ordinary horses. Its magical bridle should be taken off and kept safely. According to legend, the Scottish Macgregor clan had a Kelpie bridle that held great magical powers to grant wishes. The bridle was handed down through generations after an early ancestor obtained the bridle by capturing a kelpie horse near Loch Sloch. It is said that kelpies howl to warn of an approaching storm.[9]

BÄCKAHÄSTEN, OR WATER HORSES

In Scandinavia and Poland, Nixes, or Nacken, can appear as white or gray horses apparently abandoned close to rivers or lakes, especially when it is misty. Anyone who climbed onto the horse's back would not be able to get off again, and the horse would jump into the river, drowning the rider. In the Middle Ages, it was said that the rider might escape by saying three times, "Bäckahästen, go back to your watery places and set me free, in the name of our Lady and the Holy Trinity."

WATER NIXES, OR NACKEN

Throughout the lands of northern Europe: Sweden, Norway, Finland, and Iceland, unfriendly water spirits are called *nacken* and can take mortal forms, including a horse. The females are beautiful, with the tail of a fish, but can also appear totally human apart from the wet hem of their green gowns that will never dry, even in the sun. The less friendly ones attempt to lure men to their watery homes. The male water spirits are skilled musicians who lure women and children into lakes, rivers, or streams while playing enchanted songs on their violins. They do this in order to make the women their wives and to have children by the mortals who would have a soul—something the nixes did not have. Their music is believed to herald a drowning within twenty-four hours. Males also turn themselves into treasure floating on water to lure the unsuspecting to wade in and try to retrieve it. They may also pretend to be drowning youths and drag their rescuer down beneath the water.

But they can also, it is said, have a better side. It was said that tobacco chews could be dropped into the water in exchange for music lessons. Other myths tell of their sadness that they can never have a soul.

Nixes are most clearly seen on Midsummer Eve and Night, Christmas Eve, the old Midwinter Solstice Eve around December 21, and on Thursdays.

KRAKEN

A cross between a sea monster and a malevolent water spirit, the Scandinavian Kraken is reputedly as large as an island and takes the form of either a serpent or a giant octopus or squid. It either encircles boats with its tentacles and tips them out of the water, creating a powerful whirlpool, or lies with its back facing up, leading sailors to believe it to be an island. Once the sailors land on the surface, it will descend into the waters, drowning them or eating them. The English Victorian poet Alfred Lord Tennyson wrote a sonnet in 1830 about the belief that the Kraken will rise to the surface at the end of the world and bring chaos:

> Below the thunders of the upper deep,
> Far, far beneath in the abysmal sea,
> His ancient, dreamless, uninvaded sleep
> The Kraken sleepeth . . .
> There hath he lain for ages, and will lie
> Battening upon huge sea-worms in his sleep,
> Until the latter fire shall heat the deep;
> Then once by man and angels to be seen,
> In roaring he shall rise and on the surface die.

Accounts of the Kraken, apparently factual, date from 1000 CE in seafaring Norway. In 1752, when the Bishop of Bergen, Erik Ludvigsen Pontoppidan, wrote *The Natural History of Norway*, he described the Kraken as the largest sea creature in the world.[10] He estimated it was one and a half miles long with arms like a starfish. However, because it attracted fish, sometimes sailors would venture too close. It was probably a member of an extremely large squid family of the kind described earlier in the chapter able to tip ships which were quite small at the time.

THE WATER SPIRITS OF THE FAR EASTERN TRADITION

THE NAGA, OR NAGAS

The Naga are Indian sea serpents who are especially revered by Hindus in southern India. They live in the underwater realms called Patalal and are ruled by Varuna, god of storms. The Naga also have their serpentlike kings and queens. Nagas are the children of the wise man Kasyapa and his wife Kadru. With his other wife Kasyapa had Garuda and various magical birds and reptiles.

The Nagas attained immortality when Garuda brought them *amrita*, a sacred honeylike elixir from the deities, in return for his own mother's release. This incident is discussed in Chapter 4. Though the god Indra took the amrita back when he discovered the theft, the amrita the Naga had drunk was so powerful it split their tongues, the reason it is said snakes have forked tongues.

Nagas are natural guardians of nature, springs, wells, and rivers, and they dwell in watercourses of all kinds, or beneath sacred trees near water. They bring fertility, good luck, money, and the cooling rain if people respect and care for the land. However, they can behave vengefully, bringing floods or drought if angered. They are regarded as semidivine beings. The entrances to their subterranean palaces are at the bottom of wells, deep lakes, and rivers.[11]

Called the first inhabitants of the Kashmir region, they have temples dedicated to them close to sacred springs. One of their kings, Nila, is honored when snow falls for the first time in winter. Their images appear in temples, shrines, and in homes throughout India and Tibet. They are also requested for abundant harvests. They include large cobras or water pythons; serpents with many snake heads; half-human, half-snake; or as a gigantic snake large enough to swallow an elephant.

STRANGE WATER CREATURES IN CLASSICAL MYTH

The medieval bestiaries record strange beasts such as the Hippocampus— an aquatic monster. Known as a sea horse, it has the head and forefeet of a horse and the tail of a dolphin. Its horselike forefeet, however, end as flippers rather than hooves. Hippocampus is a Roman name, as well as the zoological name given to some pygmy sea horses. Hippocampi drew the chariot of Poseidon, the sea god in Greek legend, who was Neptune to the Romans. Occasionally, Poseidon/Neptune rode on the back of a hippocampus.[12] Leonardo da Vinci painted Poseidon and his sea horses in 1511, showing the horses with both fish tails and spiral tails instead of legs. The picture is in the Windsor Royal Library that is part of Queen Elizabeth's Windsor Palace, near London. The name comes from the Greek *hippos*, which means horse, and *kampos*, meaning sea monster.

HYDRA

According to Greek myth the Hydra was a monster that lived in the watery area near the ancient city of Lerna in Argolis. It was a child of the serpent woman Echidna and Typhon. The Hydra had the body of a serpent and nine heads, though some versions say she had up to a hundred heads. One head was immortal and could not be destroyed by any weapon. If any of the other heads were cut off, two would grow in its place. She spewed out a deadly venom and devoured cattle and people indiscriminately.[13]

As part of his second Labor, Heracles was ordered to kill the Hydra. He took his nephew Iolaus with him. Heracles used fiery arrows to drive the monster from its underground lair. Because each time he cut off a head two heads grew, Iolaus burned away the neck beneath each head so that it could not regrow. To destroy the indestructible head, Heracles smashed it with his club, ripped it off with his hands, and buried it in the ground with a huge boulder on top. He dipped his arrows in the spilled venom and blood to make them doubly effective in his future tasks.

SCYLLA AND CHARYBDIS

Scylla and Charybdis were two sea monsters that guarded a channel of water so narrow that it was seemingly impossible to escape one or the other when sailing past. Scylla had six hideous heads, each with three rows of razor sharp teeth, twelve doglike legs, and a fish tail. She and Charybdis would attack boats that attempted to pass through the straits. The hero Odysseus lost six of his men when Scylla caught them as his ship passed, but he took their place and managed to help the remaining crew row the boat safely away.

According to legend, Scylla was once a beautiful sea maiden seduced by Poseidon. His wife Amphitrite filled Scylla's favorite bathing pool with poisonous herbs, and Scylla became a monster. In Ovid's version Glaukos, the sea and fisherman god, fell in love with Scylla, but she did not love him and ran away. He went to the sorceress Circe to ask for a love potion so that Scylla would care for him. But Circe also desired him and she was so furious when he rejected her that she poured poison into Scylla's bathing pool. Scylla was so distressed at her hideous appearance when she looked into the water that she took revenge on whoever passed because she could not bear them to see her.

Charybdis, or Kharybdis, was described as a huge whirlpool, a gigantic mouth through which she swallowed and spewed out seawater three times a day to create constantly bubbling whirlpools that dragged boats down and engulfed anything that came near. She lived beneath a huge fig tree on the banks of the Straits of Messina, between Italy and Sicily, where there are natural whirlpools and a rock into which Scylla was later transformed. Some scholars have suggested the straits may be near Cape Skilla in northwest Greece. Charybdis was the daughter of the sea god Poseidon and the earth mother Gaia. Like Scylla, she was once a beautiful sea nymph, a *naiad*, and helped her father to increase his kingdom by flooding the land. But her uncle Zeus, the god of the earth and sky, was furious and turned her into a hideous mouthlike chasm. She was condemned to always be thirsty and to suck in seawater three times a day and regurgitate it with her thirst unsatisfied.

THE WATER MEN AND WOMEN OF MYTH

THE MORGANS, OR MORGANA

In Brittany, there are tales of the Morgana, powerful sea fairies who cause storms and drag sailors to their deaths beneath the waves, in unsuccessful attempts to satisfy their own passions, because the sailors they captured could not breathe beneath the water.

The Morgana legends first appeared when Brittany was Christianized in the fifth century CE. Druidesses, pagan priestesses, and noblewomen would not convert to the new religion and so may have been drowned for their disobedience. The first Morgan was called Dahut, daughter of Gradlon, the king of Cornouaille in Brittany. Gradlon created Ys, a beautiful city in Finistere on the northwest coast of Brittany. The city was built below sea level with walls to keep back the water. A dyke was opened to allow the fishing boats to leave and enter.

Dahut probably continued to worship the pagan deities and so was in constant conflict with Corentin, the bishop of Quimper. According to the local legends, Dahut was accused of bringing disrepute to the city with her unbridled passions and causing the destruction of the city by handing the keys to the dyke (that she had stolen from her father) to her lover—the Devil, or Satan. Satan flooded the town and the waves drowned all the citizens except for Gradlon, Corentin, and Dahut, who clung to the back of her father's horse. But the bishop told Gradlon to cast his wicked daughter into the sea or he too would be drowned. So Gradlon pushed his daughter into the sea, leaving her to perish. Dahut did not die, it is said, but was transformed into the vengeful Marie Morgana. Other versions of the tale assign the role of the condemning cleric to St Guenole, who was the first missionary in the area. This is obviously a Christianized account of an actual town with poor sea defenses that was submerged in the fifth century. The area is often shrouded in mist, and locals say they can hear the bells of the city beneath the waves. Fishermen out early see the Morgana, who became known as sea sisters, sitting on the rocks and combing their hair. They wait to lure boats onto the rocks in the mist and claim their lovers. The coast is rocky and treacherous.

In fact the Fata Morgana, as they are called, are also reported around the Messina Straits in Italy. They are powerful mirages, in which the image appears above the observer, especially over the sea around coastal areas. These mirages may create false images of mountain ranges, phantom ships, or in modern interpretation, UFOs. The Messina Straits are an area where these mirages are quite common.

Fata Morgana mirages are so called because it was believed they were created by witches and sorcerers to mislead unsuspecting travelers. They have been named after Morgan le Fay, the sorceress and half-sister of King Arthur, who was also associated with Brittany as one of the mythical Ladies of the Lake.

THE SELKIES, OR SEAL PEOPLE

Selkies, seal-like men and women, are associated with the folklore of the Orkneys, the Western Isles, Ireland, and the north and western coasts of Scotland. Selkies are also called silkies, or selchie. According to legend, they often mated with or married mortals. Nineteenth-century Orkney folklore, mixing legend with apparent factual accounts, spoke of families with Selkie ancestry and even children born with webbed hands and feet. As described in the following section on Mer people, there are many types of physiological conditions that were untreatable until thirty years ago. When a child, or indeed a family, was born with an unusual physical condition, it was common to blame the fairies or a fairy condition; naturally webbed feet and hands seem linked to seal people.[14] An unexpected pregnancy out of wedlock could be explained as a Selkie child. Because seals were so common around the shores and a seal head can look like a human, it was perhaps easy for Selkie legends to grow. Midsummer Eve was one common time for Selkies to be reported coming to shore to take off their sealskins and dance. If they lost their sealskins, they had to remain in human form. This is why in a number of Selkie legends the mortal husband, or less frequently the wife, would lock away the sealskin after wooing the Selkie.

One typical example tells of a fisherman of the McCodrum clan who found seven beautiful Selkie sisters dancing on the shore. Nearby on rocks were seven sealskins. By stealing one of the skins he was able to capture a Selkie who lived with him in her mortal form. They had two children. As years went on, she lost her beauty, her skin became dry, and she became so exhausted that she could hardly move. So she searched for her sealskin, for she knew only by returning to the water could she survive. At last the Selkie discovered her sealskin locked in a cupboard, wrapped herself in it and returned to the waves. In some versions of the myth, her only son finds the skin, restores it to his mother, and dives into the waves with her and meets his grandfather. Though he returns to live with his father, the boy often sits on the rocks while his mother sings to him. The clan, it is said, was thereafter called McCodrum of the Seals. They were gifted with the second sight of the fairy people and reputed to be as at home on the water as on land.

The male Selkie fared better in myth and would return to the waters, usually after the first child was born. However, his partner on land would light a candle in the window to tell her lover she was missing him and he would return for a while.[15]

MERMAIDS AND MERMEN

Mer people are usually regarded as beautiful, with human heads and bodies to the waist, but fish tail below the waist. Identified with seals or various other sea creatures, they nevertheless are one of the most persistent sea people reported by sailors over the centuries and worldwide. Usually they are helpful, saving drowning sailors and guiding ships away from rocks, though occasionally they can be malevolent or, like the Morgana, drown a would-be lover because they do not realize he or she cannot breathe below the water. Mermaids live for 300 years.

THE LITTLE MERMAID OF DENMARK

Mermaids have, according to myth, married mortal men, usually through trickery on the part of the human who steals one of their possessions, such as a pearl mirror or comb, as they sit sunning themselves on the rocks. This object binds the mermaid to dry land until she can retrieve it. However, in the most famous mermaid story of all time, told by Hans Christian Andersen, it was the mermaid who was rejected by the mortal. If you go to Copenhagen, you will see the Little Mermaid statue in the harbor at Langelinie. It was erected in 1913 in memory of Andersen, Denmark's most famous son, and has since then become a symbol of Denmark.

Hans Andersen's Little Mermaid is the story of how the mermaid, on her first visit to the surface of the water at the age of fifteen, saves the life of a shipwrecked prince and falls in love with him. She goes to a sea witch who promises her human legs and says that if the prince loves her more than any other, the mermaid will gain a soul. But to become human, the price is very high. In return for her legs, the mermaid has to give the witch her lovely voice, and every step she takes on land is like walking on red-hot needles. In spite of her sacrifice, the prince marries a human princess and the mermaid cannot return to the sea except as foam, unless she kills the prince before his marriage. She refuses to do so and plunges into the sea. However, her goodness is rewarded and she is taken up to the clouds by the sylphs, the archetypal air spirits, and gains the chance of earning a soul by good deeds as an air spirit.[16]

THE MERMAID, OR HAVFREUI, IN GOTLAND

The Gotland mermaid, or Havfreui, was immortalized in a folktale about some local fishermen who were setting their nets at sea off Gotland, a historic island off the east coast of Sweden. The legend dates back to the 1800s. A beautiful mermaid with huge eyes swam near the boat and held out her hands. She was wearing one glove, and because the weather was chill, she asked the fishermen for another glove. One of them tossed his glove to her, saying: "You are welcome, beautiful Havfreui. Take the glove in friendship." Months later he was out fishing alone when the mermaid swam up to the boat and told him to head for shore because a bad storm was coming. She called him her glove friend. The lone fisherman hauled in his nets, which were unusually full, and reached shore just as the storm broke. Many other fishermen from the area perished in the storm.

MELUSINE, THE FRENCH MERMAID

A French medieval tale from the end of the twelfth century tells of the fairy queen Melusine, of the forest of Colombiers in the French region of Poitou. She married Raymond or Guy of Poitou, brought him great wealth, and magically built the castle at Lusginan overnight. They had ten children and founded the dynasty of Lusignan, though each child had a strange physical characteristic. For example, her son Geoffrey had one huge tooth. Melusine made her husband promise when they married that he would never see her in the bath on a Saturday. But when his brother visited and questioned this, he became curious. He spied on her and discovered her in mermaid form. In some versions she has a serpent tail. Melusine saw her husband and instantly disappeared but returned every night in mermaid form to feed her youngest child. In another account, Raymond revealed he knew the secret years later and she instantly took the form of a dragon or serpent and flew out of the window.

One painting of a series of sixteen about her life by Guillebert de Mets, painted around 1410–20, shows her husband peeping into the bathhouse and seeing Melusine in mermaid form. This picture is in the Bibliothèque Nationale de France. Another painting in the series shows her in mermaid form returning to feed her youngest child at night.

According to myth, she returns crying whenever a count of Lusignan is about to die or a new one is to be born, and it has been prophesied the line would continue until the end of time.[17]

THE GERMAN MERMAID TALE

A strange story comes from Germany, though I have not been able to date it except to the later 1800s. I was told the story by a German teacher I met about fifteen years ago in southwest England when she was staying with my husband's aunt. A man named Brauhard, who was a sailor, returned home to his native Lautenberg with a mermaid wife. He built her a huge tub of water in the house so she could still swim when she wanted. But local people became very angry at one of their own kind living with this strange creature and the mermaid was mysteriously poisoned. Brauhard was grief-stricken, for he loved his beautiful mermaid very much. He used the money given by her Mer father to help the local poor. This wealth started the Brauhard Fund, which even today exists for the benefit of local people in need. Of course, Brauhard could have acquired the wealth by trading, but many believe the story.

MERROW

In Ireland, the Mer people are called the Merrow and live off the wild coasts of Ireland. The Merrow women are beautiful and sometimes inter-marry with humans. Occasionally, they take the form of small hornless cows seen walking on the seashore at low tide. The Merrow males are ugly and have green teeth, green hair, red noses, and webbed hands. They appear as a warning of coming gales and bad storms. Men and women wear red feather caps that enable them to dive beneath the waves. As with the Selkies' seal skins, merrows without their red caps were condemned to living on land.

DO MERMAIDS EXIST?

It has been suggested that mermaids and mermen may actually be Sire-nias, sea mammals that include the sea cow and the manatee, which has two forward flippers, a flat seal-like tail, and can grow up to fifteen feet long. Manatees are said to hold their young in their flippers the way a human mother cradles her child, and the long flowing hair may in fact have been seaweed draped around them as they rose to the surface. At a distance, a group of these creatures near rocks might have been interpreted as mer-maids. Indeed, the Italian explorer Christopher Columbus, who sailed across the Atlantic Ocean in the early 1490s, commented that he had seen mermaids but they were not as beautiful as he had imagined. Maybe he saw manatees.

Another explanation for those mermaids apparently displayed in freak shows during the 1800s, may have been people suffering from Sirenomelia, or mermaid syndrome, in which an infant is born with his or her legs joined together like a tail. Only very recently and rarely has it been possible to oper-ate on the legs.

BIBLIOGRAPHY

1. Montgomery, C. *The Shark God: Encounters with Myth and Magic in the South Pacific*. London: Fourth Estate, 2006.
2. Swire, O. F. *The Outer Hebrides and Their Legends*. Edinburgh, Scotland: Oliver and Boyd, 1966.
3. Lewis, S. *Mexico and Peru: Myths and Legends*. London: Senate Books, 1994.
4. Smith, Richard G. *Ancient Tales and Folklore of Japan*. Whitefish, MT: Kessinger Publishing, 2003.

5. Hahner-Herzog, I., M. Kecskesi, and L. Vajda. *African Masks: The Barbier-Mueller Collection.* 2 vols. London: Prestel Publishing, 2002.
6. Radford, B., and J. Nickell. *Lake Monster Mysteries: Investigating the World's Most Elusive Creatures.* Lexington: University Press of Kentucky, 2004.
7. Binns, R. *The Loch Ness Mystery Solved.* Buffalo, NY: Prometheus Books, 1984.
8. Ellis, R. *Monsters of the Sea.* Guilford, CT: Lyons Press, 2006.
9. Briggs, K. *Encyclopedia of Fairies, Hobgoblins, Brownies, Bogies and Other Supernatural Creatures.* Pantheon Fairy Tale and Folklore Library American Edition. New York: Pantheon, 1978.
10. Pontoppidan, E. *Natural History of Norway* [translated from the Danish original]. London: A Linde, 1775. (Rare but worth seeing if possible.)
11. Vogel J. *Indian Serpent Lore or the Nagas in Hindu Legend and Art. Whitefish*, MT: Kessinger Publishing, 2005.
12. Baxter, R. *Bestiaries and Their Uses in the Middle Ages.* Stroud, Gloucestershire, England: Alan Sutton Publishing, 1998.
13. Graves, R. *The Greek Myths: Complete Edition.* London and New York: Penguin, 1993.
14. See note 13.
15. Williamson, D. *Tales of the Seal People: Scottish Folk Tales.* Northampton, MA: Interlink Books, 1998.
16. Andersen, H. C. *Complete Hans Andersen Fairy Tales.* New York: Gramercy Books, 1993.
17. Maddox, D., and S. Sturm-Maddox, eds. *Melusine of Lusignan: Founding Fiction in Late Mediaeval France.* Athens: University of Georgia Press, 1996.

CHAPTER 9

Animals and Prophecy

The movements, calls, and unusual behavior of animals and birds formed one of the earliest forms of prophecy. This may be because animals and birds are so closely tuned in to natural and cosmic energies that any sudden change in behavior forewarned humans of imminent danger such as an earthquake or tsunami. This has been the case in many lands throughout the ages.

The ancient Egyptians, Greeks and Romans, the Far East people, and people in surviving indigenous societies today have studied what they consider omens or prophetic signs from nature. They have frequently regarded certain species or individual members of a species sacred because these creatures seem able to convey the will of the deities; or in modern psychological terms, trigger access to the wise part of every human that may be obscured by anxiety about an issue or conflicting opinions.

It has been speculated that the unusual behavior, for example, of a flock of birds may reflect some intangible cosmic change of energies that could also make people act more unpredictably. This could, in the ancient world, indicate a surge of power that might make a battle or bid for leadership successful at the time of the divination. Divination means the wisdom of a divus or diva, a god or goddess. This could be, in psychological terms, the higher part of every person's human consciousness that may seem hard to access in the modern, fast-paced world.

Birds especially were regarded as messengers from the deities or even deities in disguise. Early natural bird divination and that using other sacred animals (such as the Bull of Apis in ancient Egypt) could indicate the intentions and favor of the deities toward a person, the state, a battle, or even a new building.

It may be that observing animal and bird behavior patterns does help an individual tune into his or her own instincts or intuition. Though it is hard to measure intuition scientifically, many people do seem to know instinctively whether or not a person is trustworthy, for example. Mothers especially are very tuned into a young child even when the mother is asleep or absent.[1]

When the person studying the creatures was an expert diviner, these instincts would be very well developed. The relationship between the actual behavior observed and the predictions made is complex and hard to assess scientifically.

ANIMALS AND PREDICTING NATURAL DISASTERS

It is remarkably difficult to measure an animal's predictive powers in the laboratory. However, there has been a lot of anecdotal evidence of animals, birds, and even fish acting strangely before the onset of an earthquake, most dramatically in the twenty-four hours before the quake strikes. One example of a natural forewarning was recorded in the United States on August 17, 1959, when thousands of terns, gulls, and other waterfowl that had been observed living on Montana's Lake Hegben for several months suddenly flew away in the afternoon, though the lake water remained smooth and motionless. Just before midnight the same day, earthquakes hit the region. The dam wall of the lake was breached by the tremors from a 7.5 quake, and the canyon below it collapsed. It was feared the whole dam wall would give way. This could, of course, be regarded as coincidence except that this panic reaction of creatures before a natural disaster—and even before it is predicted by artificial measuring devices—has been commonly observed.

This seeming ability of animals and birds to predict earthquakes is not new. As early as 373 BCE, animals, including rats, snakes, and weasels, left the Greek city of Helice in large numbers days before an earthquake destroyed the town. The ancient Greeks also reported that bees swarmed from their hives before the earthquake. This omen was taken very seriously as a warning from Artemis, the bee and hunting goddess, that people should leave the area at once.

Undomesticated creatures and strays seem particularly in tune with incipient earthquakes. For example, before the earthquake in Morocco in 1960, stray animals, including dogs, were seen streaming from the port in large numbers up to twenty-four hours before the shock that killed 15,000 people.

LISTENING TO THE ANIMALS

On February 4, 1975, the Chinese cleared the city of Haicheng because of signs of unusually disturbed animal behavior. A few hours later, a 7.3 earthquake hit the area. Although there was extensive damage to buildings, it is estimated that 90,000 lives were saved because the animals' early warning system was recognized.

The Chinese and Japanese take natural warning signs seriously, and zoo animals are carefully studied regularly for sudden mass unusual behavior. The earthquake bureau in Nanning, capital of the Guangxi province in China, has set up 24-hour video observation of snakes on snake farms to monitor any collective adverse reactions. "Of all the creatures on Earth, snakes are perhaps the most sensitive to earthquakes," the earthquake bureau director Jiang Weisong told Reuters news agency. "When an earthquake is about to occur, snakes will move out of their nests, even in the cold of winter. If the earthquake is a big one, the snakes will even smash into walls while trying to escape." He states that snakes can sense an earthquake from 120 kilometers away, three to five days before it happens. Other experts think that the more extreme the animals' behavior, the stronger the quakes will be. Mice become dazed before an earthquake and can easily be caught by hand. Even deep-sea fish are affected by pre-earthquake panic. No one knows precisely how animals, birds, reptiles, and fish sense earthquakes coming. Theories suggest variously that they may become aware of changes in the earth's electrical or magnetic field, gases released from the earth prior to a quake, or seismic preshocks that are undetectable at present by even the most sensitive human-made instruments.[2]

ANIMALS AND TSUNAMIS

In the tragic tsunami tidal wave in Southeast Asia on December 26, 2004, not a single animal was killed. Not even a rabbit carcass was recovered, though almost a quarter of a million people lost their lives in the gigantic waves along the Indian Ocean coast. Elephants in Sri Lanka, Sumatra, and Thailand were seen moving on to high ground in the hours before the giant waves struck and were heard trumpeting loudly as they went. Indeed, where people took notice of the animals' unusual behavior, they were also saved.

Rupert Sheldrake, a former Fellow of Clare College, Cambridge University, Research Fellow of the Royal Society in biochemistry, and currently Fellow of the Institute of Noetic Sciences in Petaluma, California, has studied the phenomena of animals and birds anticipating earthquakes, tsunamis, and other natural disasters. He describes in recent research how in Ban Koey, a village in Thailand, a herd of buffalo were grazing near the beach on December 26 when they suddenly lifted their heads and looked out to sea, their ears standing upright. They turned and stampeded up the hill. The villagers followed and survived. It seems unlikely that the land animals responded to the tremors of an underwater earthquake.

In India, too, in Cuddalore District in Tamil Nadu, in the hours before a tsunami struck, Sheldrake reported that creatures including buffaloes, goats, and wild dogs fled the beaches and that nesting flamingos left for higher ground.

ANIMALS AND WARNINGS OF OTHER NATURAL DISASTERS

It has been observed by naturalist Wild Lyle that, when turtles in Florida lay their eggs particularly high up in the riverbanks, it foretells a bad hurricane season.

Animals can also anticipate avalanches. On February 22, 1999, in the area around Galtür village, in the Austrian Tyrol region, the chamois antelopes suddenly left the mountains for the shelter of the valleys. The following day an avalanche occurred, killing a number of people. The area was officially considered to be a safe, avalanche-free zone. The avalanche occurred because of freak weather conditions. Mountain goats also seem able to anticipate avalanches. It has been suggested this may be an innate survival mechanism among creatures that live on mountains.

THE APPARENT ABILITY OF PETS TO ANTICIPATE WHEN AN OWNER IS RETURNING HOME

The most common example of animals' predictive powers that has been studied formally using observational methods is the apparent ability of pets to anticipate when owners are returning home. Sheldrake has studied this phenomenon extensively, and many people have firsthand experience of this. He reports that 51 percent of dog owners and 30 percent of cat owners in America and the UK, interviewed as part of random household surveys, said that their pets regularly knew when they were coming home.[3] In both surveys, most of the dogs that anticipated the return of a family member did so less than five minutes before the person arrived home. Sixteen percent of the dog owners in England and 19 percent in California said that the dogs reacted more than ten minutes before the human arrival.

I regularly experience this with my old half-blind cat Jenny. Whenever I go away from my home on the Isle of Wight in southern England for three weeks or more to Sweden, France, or the UK mainland, or even if I go out for the day, Jenny is always sitting on the front wall waiting for me when I return. I am assured by people who care for my two cats in my absence that Jenny does not spend the entire three weeks sitting on the wall and indeed rarely goes out of the house. However, even when I return after midnight on a rainy night, the first thing I hear on getting out of my car or a taxi is Jenny's loud meowing. Often, I cannot park my car outside the house and have to leave it some distance away. Then Jenny will come bounding toward me, getting under my feet as I struggle with my bags, even though I generally do not pass the house before parking. Jenny's daughter Molly Mole does not react in this way.

Though my experience is pure anecdote, the following story intrigues me. Sheldrake studied in detail a terrier called Jaytee, owned by Pamela Smart, who lived in Ramsbottom, Greater Manchester. Jaytee seemed to anticipate his owner's *intention* to come home, up to about forty-five minutes before her arrival. Pam adopted Jaytee from Manchester Dogs' Home in 1989 when he was still a puppy and feels she has a very close link with him, a factor that is often reported in anecdotal evidence. Her parents reported over a number of years that Jaytee anticipated her homecoming, even after she was laid off in 1993 and had irregular hours of absences. From 1994, Sheldrake videotaped, in over 100 experiments, the area by the French window where Jaytee waited during Pamela's absences. She used different modes of transport to rule out sounds of the car approaching. In other experiments, Pam was alerted by radio pager of different times she should return, unknown to anyone in the house who might have been communicating unconsciously by nonverbal signals with the animal. In every case Jaytee would go to the window when Pamela left for home. Odds against this were estimated at more than 100,000 to 1. Jaytee seemed to react to Pam's intention to come home even when she was many miles away.

Sheldrake has also carried out experiments concerning the apparent ability of dogs to know when they are going to be taken for walks. During the experiments, the dogs were kept in familiar, separate rooms or outbuildings where they relaxed and were under constant videotaped surveillance. The owners randomly selected a time, thought hard about taking the dog for a walk and would go to the dog five minutes later. The videotapes showed the dogs becoming excited at the precise time the owner was picturing the walk but before the owner had moved; the excitement was manifest when the owner was only anticipating the walk. Such research opens up possibilities for future studies into the mind link between humans and animals.[4]

PROPHETIC BIRDS IN ANCIENT ROME

The Roman historian Livy recounts that in 390 BCE, geese sacred to Juno cackled in the courtyard of the temple of Carmentis when the Gauls sent armed scouts to the city under cover of darkness to climb the cliff of Capitol Hill; thanks to the geese the city was saved. They responded when human guards of the city did not hear the intruders.[5] Even the dogs in the city were not aware of the intruders. The honking of the geese and the flapping of their wings woke Manlius, who had been a consul three years before, and he, assisted by other soldiers who arrived soon after, drove the Gauls back down the steep slopes. This, of course, was not strictly prophecy because the invaders were actually present, but it does show how even a creature considered not very intelligent can be tuned into a sound that heralded danger, through the ordinary noises of guards and others walking round the city.

AUSPICY, OR BIRD DIVINATION, IN ANCIENT ROME

Omens were taken very seriously in ancient Rome, especially those that deliberately sought to understand the will of the deities about significant issues. One of the most highly regarded methods in Rome was observing the flight pattern and call of birds, or *taking the auspices*. Another favored divinatory observation was the pecking behavior of the sacred chickens that were taken in coops when the legions moved throughout the empire. The chickens were used for answering questions about battle strategy or the favorable outcome of a planned attack or about domestic affairs. The chickens indicated the right option by first pecking corn from a number of separate areas labeled with letters or special signs to indicate the choices. Of course, this could be entirely random, but psychologically once a choice was made, people worked hard to make it a success because they believed the will of the deities was with them, a kind of self-fulfilling prophecy.

One of the most famous auspice or bird-flight divination stories is connected with the founding of Rome. It is told that in 753 BCE the twins Romulus and Remus arrived at Palatine Hill but could not agree where to found the city. Romulus believed that the best site was the Palatine Hill. However, Remus insisted that the Aventine Hill could be more easily defended, so they decided to use auspicy, bird divination, to receive the will of the gods on the matter. Each brother sat on the ground and looked upward into a specified area. Remus saw six vultures, an excellent omen, while Romulus saw twelve, which was even better. However, Remus insisted that he had seen his vultures first and in the subsequent dispute over digging the boundaries, Remus was killed, some accounts say by his brother Romulus.[6]

BIRD DIVINATION CONSIDERED

How could this kind of divination possibly work? The Romans, though superstitious, were also logical people and would not risk totally inaccurate predictions.

Farmers and those who work on the land are gifted in *reading* animal patterns (and many are expert meteorologists). Bird augury may work on the principle that birds, being closer to nature than humans and more sensitive to invisible energies, express by their physical actions, approaching energy before even the most psychic human is aware of it (as in the case of earthquakes). The physical actions of the birds are interpreted and related to human questions by the intuition of the diviner. This is a valuable psychological device for accessing our highly knowledgeable but relatively inaccessible deep stores of knowledge that the trained diviner can more easily interpret.

The premise behind bird divination is expressed by the psychotherapist Carl Gustav Jung in his theory of synchronicity, or meaningful coincidence: no action or event is accidental or random. The bird flight or call that is seen or heard at the same moment a particular question is asked can shed light on the problem. For example, if an owl whose call was unfavorable flew in, or the cry of an owl was heard from the left, which was considered a favorable omen, there were both good and bad factors involved in going ahead. The advice would be to proceed with caution but watch out for someone ill-intentioned.[7]

This deep information might not have been consciously available, even considering the known facts, because the divinatory process occurs within what Jung called the collective unconscious: the wisdom of all people in all places built into the deep unconscious that can give clues to the best possible future path to follow. All this is very vague, and no one really knows the way oracles work.

Augury, which refers to the observation of all kinds of natural phenomena, was primarily used in Rome to decide if a certain date and location was auspicious for the site of a new public building, to receive or send an ambassador, sign a treaty, or go to war. The flight patterns, kinds of birds, and so on were basically an elaborate form of yes/no replies rather than telling the future and were taken as an indication of the pleasure or displeasure of the deities.

The use of the flights of birds as omens was common in ancient Greece; among the Etruscans (the people of ancient Italy who were taken over by the Romans), and the Near East.

For state affairs the *auspicia publica*, the highest-ranking magistrates, would undertake the augury because it was believed that only they were important enough to mediate with the gods. However, they were helped by trained augurs, at first two but increased to nine by 300 BCE. The task of the augurs was to assist in establishing a *templum*, the official divination area, and to help with interpretations of omens, though in practice they probably did the actual work and the officials took the credit.[8]

Apart from state augury, the most senior male family member would undertake the divination for domestic matters in Rome. For example, on marriages or property matters, he might call on Juno, the goddess of marriage whose sacred bird was the peacock, or for matters of lawsuits he would consult Minerva, goddess of wisdom and justice. Minerva's sacred bird was the owl. These would be seen as very lucky signs for the matter under question, in spite of the owl's dubious reputation. A dove might be sought to answer questions on matters of love or family, ruled by Venus.

PERFORMING AN AUGURY WITH BIRDS

Auspices, bird flight divination, always took place on high ground. To establish a templum or divinatory area that was drawn on the ground, the east-west cardo line was marked first. This is the point on the horizon where the sun rises and sets on the day of the divination. This position of course changed through the seasons. The north-south axis, Decumanus, was aligned by the polestar, Polaris. A rectangle was formed of parallel lines in the proportion of 6:5, and in the center was the *tabernaculum*, a square tent with an opening facing south. The magister (presiding magistrate) or augur sat in front of the tent, near the edge of the top of the hill so he could focus on the sky ahead without distraction. The auspices, the official diviners, were beside him as were the obligatory flautists who played throughout the ceremony.

The ceremony began by making an offering of wine to Jupiter, the supreme god, and asking that he would send birds to indicate his approval of the purpose under question. The magistrate would next draw an imaginary templum in the sky, marked as before into four quadrants, using a hazel or ash wand called a *lituus*. The omens to be studied would hopefully appear within the sky and earth templum and the magistrate would define in advance the signs he wanted, for example, the kind of birds. He then waited and watched the designated area of the sky.

The most popular birds chosen were eagles, vultures, or osprey. If the bird call and flight were to be considered, owls, ravens, crows, or woodpeckers were chosen. Bird flight direction was an important consideration and because the auger always faced south, east was on the left. Birds coming from the east or south, straight to the front, were most auspicious, whereas birds coming from the north, behind the augur, or to the right, were considered unfavorable. The same is true for the calls of birds considered good omens, but not always. The higher the flight of the bird, the more favorable the omen. However, if a bird suddenly changed direction, there might be inconstancy or false friends. If a songbird sang or a bird uttered a cry as it took flight, it was a good sign to go ahead at once with any matter. A bird who calls as it lands may have indicated that caution was needed. If a dark bird or a bird of prey screamed as it circled, unless near its nest, there might be unexpected opposition to overcome.

There were considerable variations in the interpretation of bird call depending on the season, the sound, and circumstances, so an auger and the auspices had to be very experienced in the habits of local birds and alert to any unusual behavior. Variations also depended on the deity invoked: for example, the appearance of Jupiter's sacred eagle within the templum would indicate the highest favor.

BULLS AND PROPHECY

THE BULL OF APIS

In Ancient Egypt, the sacred Apis bull of Memphis (near modern-day Cairo) was believed to be an earthly manifestation of the creator god Ptah, and its soul was identified with his soul, or *ka* in life. Some images and statues show the bull with the sun disk between his horns and the royal *uraeus*, cobra image, on its forehead to indicate that the bull also represented the power of the pharaoh. When the bull was paraded covered in jewels and flowers, it was considered to bring blessings on the people and land and it was called the herald or messenger of Ptah. By its actions, it could reveal Ptah's will. Its breath was thought to cure any disease, and if the bull snorted at a child, that child would be endowed with the gifts of prophecy.

The bull resided within Ptah's sacred dwelling at Memphis in a specially constructed temple with two sacred areas as well as an exercise courtyard. People were able to ask questions, which the bull would answer by moving into one of the two pens in the outside area, designated as yes or no. More fortunate, wealthy, or powerful petitioners were allowed to offer him food, and if he refused, the venture about which they asked was considered inauspicious.

In Egypt, the oracle of Apis was regarded by both great and humble as an important part of decision making, and it (and other oracular methods) was a way that the priesthood was able to control a weak king (by informing him through oracles of the will of the gods). During the New Kingdom, which spanned the eighteenth to the twentieth dynasties and lasted from 1570 to 1070 BCE, the priests of Amun-Ra increasingly dictated through oracles the way the gods wished the pharaoh to rule. But even in times of a strong king, the oracles influenced state and personal matters such as choosing the heir to the throne, giving legal judgments, and determining the best time and place to plant the crops or to site a temple.

According to the Greek historian Herodotus of Halicarnassus (484–425 BCE), who provided a great deal of information on Ancient Egypt, an Apis bull was always black and was chosen for its distinctive markings. It had twenty-nine markings in all, including a white triangle on its forehead, another white mark in the shape of an winged vulture across its shoulders, and a piece of flesh in the shape of a scarab under its tongue.[9] The bull came from a cow who, it was said, conceived the bull calf when a flash of light came down from heaven to impregnate her and after its birth she never calved again.

After death, the bull of Apis was given an elaborate burial, when it was called Osiris–Apis and became associated with the resurrection and harvest Father god Osiris. The bull was embalmed and buried in underground galleries (known as the Serapeum) in the Memphite Saqqara necropolis. After death the *ka*, or soul, of Ptah passed into the next chosen Apis bull.

How might this form of oracle have a valid basis? To the Ancient Egyptians the movements of the bull indicated the will of Ptah. Maybe the petitioner knew the right course deep down, but needed an outward sign so that he or she would be able to make it work because it was believed to be right.

But the actual oracle of the bull was only the first part of what was a more profound psychological process. While the seeker was traveling home, maybe in the shimmering heat of day, or in dreams at night, the petitioner, who might have traveled hundreds of miles to see the bull, envisioned or imagined a seemingly stark yes or no message in an expanded, meaningful form. The decision would also have been mitigated or expanded by a priest or priestess at the temple so that it acted as a spur for natural creative and logical processes.

To the Greeks, the Osiris–Apis aspect of the bull became most important, and he was identified with their god Serapis. Egypt became part of the Greek world when Alexander the Great conquered it in the fourth century BCE. Alexander's successors, the Ptolemate kings, encouraged the merging of Greek and Egyptian religions. Isis, who in Egyptian religion was the wife and sister of the god Osiris, became identified as the wife of the new supreme god of the Ptolemlies, Serapis. The cult of Serapis and Isis was brought to Greece by traders from Egypt who settled in the fourth century BCE at Piraeus, the harbor town of Athens. The worship of the Apis bull continued through Roman times in Egypt.

CELTIC DRUID ANIMAL DIVINATION

The oracles of Druidry, the Celtic nature priests and priestesses, come from listening to the sounds of the natural world. The Sicilian Greek historian Diodorus Siculus, who lived between 90 and 30 BCE and described the events of Caesar's wars in Gaul and England from 43 BCE, referred to the Druidic practice of divination and bird flight.

The most intriguing form of Druid oracular practices, described in ancient Irish literature, involves dream or trance prophecy, called the bull dream.[10] At the Tarb-feis, a sacrificial bull-feast after the ritual slaughter of the bull, a leading Druid would eat the raw meat and then wrap himself in the bull hide to induce visions in sleep. *Tarb* is the old Irish word for bull. The bull dream ritual is especially associated with the slaughter of two white bulls on the Midwinter Solstice, the old Christmas, around December 21 in the Northern Hemisphere. Other accounts link the ceremony to the Celtic fire festival at the beginning of May that heralded the summer.

However, bull skin divination would be carried out if there was an urgent need, for example, to appoint a new king or leader. One problem in obtaining accurate information about Celtic customs is that we have contemporaneous accounts only from Greek or Roman sources. They often reported the biased accounts of the Roman leaders who invaded what was to them an alien and primitive culture. The most accurate accounts of the early Celtic deities and, by inference, Druidic beliefs, come from Native Celtic mythology. The remains of an oral tradition, preserved over the centuries by Celtic bards and minstrels, were recorded by Christian monks and nuns from the eighth to thirteenth centuries and were also collected as folklore from the seventeenth century onward in areas where Celtic descendants remained.

The bull dream was linked by Pliny in his *Natural History Book XVI* to the cutting of mistletoe by a white-robed priest with a gold sickle prior to the sacrifice of the bulls. Possibly the would-be prophet drank a brew made from the newly cut mistletoe to create an altered state of consciousness (dangerous in view of the toxicity of the berries and the risks of convulsions if too concentrated a dose is taken).

A typical site where the bull ceremony, according to local legend, occurred was at the Mottistone, a local stone on the hills in the center of the Isle of Wight, a small island off the south coast of England. The stone dates from the third millennium BCE. Next to the upright monolith is a flat altar stone. To the west of these two stones is a long barrow, a passage-like grave used for storing the bones of important tribal ancestors and for ceremonies to bring a good harvest by asking the help of the ancestors. The long barrow grave dates from 3000 BCE and local lore tells us that after the bulls were slaughtered and the flesh eaten, the chosen Druid would lie within the tomb wrapped in the bull hide in darkness and silence. This induced a form of sensory deprivation known to bring hallucinations, so that it seemed the ancestors brought their wisdom to show him the year ahead and answer any urgent questions the tribe had.

The bull ceremony, it is speculated in connection with the Mottistone, may have taken place at sunset on the Midwinter Solstice, culminating with the slaughter of the bull or bulls and the feast. It may be that on the next dawn the Druid was wakened by light streaming into the long barrow as the stone covering the entrance was removed and the suffocating bull skin taken off him. The sudden breaking of the darkness and sensory deprivation created a momentary heightened awareness.

The tradition of bull dreaming appears to have survived in Ireland and Scotland through the fourth, fifth, and even sixth centuries before Christianity took hold. There are accounts of the hide of a single slain bull being used to decide matters such as the identity of the future king. The old Irish story, *The Destruction of Da Derga's Hostel*,[11] has an account of a bull divination in Erin in order to discover the identity of the future king. The diviner ate the flesh (chewing on raw meat would set up a rhythmic action to slow the conscious brain activity) and drank the broth of the slain bull in order to absorb its strength and wisdom. He slept within the bull hide. The diviner was warned that were he to speak falsely, he would be struck down by the gods. There are other accounts of choosing kings or chiefs in other parts of Ireland by the same method. Sometimes the diviner would bathe in the bull broth.

At Erin, four Druids chanted mesmerizing words over the diviner, sated with bull meat and broth. This sent him or her to sleep, covered by the bull skin, which must have been very heavy indeed and was pulled over the whole head and body. In spite of the threats of being struck down, this would seem a method open to abuse by different political factions, especially if the sleeper did not dream of a future king at all. However, it did mean that the chosen candidate would be undisputed because the will of the deities had been revealed and opposition to the apparently legitimate heir would thus end or be reduced.

There are accounts of the practice continuing secretly among individuals (rich enough to have a bull) in Scotland even into medieval times. The person would wrap himself or herself in the hide of a newly killed bull near or in a cave behind a waterfall. In the darkness, with the roar of the water obscuring all other senses, he or she would be given the answer to his or her question. If the bull hide was removed at dawn, and perhaps the diviner leaped or was pushed into the foaming white water beneath the waterfall, the contrast of light and darkness and heat and cold, may have triggered a sudden sensory hallucination. This practice may be an alternative method practiced in earlier times by the pagan priesthood.

BIBLIOGRAPHY

1. Eason, C. *The Mother Link*. Berkeley, CA: Ulysses Press, 1999.
2. Sheldrake, R. *Sense of Being Stared At: And Other Unexplained Powers of the Human Mind*. New York: Three Rivers Press, 2004.
3. Sheldrake, R. *Dogs That Know When Their Owners Are Coming Home: And Other Unexplained Powers of Animals*. New York: Three Rivers Press, 1999.
4. Eason, C. *The Psychic Power of Animals*. London: Piatkus, 2003.
5. Livy, T., S. Oakley, and A. L. de Selincourt. *The Early History of Rome*. Books I–V. London and New York: Penguin Classics, 2002.
6. Wiseman, T. P. *Remus, a Roman Myth*. Cambridge: Cambridge University Press, 1995.
7. Jung, C. G. *Synchronicity: An Acausal Connecting Principle*. Translated by R. F. C Hull, 1st Princeton/Bollingen edition. Princeton: Princeton University Press, 1973.
8. Cicero. *Cicero On Old Age, On Friendship, On Divination*. Loeb Classical Library. Cambridge: Harvard University Press, 1923.
9. Herodotus. *An Account of Egypt*. Whitefish, MT: Kessinger Publishing, 2004.
10. Powell, T. G. E. *The Celts (Ancient People and Places)*. New ed. London: Thames and Hudson, 1983.
11. Stokes, W., trans. *The Destruction of Da Derga's Hostel*. Whitefish, MT: Kessinger Publications, 2004.

Bibliography

Rather than just giving you a single page reference for material that can sometimes involve tracking down rare books to read just a line or two, I have suggested books that expand each relevant topic. They give background information and further resources. This, I feel, will be most helpful both for those interested in project or research work and for those with a general interest in myths and legends. Also enter relevant words and phrases on your web browser and you can often find material from original sources and out of print or hard-to-obtain sources as e-books.

Above all, develop your own private resource file on the computer or in notebooks when you travel, even for a day or weekend. Collect any local legends or myths concerning not only fabulous animals and monsters, but a general legend and folklore database. Look out for any news stories concerning strange creatures in lakes or forests. They may include both actual creatures, maybe in an unusual place, and those that seem like fantasy. That way you have something special to hand down to future generations. Someday you may write your own book.

If you want to contact me about any topic in this book you can mail me through: www.cassandraeason.co.uk

I especially welcome family myths and legends, or regional variations of folklore.

BIBLIOGRAPHY

Alexander, C. F. *St Patrick's Breastplate*. Belfast: Appletree Press, 1995.
Alexander, H. B. *Native American Mythology*. London and New York: Dover Publications, 2005.

Allen, L. A. *Time Before Meaning: Art and Myth of the Australian Aborigines.* New York: Ty Crowell, 1976.

Andersen, Hans Christian. *Complete Hans Christian Andersen Fairy Tales.* New York: Gramercy Books, 1993.

Anonymous. *The Saga of King Hrolf Kraki.* Translated by Jesse L. Byock. New York: Penguin Classics, 1998.

Apollonius, R. *Argonautica, Book 111.* Cambridge: Cambridge University Press, 1989.

Ashe, G. *Dawn Behind the Dawn: A Search for the Earthly Paradise.* New York: Henry Holt, 1991.

Balter, M. *The Goddess and the Bull: Çatalhöyük, An Archaeological Journey to the Dawn of Civilization.* New York: Free Press, 2004.

Barber, R. *Bestiary.* Rochester, NY: Boydell and Brewer (Boydell Press), 1993.

Baring, A., and J. Cashford. *The Myth of the Goddess: Evolution of an Image.* London: Penguin, 1993.

Barney, S. A., W. J. Lewis, J. A. Beach, and O. Berghof. *The Etymologies of Isidore of Seville.* Cambridge: Cambridge University Press, 2006. (Expensive if bought new, but beautiful.)

Baxter, R. *Bestiaries and the Uses in the Middle Ages.* Stroud, Gloucestershire, England: Alan Sutton Publishing, 1998.

Beagon, M., trans. *The Elder Pliny on the Human Animal: Natural History, Book V.* Clarendon Ancient History. Oxford: Oxford University Press, 2005.

Beer, R. R. *Unicorn: Myth and Reality.* Translated by C. M. Stern. New York: Van Nostrand Reinhold Co., 1972.

Benzaguen, A. S. *Encounters with Wild Children: Temptation and Disappointment.* Montreal: McGill-Queens University Press, 2006.

Bettelheim, B. *The Uses of Enchantment: The Meaning and Importance of Fairy Tales.* New York: Vintage Books, 1975.

Binns, R. *The Loch Ness Mystery Solved.* Buffalo, NY: Prometheus Books, 1984.

Bloomfield, M. *Cerberus the Dog of Hades.* Whitefish, MT: Kessinger Publishing, 2003.

Briggs, K. *Encyclopedia of Fairies, Hobgoblins, Brownies, Bogies and Other Supernatural Creatures.* Pantheon Fairy Tale and Folklore Library American Edition. New York: Pantheon, 1978.

Brommer, F., and S. J. S. Schwarz. *Heracles: The Twelve Labors in Ancient Art and Literature.* New York: Aristide D. Caratzas, 1986.

Budge, E. A. W. *Amulets and Superstitions.* Mineola, NY: Dover Publications, 1977.

Bulfinch, T. *Bulfinch's Mythology: Age of Chivalry and Legends of Charlemagne.* London and New York: Penguin New American Library, 1962.

Byock, J., trans. *The Saga of the Volsungs: The Norse Epic of Sigurd the Dragon Slayer.* Berkeley: University of California Press, 2002.

Byrne, P. *The Search for Bigfoot: Monster, Man or Myth.* Camarillo, CA: Acropolis Books, 1975.

Campbell, J. *The Masks of God: Volume 2, Oriental Mythology.* London: Penguin, 1991.

Cardinal Farley, J., Archbishop of New York. *The Catholic Encyclopaedia*, Vol. XI. New York: Robert Appleton Company, 1911.

Cavallo, A. S. *Medieval Tapestries in the Metropolitan Museum of Art.* New York: Metropolitan Museum of Art, 1993.

Cicero. *Cicero On Old Age, On Friendship, On Divination.* Loeb Classical Library. Cambridge, MA: Harvard University Press, 1923.

Coleman, L. L. *Mothman and Other Curious Encounters.* New York: Paraview Press, 2001.

Coleridge, S. T., and W. Keach. *The Complete Poems of Samuel Taylor Coleridge.* London: Penguin, 1997.

Coles, J. M., and E. S. Higgs. *The Archaeology of Early Man.* New York: Frederick A. Praeger Press, 1960.

Corrales, S. *Chupacabras and Other Mysteries.* Pensacola, FL: Greenleaf Publications, 1997.

Crummet, M. *Tatanka Tyotanka: A Biography of Sitting Bull.* Tucson, AZ: Western National Parks Association, 2002.

Danielou, A. *The Myths and Gods of India: The Classic Work on Hindu Polytheism from the Princeton Bollingen Series.* Rochester, VT: Inner Traditions, 1991.

Day, J. S. *Traditional Hopi Kachinas: A New Generation of Carvers.* Flagstaff, AZ: Northland Publishing, 2000.

de Voragine, J. *Golden Legend.* Translated by W. G. Ryan. Princeton, NJ: Princeton University Press, 1995.

Downes, J., and G. Davis. *Owlman and Others.* Corby, Northamptonshire, England: Domra Publications, 1998.

Doyle, A. C. *The Hound of the Baskervilles.* New York: Modern Library Classics, 2002.

Drysdale, V. L., and J. E. Brown, eds. *The Gift of the Sacred Pipe.* Norman: University of Oklahoma Press, 1995.

Eason, C. *The Mother Link.* Berkeley, CA: Ulysses Press, 1999.

_____. *The Psychic Power of Animals.* London: Piatkus, 2003.

_____. *Complete Guide to Faeries and Magical Beings.* Boston: Red Wheel/Weiser, 2004.

Ellis, B. P. *Celtic Myths and Legends.* New York: Caroll and Graf, 2002.

Ellis, R. *Monsters of the Sea.* Guilford, CT: Lyons Press, 2006.

Evans-Wenz, W. Y. *The Fairy Faith in Celtic Countries, a Facsimile of the 1911 Edition.* Gerrards Cross, Buckinghamshire, England: Colin Smythe Publishers, 1977.

Fitch, E. *In Search of Herne the Hunter.* Milverton, Somerset, England: Capall Bann Publishing, 1994.

Gaisser, J. H. *Homeric Hymn to Hermes.* Brynn Mawr Commentaries. Philadelphia: University of Philadelphia, 1983.

Geoffrey of Monmouth. *A History of the Kings of Britain.* Translated by L. Thorpe. London: Penguin Books, 1973.

_____. *Life of Merlin, Vita Merlini.* Cardiff: University of Wales, 1973. (Text in English and Latin.)

Gibson, F. *Superstitions about Animals.* Whitefish, MT: Kessinger Publishing, 2003.

Gibson, M. *Reading Witchcraft: Stories of Early English Witches.* London: Routledge, 1999.

Gimbutas, M. *The Living Goddesses*. Edited and supplemented by R. D. Miriam. Berkeley: University of California Press, 1999.

Ginzburg, C., J. Tedeschi, and A. C. Tedeschi. *Clues, Myths and Historical Methods*. Washington, DC: Johns Hopkins University Press, 1992.

Goodrich N. L. *Merlin*, New York: Harper Perennial, 2004.

Grant, R. M. *Early Christians and Animals*. London: Routledge, 2001.

Graves, R. *The Greek Myths: Complete Edition*. London and New York: Penguin, 1993.

Gregory, L. *Cuchulain of Muirthemne*. Mineola, NY: Dover Publications, 2001.

Guerber, H. A. *The Myths of Greece and Rome (Anthropology and Folklore)*. London: Dover Publications, 1993.

Guerber, H. A. *The Norsemen*. London: Senate Publishing, 1994.

Hahner-Herzog, I., M. Kecskesi, and L. Vajda. *African Masks: The Barbier-Mueller Collection*. 2 vols. London: Prestel Publishing, 2002.

Hall, J. *Half Human, Half Animal: Tales of Werewolves and Related Creatures*. Bloomington, IN: Authorhouse, 2003.

Hamilton, E. *Mythology, Timeless Tales of Gods and Heroes*. New York: Warner Books, 1999.

Heaney, S. *Beowulf, a New Verse Translation*. New York: WW Norton and Co., 2001.

Herodotus. *An Account of Egypt*. Whitefish, MT: Kessinger Publishing, 2004.

Higgins, R. *Minoan and Mycenaean Art*. London: Thames and Hudson, 1997.

Holy Bible, King James's Version of 1611. Peabody, MA: Hendrickson Publishing, 2003.

Homer. *The Odyssey*. Edited by H. Rieu. Translated by E. V. Rieu. London and New York: Penguin Classics, 2003.

Hurwitz, S. *Lilith, the First Eve: Historical and Psychological Aspects of the Divine Feminine*. Translated by G. Jacobson . Einsiedein, Switzerland: Daimon Books, 1992.

Isaacs, J. *Australian Dreaming: 40,000 Years of Aboriginal History*. Sydney: Lansdowne Press, 1995.

Jordon, M. *Encyclopedia of Gods*. London: Kyle Cathie Limited, 2002.

Jung, C. G. *Synchronicity: An Acausal Connecting Principle*. Translated by R. F. C Hull, 1st Princeton/Bollingen edition. Princeton, NJ: Princeton University Press, 1973.

Keats, J. *Complete Poems (Lamia)*. New York: Random House, 1994.

Kinsella, T., trans. *The Tain*. New York: Oxford University Press, 2007.

Kinsley, D. *Hindu Goddesses, Visions of the Divine Feminine in Religion*. Berkeley: University of California Press, 1988.

Kipling, R. *The Jungle Book*. London and New York: Penguin Books, 1996.

Krantz, G. S. *Big Footprints: A Scientific Inquiry into the Reality of Sasquatch*. Boulder, CO: Johnson Books, 1992.

Larrington, C. *The Poetic Edda*. Oxford, England: Oxford Paperbacks, 1999.

Latsch, M.-L. *Traditional Chinese Festivals, Singapore*. Singapore: Graham Brash, 1985.

Leland, C. G. *Aradia, Gospel of the Witches*. Blaine, WA: Phoenix Publishing, 1990.

Lesko, B. S. *Great Goddesses of Egypt*. Norman: University of Oklahoma Press, 1999.

Livy, T., S. Oakley, and A. L. de Selincourt. *The Early History of Rome*. Books I–V. London and New York: Penguin Classics, 2002.

Mackenzie, D. A. *Myths of Babylonia and Assyria*. Whitefish, MT: Kessinger Publishing, 2004.

Mackillup, J. A. *Dictionary of Celtic Mythology*. Oxford: Oxford University Press, 2004.

Maddox, D., and S. Sturm-Maddox, eds. *Melusine of Lusignan: Founding Fiction in Late Mediaeval France*. Athens, GA: University of Georgia Press, 1996.

Matteson Langdon, E. J. *Portals of Power: Shamanism in South America*. Edited by G. Bauer. Albuquerque: University of New Mexico University Press, 1992.

Matthews, J. *The Song of Taliesin: Stories and Poems*. Illustrated by L. Stuart. London: HarperCollins, Mandala, 1991.

McEwen, G. J. *Mystery Animals of Britain and Ireland*. London: Robert Hale, 1986.

Medicine Crow, J. *From the Heart of the Crow Country: The Crow Indians' Own Stories*. Lincoln: University of Nebraska Press/Bison Books, 2000.

Messner, R. *My Quest for the Yeti: Confronting the Himalayas' Greatest Mystery*. New York: St. Martin's Griffin, 2001.

Miller, M., and K. Taube. *The Gods and Symbols of Ancient Mexico and the Maya*. London: Thames and Hudson, 1993.

Montgomery, C. *The Shark God: Encounters with Myth and Magic in the South Pacific*. London: Fourth Estate, 2006.

Morphy, H. *Myth, Totemism and the Creation of Clans*. Sydney: Oceania (University of Sydney), 1990.

Mountford, Charles P. *Winbaraku and the Myth of Jarapiri*. Adelaide: Rigby Publishing, 1968.

Newman, P. *Lost Gods of Albion*. Stroud, Gloucestershire, England: Sutton Publishing, 1997.

Oakes, L., and L. Gahlin. *Ancient Egypt: An Illustrated Reference to the Myths, Religion, Pyramids and Temples of the Land of the Pharaohs*. New York: Hermes House Anness Publishing, 2002.

Oldfield Howey, M. *The Cat in Magic and Myth*. Mineola, NY: Dover Publications, 2003.

Ovid, *Metamorphoses*. Books 1–V111. Translated by F. J. Miller. Cambridge, MA: Harvard University Press, 1916.

Parrinder, G. *African Mythology*. New York: Bedrick Books, 1991.

Pastoreau, M. *Heraldry: Its Origins and Meaning*. London: Thames and Hudson, 1997.

Peters, E. *Magic, the Witch and the Law*. Amherst, MA: University of Massachusetts Press.

Pontoppidan, E. *Natural History of Norway* [translated from the Danish original]. London: A Linde, 1775. (Rare, but worth seeing if possible.)

Powell, T.G. E. *The Celts (Ancient People and Places)*. New ed. London: Thames and Hudson, 1983.

Radford, B., and J. Nickell. *Lake Monster Mysteries: Investigating the World's Most Elusive Creatures*. Lexington, KY: University Press of Kentucky, 2004.

Rees, E. *Celtic Saints in Their Landscape*. Gloucestershire, England: Sutton Publishing, 2001.

Sheldrake, R. *Dogs that Know When Their Owners Are Coming Home: And Other Unexplained Powers of Animals*. New York: Three Rivers Press, 1999.

Sheldrake, R. *Sense of Being Stared At: And Other Unexplained Powers of the Human Mind*. New York: Three Rivers Press, 2004.

Sims, P. *The Snake-Handlers: With Signs Following, "Can Somebody Shout Amen!"* Lexington, KY: University Press of Kentucky, 1996.

Smith, Richard G. *Ancient Tales and Folklore of Japan.* Whitefish, MT: Kessinger Publishing, 2003.

Sophocles. *The Oedipus Trilogy: Oedipus Rex, Oedipus at Colognus and Antigone.* Translated by D. Fitts and R. Fitzgerald. Fort Washington, PA: Harvest Books (Harcourt Brace imprint), 2002.

Spence, L. *Mexico and Peru: Myths and Legends.* London: Senate Books, 1994.

Stokes, W., trans. *The Destruction of Da Derga's Hostel.* Whitefish, MT: Kessinger Publications, 2004.

Sturluson, S. *King Harold's Sagas from Snorri Sturluson's Heimskringla.* Translated by M. Magnusson and H. Palsson. London: Penguin, 1976.

———. *The Prose Edda: Norse Mythology.* London and New York: Penguin Books, 2005.

Summers, M. *The Werewolf in Lore and Legend.* New York: Dove Publications, 2003.

Swire, O. F. *The Outer Hebrides and Their Legends.* Edinburgh: Oliver and Boyd, 1966.

Tacitus. *The Complete Works.* Berkshire, Maidenhead, England: McGraw Hill Higher Education Press.

Thorsson, E. *Northern Magick: Mysteries of the Norse, Germans and English.* St. Paul, MN: Llewellyn, 1998.

Virgil. *The Aeneid.* Translated by Robert Fitzgerald. New York: Vintage Books, 1990.

Virtanen, L., and T. DuBois. *Finnish Folklore [Studia Fennica Folkloristica].* Helsinki: Finnish Literature Society, 2002.

Vitebsky, P. *Reindeer People: Living with Animals and Spirits in Siberia.* San Francisco: Harper Perennial, 2005.

Vogel, J. *Indian Serpent Lore or the Nagas in Hindu Legend and Art.* Whitefish, MT: Kessinger Publishing, 2005.

Vyse, S. A. *Believing in Magic: The Psychology of Superstitions.* New York: Oxford University Press, 2000.

Wallis Budge, E.A. *The Book of the Dead.* New York: Gramercy Books, 1995.

Walters, D. *The Complete Guide to Chinese Astrology: The Most Comprehensive Study of the Subject Ever Published in the English Language.* London: Watkins, 2006.

Weidermann, A. *Religion of the Ancient Egyptians.* Boston: Adamant Media Corporation, 2001.

White, T. H. *The Book of Beasts: Being a Translation from a Latin Bestiary of Twelfth Century England.* London: Dover Publications, 1984.

Wilby, E. *Cunning Folk and Familiar Spirits: Shamanistic Visionary Traditions in Early Modern Witchcraft and Magic.* Eastbourne, East Sussex, England: Sussex Academic Press, 2005.

Wilkinson, R. *The Complete Gods and Goddesses of Ancient Egypt.* London: Thames and Hudson, 2003.

Williamson, D. *Tales of the Seal People: Scottish Folk Tales.* Northampton, MA: Interlink Books, 1998.

Wiseman, T. P. *Remus, a Roman Myth.* Cambridge: Cambridge University Press, 1995.

Woodward, S., and J. McDonald. *Indian Mounds of the Middle Ohio Valley.* Granville, OH: The McDonald & Woodward Publishing Company, 1986.

Zhang, J. A. *Translation of the Ancient Chinese Book of Burial (Zang Shu).* New York: Edwin Mellen Press, 2004.

Zimmerman, L. J. *American Indians: The First Nations, Native North American Life, Myth and Art.* London: Duncan Baird Publishers, 2003.

Index

Africa, animal gods, 15
Albatross, 63
Alerion, 58
Amphisbaena, 30
Anansi, 15
Ancient Egypt
    animal deities, 10–13
    dove, 67
    dragons, 44
    eagle, 68
    egg creation myths, 55–56
    lucky frog, 131
    magical cat, 93
    prophetic bull, 161–63
    serpents gods, 20–21
    sphinxes, 84–85
    vulture gods, 53–54
    Wild Hunt, 108
Ancient Greece. *See* Greek mythology
Animal gods, 1–6
    in Ancient Egypt, 10–13
    bear, 96
    bees, 76
    bird. *See* Bird, gods
    buffalo, 13–14
    bull, 9
    butterflies, 77–78

Celtic, 5–8
cow, 12–13
frogs, 131
goats, 10
horses, 5
jaguars, 16
owl, 71
serpents, 20–29
sow, 6–7, 95
spiders, 14–15
whale, 136
wolves, 97
Animals
    that anticipate owner's return,
        156–58
    crests, 124–25
    familiar spirits, 125–28
    and *Feng Shui*, xvi–xvii
    lucky, 130–34
    predicting natural disasters, 154–56
    and prophecy, 153–65
    rituals, viii
    and tsunamis, 155–56
Anubis, 13
Ardwinna, 95
Argos, 92
Artemis, 2, 4

Auspicy, 158
    performing an, 160–61
    premise behind, 159–60
Australia
    dreamtime, 129–30
    serpent gods, 22–23
    totetism, 128
Aztecs, animal gods, 16

Babylon, dragons, 44–46
Bäckahästen, 142
Bastet, ix, 93
Bear, magical, 96
Bee
    goddesses, 76
    in mythology, 76–77
    and the Virgin Mary, 77
Benten, 137
Benu, 58–59
Beowulf, 49
Berserkers, x, 110–12
Bestiary, 28–29, 57
Bigfoot, 115–17
Bird
    creator, 56–57
    gods, 51–55
    magical. *See* Birds with magical
        associations
    prophetic, 158–61
    soul, 57
    vultures, 52–54
Bird of paradise, 63–64
Birds with magical associations, 57–58
    albatross, 63
    bird of the paradise, 63–64
    blackbird, 64
    cockerel, 64–65
    condor, 65
    crane, 65–66
    crow, 66
    dove, 67
    duck, 68
    eagle, 67–68
    hummingbird, 68–69
    jay, 69

    kingfisher, 69–70
    kookaburra, 70
    magpies, 70–71
    owl, 71
    peacock, 72
    parrot, 72
    raven, 72–73
    robin, 73
    seagull, 73–74
    swallow, 74
    swan, 74–75
    turkey, 75–76
Blackbird, 64
Black Shuck, 104–05
The Book of the Dead, 11
Buddhism, and lucky rabbit, 133
Bulgaria, dragons, 47
Bull
    gods, 9
    and prophesy, 161–65
Bull of Apis, 161–63
Burma, temple cats of, 93–94
Butterflies, goddesses, 77–78

Cadborosaurus (Caddy), 141
Caduceus, 28–29
Cailleach, 5
Caladrius, 59
Caribou, vii–viii
Cats
    Birman temple, 93–94
    and luck, 130
    magical, 93
    and witchcraft, 127–28
Celts, 4–5
    animal divination, 163–65
    bears, 96, 97
    bird goddesses, 54–55
    blackbird, 64
    crane, 64
    creator birds, 57
    dragons, 39–40
    fairy deer, 99
    horned gods, 7–8
    and lucky rabbit, 133

magical cows, 88–89
magical horse, 86–87
Mistress of the Animals, 5–6
owl goddess, 71
raven, 73
serpents, 27–28
sow, 94–95
swan, 74–75
Wild Hunt, 105–06
Centaur, 82
Cerberus, 109
Cernunnos, 7
Cerridwen, 6–7, 95
Champ, 139–40
Charybdis, 145–46
China
    cockerel, 64–65
    dragon. *See* Chinese dragon
    duck, 68
    lucky goldfish, 134
    and the phoenix, 61
Chinese dragon
    becoming a, 37
    and festivals, 36
    kinds of, 37
Christianity, 8–9
    bees, 77
    cockerel, 64–65
    and dragons, 40–44
    eagle, 68
    griffon, 83
    and the phoenix, 60
    robin, 73
    and serpents, 20, 25–26, 27–28
    shape-shifting saints, x–xii
    Stella Maris, 137
Cinnamologus, 59
Cockerel, 64–65
Condor, 65
Cow
    gods, 12–13
    in the Hindu religion, 89–91
    magical, 88–89
Crane, 65–66
Creation myths, 55–56

Crete
    cranes, 65
    Mistress of the Animals, 3
    serpent gods, 23–24
Crow, 66
Cryptozoology, xiii–xiv
Cuchullain, 126–27

Deer, magical, 99–100
Denmark, little mermaid of, 149
Divination, 153
    bird, 158–61
Dogs
    demon, 104–05
    in Greek myth, 92
    hell hounds, 108–10
    in Irish lore, 91–92
    in Norse myths, 91
    September 11, 92
    Wild Hunt, 105–08
Domesticated creatures with magical
        associations
    cats, 93–94
    cow, 88–91
    dog, 91–93
    horse, 86–88
Dove, 67
Draco, 38
Dragon
    in Ancient Egypt, 44
    in Babylonian myths, 44
    in Bulgarian lore, 47
    of the Celtic world, 39–40
    of China. *See* Chinese dragon
    during Christian times, 40–41
    dragon-slaying saints, 40–44
    etymology, 35
    as evil, 44
    Feng Shui, xviii
    in Greek mythology, 46
    Komodo, 35
    red and white, 39
    in Scandinavian myth, 47–49
    in the stars, 38
    year of, 36

Dragonfly, 78–79
Dragon slayers
    and archangel, 42
    Beowulf, 49
    female, 43–44
    male, 40–41
Dreamtime, 129–30
Duck, 68

Eagle, 67–68
Earth Mother, 2
Earthquakes, prediction by animals,
    154–55
Eingana, 22
Elephants
    and luck, 130–31
Epona, 5
Ethiopia, parander, 84

Fabulous creatures
    centaur, 82
    griffon, 83
    hippogriff, 83–84
    manticore, 84
    parander, 84
Fafnir, 48
Familiar spirits
    in the Amazon basin, 128
    animals, 125
    in Westernized tradition, 126–27
    and witchcraft, 127–28
Feng Shui
    animals of, xvi–xviii
    description, xvi–xvii
Fenris wolf, 110
Finland
    egg creation myth, 56
    soul bird, 57
France, mermaid, 150
Frejya, x
Freyr, 8
Frogs and toads, lucky, 131–32

Garuda, 59–60
Germany, mermaid, 150

Goats, 10
Goatsucker, 117–18
Gods
    animal. *See* Animal gods
    and Christianization, 8–9
    horned, 7–9
    shape-shifting, 6–7
Goldfish, and luck, 134
Greek mythology
    bird goddesses, 55
    butterfly, 78
    centaur, 82
    crow, 66
    dogs, 92
    dove, 67
    dragons, 46
    eagle, 67–68
    magical horses in, 87–88
    and the phoenix, 60
    sea monsters, 144–46
    serpent gods, 24–25
Greyfriars Bobby, 92–93
Griffon, 83
Gwion, 6

Harpies, 55
Hathor, 12
Havfreui, 149
Hercinia, 60
Herne the Hunter, 107
Hindu milk miracle, 89–91
Hippocampus, 144–45
Hippogriff, 83–84
Horse, 5
    magical, 86–88
Hummingbird, 68–69
Hydra, 145

Iceland, berserkers, 111–12
India
    egg creation myth, 56
    manticore, 84
    sea serpents, 144
    serpent gods, 21
    swan, 75

Ireland
    dogs, 91–92
    mermaid, 151

Jaguar, 16
Japan
    cranes, 66
    creator birds, 56
    dragonflies, 78
    owlman, 119
    and the phoenix, 61
    sea goddess, 137
Jay, 69
Jormungand, 48
Judaism, and serpents, 26–27

Kelpies, 142
Khadru, 21
Kingfisher, 69–70
Kookaburra, 70
Kraken, 143–44

Lake monsters, 138–40
    in North America, 139–40
    and sea serpents, 141
Leucrota, 81
Lilith, 26–27
Loch Ness Monster, 138–39
Luck, and animals, 130–34

Magical creatures
    domesticated animals, 86–94
    psychology of, viii–ix
Magpies, 70–71
Mama Cocha, 136
Manasa, 21
Manipogo, 140
Manticore, 84
Mayans, animal gods, 16
Medusa, 24–25
Melissae, 77
Mermaids
    of Denmark, 149
    description, 148
    explanation, 151

French, 150
German, 150
in Gotland, 149
in Ireland, 151
Merrow, 151
Minoan snake goddesses, 23–24
Minotaur, 9
Mistress of the Animals, 1–3
    Celtic, 5–6
    in Crete, 3
    during the Neolithic period, 3
Moca Vampire, 118
Morgana, 146–47
Mother Earth, 53
Mothman, xv–xvi
Mut, 54

Native Americans
    animal crests, 124–25
    animal gods of, 13–15
    butterflies, 78
    creator birds, 56–57
    crow, 66
    deer, 99–100
    duck, 68
    eagle, 68
    hummingbird, 68–69
    jay, 69
    and lucky rabbit, 133
    magical birds, 62–63
    totem poles, 123–24
    turkey, 75–76
    Wild Hunt, 106–07
Nekhbet, 53–54
Nemhaim, 54
Neolithic period, Mistress of the Ani-
    mals, 3
Nidhogg, 47–48
Norse mythology
    dogs, 91
    horned gods, 8
    magical cow, 88
    magical horse, 87
    raven, 72–73
    Wild Hunt, 106

Ogopogo, 140
Owl, 71
Owlman, 118–19

Pan, 10
Parander, 84
Parrot, 72
Peacock, 72
Pegasus, 25, 87–88
Peru, sea mother, 136
Peter, Stubbe, 112–13
Phoenix, 60–61
    Feng Shui, xvii
Pigs, and luck, 131
Power symbols, ix
Puerto Rico,
    goatsucker, 117–18
    Moca Vampire, 118

Quetzalcoatl, 61–62

Rabbit, and luck, 132–33
Rainbow serpent
    creation myths, 22–23
    as mother, 22
Raven, 72–73
Robin, 73
Roc, 62
Roman myth
    bears, 97
    bird divinations, 158–61
    dove, 67
    eagle, 67–68
    magical horses in, 87–88
    owl, 71

Saint Patrick, x–xii
Satyrs, 10
Saxon mythology, Wild Hunt, 107
Scandinavia
    dragons, 47–49
    wild boars, 96
Scandinavian myth, dragons, 47–49
Scylla, 145–46
Seagull, 73–74

Sea mothers, 135–36
Selkies, 147–48
Serpent Mount, 19
Serpents, 19
    caduceus, 28–29
    in Celtic Christianity, 27–28
    in Celtic myths, 30–31
    and Christianity, 20, 25–26, 27–28
    cobra, 20–21
    in Cretan myths, 23–24
    eggs, 30–31
    and evil, 20
    in Greek mythology, 24–25
    gods, 21, 23–25
    handling, 31–32
    in Judaism, 26–27
    in medieval bestiaries, 29–30
    python, 23
    sea, 140–41, 144
Shape-shifting, ix–x
    gods, 6–7
    psychology of, xii
    saints, x–xii
    shamanic, xii–xiv
Sitting Bull, 125
Sleipnir, 87
Snake handling, 31–32
Sow
    divine, 6–7
    magical, 94–95
Sphinx, 84–85
Spider
    man, 15
    woman, 14
St. George, 40–41
St. Michael, 42
Stella Maris, 136–37
Storsjoodjuret, 139
Swallow, 74
Swan, 74–75

Thunderbird, 62–63
Tiamet, 45–46
Tiger, *Feng Shui*, xviii
Tortoise, *Feng Shui*, xvii–xviii

Totemism, 121
    in Australian Aborigines, 128–30
Totem poles, 123–24
    and animal crests, 124–25
Tsunamis, prediction by animals,
    155–56
Turkey, 75–76

Uadjet, 20–21
Unicorn, 85–86

Water nixes, 142–43
Water spirits, 138, 142–44
Werewolves, xiv–xv, 112–13
    American, 113
    possible explanations, 113–14
Whale, 136

White Buffalo Woman, 13–14
Wild boar. *See* Sow
Wild children, 98–99
Wild Hunt
    in Ancient Greece, 108
    in Celtic myth, 105–06
    and Cherokee Indians, 106–07
    in Norse myths, 106
    in Saxon mythology, 107
Wolves
    magical, 97–99
    raising children, 98
    See also Werewolves

Yeti, 117

Zonget, 2

About the Author

CASSANDRA EASON is the author of more than 75 books on all aspects of mythology, magic, the paranormal, maternal intuition, and childhood spirituality. She is a former Honorary Research Fellow at the Alister Hardy Research Center for Religious and Spiritual Experience in Oxford, England, specializing in children's spiritual and religious experiences.